The Kotel Siddur

PRAYER BOOK FOR FRIDAY NIGHT & FESTIVALS

WITH TRANSLATION, TRANSLITERATION, & INSIGHTS

מנחה לערב שבת, קבלת שבת,
ערבית לשבת ולשלש רגלים.

על פי נוסח האר״י ז״ל
עם הוספות לנוסח אשכנז

THE KOTEL SIDDUR
Prayer Book for Friday Night

FIRST PRINTING

Copyright ©2010
Rabbi Zalman Goldstein and
The Jewish Learning Group, Inc.

PUBLISHED BY

www.JewishLearningGroup.com

ISBN-10: 1-891293-22-2
ISBN-13: 978-1-891293-22-1

 הקרן למורשת
הכותל המערבי
**The Western Wall
Heritage Foundation**

*Printed and distributed to organizations visiting
the Kotel by the Western Wall Heritage Foundation.*
http://english.thekotel.org/siddur • siddur@thekotel.org
Tel. 02-627-6777

PRINTED IN ISRAEL

*"Now therefore, O our God, hear the prayer
of Your servant, and to his supplications,
and cause Your face to shine upon
Your sanctuary that is desolate..."*

Dear Worshipper,

On the old leather binding of a worn *Siddur* (prayer book) there is a metal etching. Its luster has faded, but even so you can still see the picture etched by an artist — the picture of a stone wall towering over a narrow alleyway and in front of it a number of worshippers: The Western Wall.

For Jews the world over this image served as a compass. It was this image that they carried when they whispered the prayer "*...and to Jerusalem, Your city, may You return in compassion.*" They poured their longing and yearning into the picture of this ancient stone wall and they wet it with their tears.

Our generation has merited having the Western Wall not only as a focus of yearning, but as a vivid and accessible reality. We recite the prayer "*...build Your House as at the beginning; establish Your Sanctuary upon its site...*" in the very same place that our forefathers could only imagine.

Indeed, there is a special grace to praying at the Western Wall; a grace many previous generations did not merit. Now, our forefathers are looking at us from Heaven and joining our prayers, that God will return to Zion in compassion.

Our prayers join those of our ancestors, all of which are united every day at the Western Wall and rise through the Holy of Holies, to our Father in Heaven. And we answer these prayers in the ancient Jewish tradition with "*Amen.*"

With prayers for God's salvation and the complete redemption of Israel.

Rabbi Shmuel Rabinowitz
Rabbi of the Western Wall and Holy Sites
Chanuka, 5770

Acknowledgements

Whether it's first-timers, regulars, or members of international youth groups, a visit to the Kotel on a Friday evening is a unique and moving experience.

This easy-to-use English/Hebrew prayer book will assist English speaking visitors of all backgrounds in participating more fully in the Friday evening services at the Kotel.

A special thanks to **Mr. Martin Glatt**, a friend of the management team of the **Western Wall Heritage Foundation**, who has been a promoter of this undertaking; as well as **Rabbi Shlomo Gestetner**, head of the **Mayanot Institute of Jewish Studies** in Jerusalem who has spent countless hours on its development. We are fortunate that publisher **Rabbi Zalman Goldstein**, founder and director of the **The Jewish Learning Group** in New York, developed the core data and attended to the layout and typesetting. Without the invaluable contribution of these and of many other participants, this prayer book would not be available today.

Last but not least, we pay a tribute to the committed team of the **Western Wall Heritage Foundation**, in particular **Rabbi Shmuel Rabinowitz, Dov Rabinowitz** and **Arieh Banner**.

Table of Contents

• Introduction / 9

• Transliteration Chart / 12

• *Mincha*: Friday Afternoon service / 13

• Mourner's Kaddish / 98

• Kaddish D'Rabanan / 60

• Shabbat & Festival Candle Lighting / 67

• *Yedid Nefesh* / 71

• *Kabbalat Shabbat*: Service for Welcoming the Shabbat / 75

• *Maariv*: Shabbat Evening service / 109

• *Sefirat Haomer*: Counting of the Omer / 171

• *Amidah* for Festivals: Pesach, Shavuot, and Sukkot / 182

• Selected Prayers / 203

• Selected Songs / 205

• About the Kotel — The Western Wall / 209

Introduction

Friday night is a unique time. It is the point at which the world undergoes a transformation from the mundane to the holy. As the sun sets in the horizon, Jews in every corner of the globe are called upon to participate in the sanctity of the moment. Shabbat is a time when we are able to slow down and draw closer to God.

Prayer is the Jew's channel to connecting with God — made all the more powerful through communal worship. And nowhere more so than at the very heart of our spiritual yearnings, the *Kotel*, the Western Wall of the Temple Mount, the closest remnant to the Holy Temple that once stood in Jerusalem.

Wherever Jews pray, wherever they are in the world, they face the 'Holy of Holies', the innermost sanctuary of the original Temple, which housed the ark, the Cherubim and was the place of Divine manifestation. Our Sages tell us that it is the holiest place on earth, the site where the Divine Presence of God, the *Shechina*, always dwells.

If you are standing now at this sacred place, or if you are in any other part of the world and would like to pray, this Siddur is designed as a simple guide to help you. It is an appropriate prayer book for use in any synagogue throughout the world.

The Prayers

The traditional Friday night prayer service contained in this book has been recited by Jews throughout the centuries. Expressions of joy, praise, longing and pain are encapsulated in the pages of the Siddur. God understands every language, but most powerful of all is a prayer from the heart. It is with this in mind that the prayers in this Siddur have been written both in Hebrew and English, with an additional English transliteration. Insights into the depth and significance of the prayers have also been included.

You will notice that there are many different groups that gather together to pray at the Kotel. Whether you choose to join one of these services or prefer to pray on your own, you will find this Siddur to be an easy and invaluable aid.

The Torah tells us that there are three things that can change a person's destiny: prayer, charity and acts of kindness. The power of prayer is such that it can change your life.

If, rather than follow the formal prayer service, you would prefer to say a few select prayers on your own, we have highlighted some central prayers for you. (See table of contents for 'Selected Prayers.')

We hope that the English transliteration makes it easy to read and follow the Hebrew, and that the modern translation and insights into some of the prayers adds to your experience.

The Songs

Songs are a way of expressing our deepest emotions. You will find many groups at the Kotel who include singing as part of their service. If you feel a desire to join in, you will find a selection of Friday night songs with English transliteration in this Siddur.

The Significance of the Kotel — The Western Wall

Almost every person who comes to the Western Wall reaches out a hand to touch it. When feeling the ancient stones of the Kotel, we sense that we are at the place that bridges the physical with the spiritual; the place where holiness is tangible; where the past, present and future stand before us. Our Sages explain that every prayer that is uttered from our lips ascends to God through the Temple Mount. It is known as the gateway to heaven.

Standing here, at the very place where God's presence is especially manifest, you have the opportunity to truly unite with The Infinite. May the content of the Siddur help you to open your heart and experience the beauty and power of prayer, and may we merit the rebuilding of the Third Temple in our day.

PLEASE READ THIS IMPORTANT NOTE

About the liturgical tradition of this prayer book:

Essentially all prayer books found throughout the Jewish world are the same; they all contain the same central prayers unified in the same overall structure, similar in both language and content. However, with the dispersion of the Jews to far-flung communities during the course of exile, unique prayer rites and traditions developed. These variations in the text of the prayer book are known as *nussach* (lit. style or version).

Today, the three most prominent are:

• *Nussach Ashkenaz* – The European tradition, popular amongst Jews originating from Western and Eastern Europe

• *Nussach Eidot Hamizrach* – The prayer rite of Oriental Jewry, popular amongst Jews originating from Spain, North Africa, Asia and the Balkan Countries.

• *Nussach HaAri* or *Hasidic Nussach Sephard* – This prayer rite developed with the rise of the Hassidic movement in Eastern Europe. The basic structure is *Nussach Ashkenaz* with alterations reflecting the kabbalistic teachings of Rabbi Isaac Luria, known as the Ari. This nussach eventually became the predominant prayer rite amongst major segments of Eastern European Jewry.

As the focus of this Siddur is to facilitate participation by a broad cross section of the Jewish community, we have incorporated as much as possible of the above *Nuschaot* without disturbing the flow of the prayers.

We request leaders who may have a preference for a particular Nussach to compromise in the interests of encouraging fellow Jews from different backgrounds to participate in one service, using the same Siddur.

This Siddur is based on *Nussach Ha-Ari* (Sephard) as set forth by Rabbi Shneur Zalman Liadi, with special inserts for *Nussach Ashkenaz*.

[GUIDE TO TRANSLITERATIONS ON FOLLOWING PAGE]

Hebrew:	Transliteration:	Example:
כ or ח	ch	Challah
ָ	ö	Of
־	a	Hurrah
··	ay	Today
ֶ	e	Leg
ְ	'	Avid
ֹ or וֹ	o	Tone
·	i	Key
ֻ or וּ	u	Lunar
ַי	ai	Aisle
ָי	öy	Toy

Mincha
for Friday Afternoon

מנחה לערב שבת

INSIGHT

The three daily prayers — *Shacharit*, *Mincha*, and *Maariv* — were originally instituted by our three Patriarchs, Abraham, Isaac, and Jacob, respectively.

As a result of the destruction of the 1ˢᵗ Temple and the subsequent dispersion and assimilation, the people were no longer fluent in the Hebrew Language. The sages, beginning with Ezra the Scribe, saw the need to establish a formal prayer service, the core being the Amidah prayer, which was simple, lucid, yet eloquent.

The Mincha service is especially favorable to God. This is because it is recited in the afternoon when a person has to take the trouble to interrupt work or business to concentrate on sincere and undistracted prayer.

Mincha consist of:

1. *Ashrei* — an introductory Psalm.

2. *Amidah* — the silent prayer in which we make our requests to God.

3. *Tachanun* — Supplications (a form of personal entreaty). There are certain times when Tachanun is not recited, including Friday afternoons, Shabbat and the Festivals. Consequently, it has been omitted from this Siddur.

4. *Olaynu* — the concluding prayer.

Ash-ray yosh'vay vay-sechö,	אַשְׁרֵי יוֹשְׁבֵי בֵיתֶךָ,
od y'ha-l'luchö selöh.	עוֹד יְהַלְלוּךָ סֶּלָה:
Ash-ray hö-öm she-köchö lo,	אַשְׁרֵי הָעָם שֶׁכָּכָה לּוֹ,
ash-ray hö-öm she-adonöy elohöv.	אַשְׁרֵי הָעָם שֶׁיְיָ אֱלֹהָיו:
T'hilöh l'dövid, aro-mim'chö	תְּהִלָּה לְדָוִד, אֲרוֹמִמְךָ
elohai ha-melech, va-avö-r'chöh	אֱלוֹהַי הַמֶּלֶךְ, וַאֲבָרְכָה
shim'chö l'olöm vö-ed.	שִׁמְךָ לְעוֹלָם וָעֶד:
B'chöl yom avö-r'chekö,	בְּכָל יוֹם אֲבָרְכֶךָּ,
va-aha-l'löh shim'chö l'olöm vö-ed.	וַאֲהַלְלָה שִׁמְךָ לְעוֹלָם וָעֶד:
Gödol adonöy um'hulöl m'od,	גָּדוֹל יְיָ וּמְהֻלָּל מְאֹד,
v'lig'dulöso ayn chay-ker.	וְלִגְדֻלָּתוֹ אֵין חֵקֶר:
Dor l'dor y'shabach ma-asechö,	דּוֹר לְדוֹר יְשַׁבַּח מַעֲשֶׂיךָ,
ug'vuro-sechö yagidu.	וּגְבוּרֹתֶיךָ יַגִּידוּ:
Hadar k'vod ho-dechö,	הֲדַר כְּבוֹד הוֹדֶךָ,
v'div'ray nif-l'osechö ö-sichöh.	וְדִבְרֵי נִפְלְאֹתֶיךָ אָשִׂיחָה:
Ve-ezuz no-r'osechö yo-mayru,	וֶעֱזוּז נוֹרְאֹתֶיךָ יֹאמֵרוּ,
ug'dulös'chö asap'renöh.	וּגְדֻלָּתְךָ אֲסַפְּרֶנָּה:
Zecher rav tuv'chö yabi-u,	זֵכֶר רַב טוּבְךָ יַבִּיעוּ,
v'tzid'kös'chö y'ra-naynu.	וְצִדְקָתְךָ יְרַנֵּנוּ:
Chanun v'rachum adonöy,	חַנּוּן וְרַחוּם יְיָ,
erech apa-yim ug'döl chösed.	אֶרֶךְ אַפַּיִם וּגְדָל חָסֶד:
Tov adonöy lakol,	טוֹב יְיָ לַכֹּל,
v'ra-chamöv al köl ma-asöv.	וְרַחֲמָיו עַל כָּל מַעֲשָׂיו:
Yoduchö adonöy köl ma-a-sechö,	יוֹדוּךָ יְיָ כָּל מַעֲשֶׂיךָ,
va-chasi-dechö y'vö-r'chu-chöh.	וַחֲסִידֶיךָ יְבָרְכוּכָה:
K'vod mal'chus'chö yo-mayru,	כְּבוֹד מַלְכוּתְךָ יֹאמֵרוּ,
ug'vurö-s'chö y'da-bayru.	וּגְבוּרָתְךָ יְדַבֵּרוּ:
L'hodi-a liv'nay hö-ödöm	לְהוֹדִיעַ לִבְנֵי הָאָדָם

14

אַשְׁרֵי — Happy are those who dwell in Your House; they will yet praise You forever. Happy is the people whose lot is thus; happy is the people whose God is the Lord. A Psalm of praise by David: I will exalt You, my God the King, and bless Your Name forever. Every day I will bless You, and extol Your Name forever. The Lord is great and exceedingly exalted, and there is no limit to His greatness. One generation to another will laud Your works, and tell of Your mighty acts. I will speak of the splendor of Your glorious majesty and of Your wondrous deeds. They will proclaim the might of Your awesome acts, and I will recount Your greatness. They will express the remembrance of Your abounding goodness, and sing of Your righteousness. The Lord is gracious and compassionate, slow to anger and of great kindness. The Lord is good to all, and His mercies extend over all His works. Lord, all Your works will give thanks to You, and Your pious ones will bless You. They will declare the glory of Your kingdom, and tell of Your strength. To make known to men His mighty acts, and the glorious majesty of His kingdom. Your

---

INSIGHT

אַשְׁרֵי — Psalm 145, was authored by King David (10th Century B.C.E.). The verses are written in the order of the Hebrew alphabet, known as the Aleph-Bet, symbolizing the order of creation and life. This Psalm also contains the passage *"You open Your hand and satisfy the desire of every living thing."* This acknowledges that God cares for every form of life. The great Sages of the Talmud taught that those who recite Ashrei three times a day will have a share in the world to come, and therefore it is recited twice during the Morning Prayer, and once in the Afternoon Prayer.

g'vurosöv, uch'vod hadar	גְּבוּרֹתָיו, וּכְבוֹד הֲדַר
mal'chuso. Mal'chus'chö,	מַלְכוּתוֹ: מַלְכוּתְךָ
mal'chus köl olö-mim,	מַלְכוּת כָּל עוֹלָמִים,
umem-shal-t'chö b'chöl	וּמֶמְשַׁלְתְּךָ בְּכָל
dor vödor. So-maych	דּוֹר וָדֹר: סוֹמֵךְ
adonöy l'chöl ha-nof'lim,	יְיָ לְכָל הַנֹּפְלִים,
v'zokayf l'chöl ha-k'fufim.	וְזוֹקֵף לְכָל הַכְּפוּפִים:
Aynay chol ay-lechö y'sa-bayru,	עֵינֵי כֹל אֵלֶיךָ יְשַׂבֵּרוּ,
v'atöh no-sayn löhem	וְאַתָּה נוֹתֵן לָהֶם
es öch-löm b'ito.	אֶת אָכְלָם בְּעִתּוֹ:
Posay-ach es yödechö,	פּוֹתֵחַ אֶת יָדֶךָ,
umasbi-a l'chöl chai rötzon.	וּמַשְׂבִּיעַ לְכָל חַי רָצוֹן:
Tzadik adonöy b'chöl d'röchöv,	צַדִּיק יְיָ בְּכָל דְּרָכָיו,
v'chösid b'chöl ma-asöv.	וְחָסִיד בְּכָל מַעֲשָׂיו:
Körov adonöy l'chöl ko-r'öv,	קָרוֹב יְיָ לְכָל קֹרְאָיו,
l'chol asher yikrö-u-hu ve-emes.	לְכֹל אֲשֶׁר יִקְרָאֻהוּ בֶאֱמֶת:
R'tzon y'ray-öv ya-aseh,	רְצוֹן יְרֵאָיו יַעֲשֶׂה,
v'es shav-ösöm yish-ma	וְאֶת שַׁוְעָתָם יִשְׁמַע
v'yoshi-aym. Shomayr adonöy	וְיוֹשִׁיעֵם: שׁוֹמֵר יְיָ
es köl ohavöv, v'ays köl	אֶת כָּל אֹהֲבָיו, וְאֵת כָּל
hö-r'shö-im yash-mid.	הָרְשָׁעִים יַשְׁמִיד:
T'hilas adonöy y'daber pi,	תְּהִלַּת יְיָ יְדַבֶּר פִּי,
vi-vöraych köl bösör shaym	וִיבָרֵךְ כָּל בָּשָׂר שֵׁם
köd-sho l'olöm vö-ed.	קָדְשׁוֹ לְעוֹלָם וָעֶד:
Va-anachnu n'vöraych yöh,	וַאֲנַחְנוּ נְבָרֵךְ יָהּ,
may-atöh v'ad olöm, ha-l'luyöh.	מֵעַתָּה וְעַד עוֹלָם, הַלְלוּיָהּ:

kingship is a kingship over all worlds, and Your dominion is throughout all generations. The Lord supports all who fall, and makes erect all who are bent. The eyes of all look expectantly to You, and You give them their food at the proper time. You open Your hand and satisfy the desire of every living thing. The Lord is righteous in all His ways, and benevolent in all His deeds. The Lord is close to all who call upon Him, to all who call upon Him in truth. He fulfills the desire of those who fear Him, hears their cry and delivers them. The Lord watches over all who love Him, and will destroy all the wicked. My mouth will utter the praise of the Lord, and let all flesh bless His holy Name forever. And we will bless the Lord from now to eternity. Praise the Lord.

DID YOU KNOW?

Prayer is one of the primary channels through which Jews connect to God. God is our Father and we are His children, and prayer is the medium through which we give thanks, praise, and pour out our heart in times of need.

On this, Maimonides wrote: *"We are told to offer up prayers to God, in order to establish firmly the true principle that God takes notice of our ways, that He can make them successful if we serve Him, or disastrous if we disobey Him; that success and failure are not the result of chance or accident."*

As is the case with all other commandments that God has given the Jewish people, the commandment to pray is not for His sake but for ours.

God does not 'need' our prayers. It is us who cannot do without our prayers. Our lives are enhanced when we acknowledge our dependence on God: including our health, our daily bread, our general welfare and our very lives.

The leader recites Half-Kaddish. We follow with the *Amidah* prayer.

HALF-KADDISH

It is customary for the one saying Kaddish to bow the head while reciting certain words. These words are bracketed below by the following symbol: "°". When the symbol appears before a word, bow the head, and remain bowed until the word that ends with the same symbol, then raise the head.

Yis-gadal v'yis-kadash °sh'may rabö°.

יִתְגַּדַּל וְיִתְקַדַּשׁ °שְׁמֵהּ רַבָּא°:

(Cong.: Ömayn.)

אמן

STANDING

B'öl'mö di v'rö chir'u-say

בְּעָלְמָא דִּי בְרָא כִרְעוּתֵהּ

v'yam-lich mal'chusay,

וְיַמְלִיךְ מַלְכוּתֵהּ,

Nussach Sfard: v'yatz-mach pur-könay

נוסח ספרד: וְיַצְמַח פּוּרְקָנֵהּ

°vikö-rayv m'shi-chay°.

°וִיקָרֵב מְשִׁיחֵהּ°:

(Cong.: Ömayn.)

אמן

B'cha-yay-chon uv'yomay-chon uv'cha-yay

בְּחַיֵּיכוֹן וּבְיוֹמֵיכוֹן וּבְחַיֵּי

d'chöl bays yisrö-ayl, ba-agölö uviz'man

דְּכָל בֵּית יִשְׂרָאֵל, בַּעֲגָלָא וּבִזְמַן

köriv °v'im'ru ömayn°.

קָרִיב °וְאִמְרוּ אָמֵן°:

(Cong.: Ömayn. Y'hay sh'may rabö m'vörach

אמן. יְהֵא שְׁמֵהּ רַבָּא מְבָרַךְ

l'ölam ul'öl'may öl'ma-yö.

לְעָלַם וּלְעָלְמֵי עָלְמַיָּא:

Yisböraych)

יִתְבָּרַךְ:

°Y'hay sh'may rabö m'vörach

°יְהֵא שְׁמֵהּ רַבָּא מְבָרַךְ

l'ölam ul'öl'may öl'ma-yö.

לְעָלַם וּלְעָלְמֵי עָלְמַיָּא:

Yis-böraych° °v'yish-tabach, v'yispö-ayr,

יִתְבָּרַךְ° °וְיִשְׁתַּבַּח, וְיִתְפָּאַר,

v'yis-romöm, v'yis-nasay,

וְיִתְרוֹמַם, וְיִתְנַשֵּׂא,

v'yis-hadör, v'yis-aleh, v'yis-halöl°,

וְיִתְהַדָּר, וְיִתְעַלֶּה, וְיִתְהַלָּל°,

°sh'may d'kud-shö b'rich hu°.

°שְׁמֵהּ דְּקֻדְשָׁא בְּרִיךְ הוּא°:

(Cong.: Ömayn.)

אמן

L'aylö min köl bir'chösö v'shi-rösö,

לְעֵלָּא מִן כָּל בִּרְכָתָא וְשִׁירָתָא,

tush-b'chösö v'neche-mösö,

תֻּשְׁבְּחָתָא וְנֶחֱמָתָא,

da-amirön b'öl'mö,

דַּאֲמִירָן בְּעָלְמָא,

°v'im'ru ömayn°.

°וְאִמְרוּ אָמֵן°:

(Cong.: Ömayn.)

אמן

INSIGHT

יִתְגַּדֵּל — The Kaddish is one of the most profound prayers. It praises God and expresses our complete faith in Him — even though His name does not appear even once. In the times of the Talmud when the Kaddish was formulated, it was written in Aramaic, the common language of the time, which has endured throughout the centuries.

The word Kaddish means holy. Reciting it reinforces the holiness of God's name and brings holiness to all those who respond *"Amen"*. In essence, the Kaddish declares that God is the Creator and ruler of the world.

During the prayer service there are four versions of the Kaddish:

1) The abbreviated form, called the *"Half Kaddish."* 2) The *"Complete Kaddish"* is used to conclude a major part of the service. 3) The *"Rabbi's Kaddish"* is used as an epilogue to the study of rabbinic literature. 4) The *"Mourner's Kaddish"* is recited for the first eleven months after the passing, and on each yahrtzeit (anniversary of the passing) thereafter.

The leader recites Half-Kaddish. We follow with the *Amidah* prayer.

STANDING   **HALF-KADDISH**

יִתְגַּדֵּל — Exalted and hallowed be His great Name. (Cong.: Amen)

בְּעָלְמָא — Throughout the world which He has created according to His Will. May He establish His kingship, (Nussach Sfard: and bring forth His redemption and hasten the coming of His Moshiach. (Cong.: Amen))

בְּחַיֵּיכוֹן — In your lifetime and in your days and in the lifetime of the entire House of Israel, speedily and soon, and say, Amen. (Cong.: Amen. May His great Name be blessed forever and to all eternity. Blessed)

יְהֵא — May His great Name be blessed forever and to all eternity. Blessed and praised, glorified, exalted and extolled, honored, adored and lauded be the Name of the Holy One, blessed be He. (Cong.: Amen).

לְעֵלָּא — Beyond all the blessings, hymns, praises and consolations that are uttered in the world; and say, Amen. (Cong.: Amen)

THE AMIDAH
The Amidah is recited quietly to oneself, while standing with both feet together. Before beginning, take three steps back, then three steps forward, and say:

Adonöy, s'fösai tif-töch ufi   אֲדֹנָי, שְׂפָתַי תִּפְתָּח וּפִי

yagid t'hilö-sechö.   יַגִּיד תְּהִלָּתֶךָ:

STANDING

At the word "*Böruch*" bend the knee; at "*Atöh*" bow forward; and at "*Adonöy*" straighten up.

RECALLING OUR PATRIARCHS

Böruch atöh adonöy elo-haynu   בָּרוּךְ אַתָּה יְיָ אֱלֹהֵינוּ

vay-lohay avosaynu,   וֵאלֹהֵי אֲבוֹתֵינוּ,

elo-hay avröhöm, elo-hay   אֱלֹהֵי אַבְרָהָם, אֱלֹהֵי

yitzchök, vay-lohay ya-akov,   יִצְחָק, וֵאלֹהֵי יַעֲקֹב,

hö-ayl ha-gödol ha-gibor   הָאֵל הַגָּדוֹל הַגִּבּוֹר

v'hanorö, ayl el-yon, gomayl   וְהַנּוֹרָא, אֵל עֶלְיוֹן, גּוֹמֵל

cha-södim tovim, ko-nay ha-kol,   חֲסָדִים טוֹבִים, קוֹנֵה הַכֹּל,

v'zochayr chas'day övos,   וְזוֹכֵר חַסְדֵי אָבוֹת,

umay-vi go-ayl liv'nay v'nayhem   וּמֵבִיא גוֹאֵל לִבְנֵי בְנֵיהֶם

l'ma-an sh'mo b'ahavöh.   לְמַעַן שְׁמוֹ בְּאַהֲבָה:

Between Rosh Hashana and Yom Kippur add:

Zöch'raynu l'cha-yim, melech chöfaytz   זָכְרֵנוּ לְחַיִּים, מֶלֶךְ חָפֵץ

ba-cha-yim, v'chös'vaynu b'sayfer   בַּחַיִּים, וְכָתְבֵנוּ בְּסֵפֶר

ha-cha-yim, l'ma-an'chö elohim cha-yim.   הַחַיִּים, לְמַעַנְךָ אֱלֹהִים חַיִּים.

At the word "*Böruch*" bend the knee; at "*Atöh*" bow forward; and at "*Adonöy*" straighten up.

Melech ozayr   מֶלֶךְ עוֹזֵר

umo-shi-a umö-gayn.   וּמוֹשִׁיעַ וּמָגֵן:

Böruch atöh adonöy,   בָּרוּךְ אַתָּה יְיָ,

mö-gayn avröhöm.   מָגֵן אַבְרָהָם:

20

INTRODUCTION

The Amidah is the central prayer of the service. *'Amidah'* means standing, for we stand and recite it quietly and with devotion, because it is a personal request to God. It is also known as the 'Eighteen Benedictions' because the weekday Amidah originally comprised of eighteen blessings. The Amidah addresses every aspect of our faith, as well as our personal and communal needs. It opens with the affirmation that God is our father, and ends with the acknowledgement that God blesses His people with peace.

THE AMIDAH

The Amidah is recited quietly to oneself, while standing with both feet together. Before beginning, take three steps back, then three steps forward, and say:

STANDING אֲדֹנָי — My Lord, open my lips, and my mouth shall declare Your praise.

At the word "Blessed" bend the knee; at "You" bow forward; and at "Lord" straighten up.

RECALLING OUR PATRIARCHS

בָּרוּךְ — **Blessed** are **You**, **Lord** our God and God of our fathers, God of Abraham, God of Isaac and God of Jacob, the great, mighty and awesome God, exalted God, Who bestows bountiful kindness, Who creates all things, Who remembers the piety of the Patriarchs, and Who, in love, brings a redeemer to their children's children, for the sake of His Name.

Between Rosh Hashana and Yom Kippur add:

זָכְרֵנוּ — Remember us for life, King Who desires life; inscribe us in the Book of Life, for Your sake, O living God.

At the word "Blessed" bend the knee; at "You" bow forward; and at "Lord" straighten up.

O King, [You are] a helper, a savior and a shield. Blessed are **You Lord**, Shield of Abraham.

21

Atöh gibor l'olöm adonöy,   אַתָּה גִבּוֹר לְעוֹלָם אֲדֹנָי,

m'cha-yeh maysim atöh,   מְחַיֶּה מֵתִים אַתָּה,

rav l'hoshi-a.   רַב לְהוֹשִׁיעַ:

In summer say: Morid ha-töl.   בקיץ: מוֹרִיד הַטָּל:

In winter say: Mashiv höru-ach   בחורף: מַשִּׁיב הָרוּחַ

umo-rid ha-geshem.   וּמוֹרִיד הַגֶּשֶׁם:

M'chal-kayl cha-yim b'chesed,   מְכַלְכֵּל חַיִּים בְּחֶסֶד,

m'cha-yeh may-sim b'racha-mim   מְחַיֶּה מֵתִים בְּרַחֲמִים

rabim, so-maych nof'lim,   רַבִּים, סוֹמֵךְ נוֹפְלִים,

v'rofay cholim, uma-tir   וְרוֹפֵא חוֹלִים, וּמַתִּיר

asu-rim, um'ka-yaym emu-nöso   אֲסוּרִים, וּמְקַיֵּם אֱמוּנָתוֹ לִישֵׁנֵי

li-shaynay öför, mi chö-mochö   עָפָר, מִי כָמוֹךְ

ba-al g'vuros umi do-meh löch,   בַּעַל גְּבוּרוֹת וּמִי דוֹמֶה לָּךְ,

melech may-mis um'cha-yeh   מֶלֶךְ מֵמִית וּמְחַיֶּה

umatz-mi-ach y'shu-öh.   וּמַצְמִיחַ יְשׁוּעָה:

Between Rosh Hashana and Yom Kippur add:

Mi chömochö öv hörachamön zochayr   מִי כָמוֹךָ אָב הָרַחֲמָן זוֹכֵר

y'tzuröv l'cha-yim b'racha-mim.   יְצוּרָיו לְחַיִּים בְּרַחֲמִים:

V'ne-emön atöh l'ha-cha-yos   וְנֶאֱמָן אַתָּה לְהַחֲיוֹת

may-sim. Böruch atöh adonöy,   מֵתִים: בָּרוּךְ אַתָּה יְיָ,

m'cha-yeh ha-amaysim.   מְחַיֶּה הַמֵּתִים:

THE *KEDUSHA*
**The Kedusha is recited during the leader's repetition of the Amidah.
Like Kaddish, *Kedusha* also means holy, elevating this section to a special
status. The Kedusha is a responsive prayer, recited line by line, with the
congregation saying one statement and the leader responding.**

GOD'S MIGHT

אַתָּה — You are mighty forever, my Lord; You resurrect the dead; You are powerful to save.

In summer say: He causes the dew to descend.

In winter say: He causes the wind to blow and the rain to fall.

He sustains the living with lovingkindness, resurrects the dead with great mercy, supports the falling, heals the sick, releases the bound, and fulfills His trust to those who sleep in the dust. Who is like You, mighty One! And who can be compared to You, King, Who brings death and restores life, and causes deliverance to spring forth!

Between Rosh Hashana and Yom Kippur add:

מִי — Who is like You, merciful Father, Who in compassion remembers His creatures for life.

וְנֶאֱמָן — You are trustworthy to revive the dead. Blessed are You Lord, Who revives the dead.

DID YOU KNOW?
Essential to prayer is *kavanah* (concentration and inner devotion). Entering into prayer is, in fact, stepping into another kind of reality, detaching ones mind from the mundane and striving to connect to the Infinite.

THE *KEDUSHA*
The Kedusha is recited during the leader's repetition of the Amidah. Like Kaddish, *Kedusha* also means holy, elevating this section to a special status. The Kedusha is a responsive prayer, recited line by line, with the congregation saying one statement and the leader responding.

THE "KEDUSHA" (Nussach Sfard/Ari)

STANDING

Cong. then leader: Nak-dishŏch v'na-ari-tzŏch k'no-am si-ach sod sar'fay kodesh, ha-m'shal'shim l'chŏ k'dushŏh, ka-kŏsuv al yad n'vi-echŏ v'körö zeh el zeh v'ömar.

קהל וחזן: נַקְדִּישָׁךְ וְנַעֲרִיצָךְ כְּנֹעַם שִׂיחַ סוֹד שַׂרְפֵי קֹדֶשׁ, הַמְשַׁלְּשִׁים לְךָ קְדֻשָּׁה, כַּכָּתוּב עַל יַד נְבִיאָךְ וְקָרָא זֶה אֶל זֶה וְאָמַר:

Cong. then leader: Kŏdosh, kŏdosh, kŏdosh, adonŏy tz'vŏ-os, m'lo chöl hö-öretz k'vodo.

קהל וחזן: קָדוֹשׁ, קָדוֹשׁ, קָדוֹשׁ, יְיָ צְבָאוֹת, מְלֹא כָל הָאָרֶץ כְּבוֹדוֹ:

Leader: L'umösöm m'shab'chim v'om'rim.

חזן: לְעֻמָּתָם מְשַׁבְּחִים וְאוֹמְרִים:

Cong. then leader: Böruch k'vod adonöy mim'komo.

קהל וחזן: בָּרוּךְ כְּבוֹד יְיָ מִמְּקוֹמוֹ:

Leader: Uv'div-rei köd-sh'chö kösuv lay-mor.

חזן: וּבְדִבְרֵי קָדְשְׁךָ כָּתוּב לֵאמֹר:

Cong. then leader: Yimloch adonöy l'olöm eloha-yich tziyon l'dor vö-dor, ha-l'luyöh.

קהל וחזן: יִמְלֹךְ יְיָ לְעוֹלָם אֱלֹהַיִךְ צִיּוֹן לְדֹר וָדֹר, הַלְלוּיָהּ:

MAY BE SEATED

THE "KEDUSHA" (*Nussach Ashkenaz*)

STANDING

Cong. then leader: N'ka-daysh es shim'chö bö-olöm, k'shaym she-makdishim oso bish'may mŏrom, ka-kösuv al yad n'vi-echö v'körö zeh el zeh v'ömar.

קהל וחזן: נְקַדֵּשׁ אֶת שִׁמְךָ בָּעוֹלָם, כְּשֵׁם שֶׁמַּקְדִּישִׁים אוֹתוֹ בִּשְׁמֵי מָרוֹם, כַּכָּתוּב עַל יַד נְבִיאָךְ וְקָרָא זֶה אֶל זֶה וְאָמַר:

Cong. then leader: Kŏdosh, kŏdosh, kŏdosh, adonŏy tz'vŏ-os, m'lo chöl hö-öretz k'vodo.

קהל וחזן: קָדוֹשׁ, קָדוֹשׁ, קָדוֹשׁ, יְיָ צְבָאוֹת, מְלֹא כָל הָאָרֶץ כְּבוֹדוֹ:

Leader: L'umösöm böruch yo-mayru.

חזן: לְעֻמָּתָם בָּרוּךְ יֹאמֵרוּ:

Cong. then leader: Böruch k'vod adonöy mim'komo.

קהל וחזן: בָּרוּךְ כְּבוֹד יְיָ מִמְּקוֹמוֹ:

Leader: Uv'div-rei köd-sh'chö kösuv lay-mor.

חזן: וּבְדִבְרֵי קָדְשְׁךָ כָּתוּב לֵאמֹר:

Cong. then leader: Yimloch adonöy l'olöm eloha-yich tzi-yon l'dor vö-dor, ha-l'luyöh.

קהל וחזן: יִמְלֹךְ יְיָ לְעוֹלָם אֱלֹהַיִךְ צִיּוֹן לְדֹר וָדֹר, הַלְלוּיָהּ:

Leader: L'do vödor na-gid g'dölechö u-l'naytzach n'tzöchim k'du-shös'chö nakdish, v'shiv-chachö elohaynu mipi-nu lo yömush l'olöm vö-ed, ki ayl melech gödol v'ködosh ötöh. Böruch atöh adonöy, *hö-ayl (*Between Rosh Hashana and Yom Kippur substitute: Ha-melech) ha-ködosh.

חזן: לְדוֹר וָדוֹר נַגִּיד גָּדְלֶךָ וּלְנֵצַח נְצָחִים קְדֻשָּׁתְךָ נַקְדִּישׁ, וְשִׁבְחֲךָ אֱלֹהֵינוּ מִפִּינוּ לֹא יָמוּשׁ לְעוֹלָם וָעֶד, כִּי אֵל מֶלֶךְ גָּדוֹל וְקָדוֹשׁ אָתָּה: בָּרוּךְ אַתָּה יְיָ, הָאֵל (בעשי"ת הַמֶּלֶךְ) הַקָּדוֹשׁ:

STANDING

THE "KEDUSHA" (Nussach Sfard/Ari)

נַקְדִּישָׁך — Cong. then leader: We will hallow and adore You as the sweet words of the assembly of the holy Seraphim who thrice repeat "holy" unto You, as it is written by Your prophet: And they call one to another and say.

קָדוֹשׁ — Cong. then leader: "Holy, holy, holy is the Lord of hosts; the whole earth is full of His glory."

לְעֻמָּתָם — Leader: Those facing them offer praise and say.

בָּרוּךְ — Cong then Leader: "Blessed be the glory of the Lord from its place." Leader: And in Your holy Scriptures it is written thus:

יִמְלֹךְ — Cong. then leader: The Lord shall reign forever; your God, O Zion, throughout all generations. Praise the Lord.

STANDING

THE "KEDUSHA" (*Nussach Ashkenaz*)

Cong. then leader: We will hallow Your Name in this world, just as they sanctify it in the Heavans above, as it is written by Your prophet: And they call one to another and say.

Cong. then leader: "Holy, holy, holy is the Lord of hosts; the whole earth is full of His glory."

Leader: Those facing them say "Blessed."

Cong then Leader: "Blessed be the glory of the Lord from its place." Leader: And in Your holy Scriptures it is written thus:

Cong. then leader: The Lord shall reign forever; your God, O Zion, throughout all generations. Praise the Lord.

Leader: From generation to generation we shall recount Your greatness and forever shall we proclaim Your holiness. Your praise, our God, shall not cease from our mouth forever and ever, for You, God, are a great and holy King. Blessed are You Lord, *the holy God. (*Between Rosh Hashana and Yom Kippur substitute: the holy King.)

MAY BE SEATED

INSIGHT

קָדוֹשׁ — "*Holy, holy, holy.*" Our Sages tell us that the angels utter praises to God after we recite our prayers on earth in the morning. The word holy is stated three times to reinforce that God is holy in the Heavens above, holy on earth, and holy forever and ever.

Continue Here

HOLINESS OF GOD'S NAME

Atöh ködosh v'shim'chö אַתָּה קָדוֹשׁ וְשִׁמְךָ
ködosh uk'doshim b'chöl yom קָדוֹשׁ וּקְדוֹשִׁים בְּכָל יוֹם
y'ha-l'luchö selöh. Böruch atöh יְהַלְלוּךָ סֶּלָה. בָּרוּךְ אַתָּה
adonöy, *hö-ayl ha-ködosh. יְיָ, הָאֵל הַקָּדוֹשׁ:
(*Between Rosh Hashana and Yom Kippur (בעשי״ת:
substitute: Ha-melech ha-ködosh.) הַמֶּלֶךְ הַקָּדוֹשׁ)

UNDERSTANDING

Atöh chonayn l'ödöm da-as, אַתָּה חוֹנֵן לְאָדָם דַּעַת,
um'lamayd le-enosh binöh, וּמְלַמֵּד לֶאֱנוֹשׁ בִּינָה,
chönaynu may-it-chö חָנֵּנוּ מֵאִתְּךָ
chöch-möh binöh vödö-as. חָכְמָה בִּינָה וָדָעַת:
Böruch atöh adonöy, בָּרוּךְ אַתָּה יְיָ,
chonayn hadö-as. חוֹנֵן הַדָּעַת:

REPENTANCE

Hashi-vaynu övinu הֲשִׁיבֵנוּ אָבִינוּ
l'sorö-sechö, v'körvay-nu לְתוֹרָתֶךָ, וְקָרְבֵנוּ
mal-kaynu la-avodö-sechö, מַלְכֵּנוּ לַעֲבוֹדָתֶךָ,
v'hacha-ziraynu bis'shuvöh וְהַחֲזִירֵנוּ בִּתְשׁוּבָה
sh'laymöh l'fönechö. שְׁלֵמָה לְפָנֶיךָ:
Böruch atöh adonöy, בָּרוּךְ אַתָּה יְיָ,
hörotzeh bis'shuvöh. הָרוֹצֶה בִּתְשׁוּבָה:

FORGIVENESS

S'lach lönu övinu, סְלַח לָנוּ אָבִינוּ,
ki chötönu, m'chol lönu כִּי חָטָאנוּ, מְחוֹל לָנוּ
mal-kaynu, ki föshö-nu, מַלְכֵּנוּ, כִּי פָשָׁעְנוּ,

Continue Here

HOLINESS OF GOD'S NAME

אַתָּה — You are holy and Your Name is holy, and holy beings praise You daily for all eternity. Blessed are You Lord, *the holy God. (*Between Rosh Hashana and Yom Kippur substitute: the holy King.)

UNDERSTANDING

אַתָּה — You graciously bestow knowledge upon man and teach mortals understanding. Graciously bestow upon us from You, wisdom, understanding and knowledge. Blessed are You Lord, Who graciously bestows knowledge.

REPENTANCE

הֲשִׁיבֵנוּ — Cause us to return, our Father, to Your Torah; draw us near, our King, to Your service; and bring us back to You in whole-hearted repentance. Blessed are You Lord, Who desires penitence.

FORGIVENESS

סְלַח — Pardon us, our Father, for we have sinned; forgive us, our King, for we have transgressed; for You are a good and forgiving

INSIGHT

הֲשִׁיבֵנוּ — Our Sages advise that before we request material matters from God, it is wise to strengthen our spiritual state. This requires introspection and self-improvement. The human being is a spiritual creature in a physical world — part angel and part physical. So it is equally important (if not more so) to nourish our spiritual side as well as the physical. Therefore we petition God to give us the resolve to accomplish this.

ki ayl tov v'salöch ötöh.   כִּי אֵל טוֹב וְסַלָּח אָתָּה:

Böruch atöh adonöy,   בָּרוּךְ אַתָּה יְיָ,

chanun ha-mar-beh lislo-ach.   חַנּוּן, הַמַּרְבֶּה לִסְלֹחַ:

REDEMPTION

R'ay nö v'ön-yaynu   רְאֵה נָא בְעָנְיֵנוּ

v'rivöh rivaynu,   וְרִיבָה רִיבֵנוּ,

ug'ölay-nu m'hayröh   וּגְאָלֵנוּ מְהֵרָה

l'ma-an sh'mechö,   לְמַעַן שְׁמֶךָ,

ki ayl go-ayl chözök ötöh.   כִּי אֵל גּוֹאֵל חָזָק אָתָּה:

Böruch atöh adonöy,   בָּרוּךְ אַתָּה יְיָ,

go-ayl yisrö-ayl.   גּוֹאֵל יִשְׂרָאֵל:

HEALING

R'fö-aynu adonöy v'nayrö-fay,   רְפָאֵנוּ יְיָ וְנֵרָפֵא,

hoshi-aynu v'nivöshay-öh,   הוֹשִׁיעֵנוּ וְנִוָּשֵׁעָה,

ki s'hilö-saynu ötöh,   כִּי תְהִלָּתֵנוּ אָתָּה,

v'ha-alay aruchöh ur'fu-öh   וְהַעֲלֵה אֲרוּכָה וּרְפוּאָה

sh'laymö l'chöl mako-saynu.   שְׁלֵמָה לְכָל מַכּוֹתֵינוּ:

Ki ayl melech rofay ne-emön   כִּי אֵל מֶלֶךְ רוֹפֵא נֶאֱמָן

v'rachamön ötöh.   וְרַחֲמָן אָתָּה:

Böruch atöh adonöy,   בָּרוּךְ אַתָּה יְיָ,

rofay cho-lay amo yisrö-ayl.   רוֹפֵא חוֹלֵי עַמּוֹ יִשְׂרָאֵל:

PROSPERITY

Böraych ölaynu adonöy elo-haynu   בָּרֵךְ עָלֵינוּ יְיָ אֱלֹהֵינוּ

es hashönöh hazos, v'ays köl   אֶת הַשָּׁנָה הַזֹּאת, וְאֶת כָּל

minay s'vu-ösöh l'tovöh,   מִינֵי תְבוּאָתָה לְטוֹבָה,

God. Blessed are You Lord, gracious One Who pardons abundantly.

REDEMPTION

רְאֵה — Behold our affliction and wage our battle; redeem us speedily for the sake of Your Name, for You God are a mighty Redeemer. Blessed are You Lord, Redeemer of Israel.

HEALING

רְפָאֵנוּ — Heal us, O Lord, and we will be healed; help us and we will be saved; for You are our praise. Grant complete cure and healing to all our wounds; for You, Almighty King, are a faithful and merciful healer. Blessed are You Lord, Who heals the sick of His people Israel.

PROSPERITY

בָּרֵךְ — Bless for us, Lord our God, this year and all the varieties of its produce for good; and bestow:

INSIGHT

בָּרֵךְ עָלֵינוּ — The blessings of the Amidah deal mainly with practical issues in daily life including the need to earn our daily bread.

Böraych means bless. In this section of the Amidah, we ask God to bless us with a good year through the fruits of our labor, or in the words of the prayer, "for good" and "for blessing."

Because Judaism is a life-long guide to spiritual growth, work *per se* should never be seen as an end in itself, but as a conduit for good.

We work to make a positive difference to ourselves as well as to others. When we accomplish this, our work does indeed become a blessing.

Mincha Services

In summer say: בקיץ:

v'sayn b'röchö   וְתֵן בְּרָכָה

In winter say: בחורף:

v'sayn tal umötör liv-röcho   וְתֵן טַל וּמָטָר לִבְרָכָה

al p'nay hö-adömö,   עַל פְּנֵי הָאֲדָמָה,

v'sab'aynu mituvechö,   וְשַׂבְּעֵנוּ מִטוּבֶךְ,

uvöraych sh'nösaynu   וּבָרֵךְ שְׁנָתֵנוּ

ka-shönim ha-tovos liv-röchöh,   כַּשָּׁנִים הַטּוֹבוֹת לִבְרָכָה,

ki ayl tov umay-tiv atöh   כִּי אֵל טוֹב וּמֵטִיב אַתָּה

um'vöraych ha- shönim.   וּמְבָרֵךְ הַשָּׁנִים:

Böruch atöh adonöy,   בָּרוּךְ אַתָּה יְיָ,

m'vöraych ha-shönim.   מְבָרֵךְ הַשָּׁנִים:

INGATHERING OF EXILES

T'ka b'shoför gödol   תְּקַע בְּשׁוֹפָר גָּדוֹל

l'chayru-saynu, v'sö nays   לְחֵרוּתֵנוּ, וְשָׂא נֵס

l'kabaytz gölu-yosaynu,   לְקַבֵּץ גָּלֻיּוֹתֵינוּ,

v'kab'tzaynu yachad   וְקַבְּצֵנוּ יַחַד

may-arba kan'fos   מֵאַרְבַּע כַּנְפוֹת

hö-öretz l'artzaynu.   הָאָרֶץ לְאַרְצֵנוּ:

Böruch atöh adonöy,   בָּרוּךְ אַתָּה יְיָ,

m'ka-baytz nid-chay   מְקַבֵּץ נִדְחֵי

amo yisrö-ayl.   עַמּוֹ יִשְׂרָאֵל:

RESTORATION OF TORAH-TRUE JUSTICE

Hö-shivöh shof'taynu   הָשִׁיבָה שׁוֹפְטֵינוּ

k'vöri-shonöh v'yo-atzay-nu   כְּבָרִאשׁוֹנָה, וְיוֹעֲצֵינוּ

k'vat'chilöh, v'hö-sayr mi-menu   כְּבַתְּחִלָּה, וְהָסֵר מִמֶּנּוּ

In summer say: Blessing

In winter say: Dew and rain for blessing

upon the face of the earth. Satisfy us from Your bounty and bless our year like other good years, for blessing; for You are a generous God Who bestows goodness and blesses the years. Blessed are You Lord, Who blesses the years.

INGATHERING OF EXILES

תְּקַע — Sound the great shofar for our freedom; raise a banner to gather our exiles, and bring us together from the four corners of the earth into our land. Blessed are You Lord, Who gathers the dispersed of His people Israel.

RESTORATION OF TORAH-TRUE JUSTICE

הָשִׁיבָה — Restore our judges as in former times, and our coun-selors as of yore; remove from us sorrow and sighing, and reign

---

INSIGHT

תְּקַע — As a people, we are not whole until our brethren are gathered together and "returned from the four corners of the earth into our land" — united again in the Land of Israel.

Allegorically 'the four corners of the earth' represent disparate spiritual corners in which people may find themselves.

Thus, we beseech God to help us see the truth in His Torah and the unity of its path so that we can stand united as one, serving God in ultimate unity.

yögon va-anöchöh, um'loch	יָגוֹן וַאֲנָחָה, וּמְלֹךְ
ölaynu atöh adonöy l'vad'chö	עָלֵינוּ אַתָּה יְיָ לְבַדְּךָ
b'chesed uv'ra-chamim,	בְּחֶסֶד וּבְרַחֲמִים,
b'tzedek uv' mishpöt.	בְּצֶדֶק וּבְמִשְׁפָּט:
Böruch atöh adonöy,	בָּרוּךְ אַתָּה יְיָ,
*melech ohayv tz'dököh	*מֶלֶךְ אוֹהֵב צְדָקָה
umish-pöt.	וּמִשְׁפָּט:
(*Between Rosh Hashana and Yom Kippur	(בעשי״ת:
substitute: Ha-melech ha-mish-pöt.)	*הַמֶּלֶךְ הַמִּשְׁפָּט):

AGAINST HERETICS

V'la-mal-shinim al t'hi sik-vöh,	וְלַמַּלְשִׁינִים אַל תְּהִי תִקְוָה,
v'chöl ha-minim v'chöl	וְכָל הַמִּינִים וְכָל
ha-zaydim k'rega yo-vaydu,	הַזֵּדִים כְּרֶגַע יֹאבֵדוּ,
v'chöl o-y'vay am'chö	וְכָל אוֹיְבֵי עַמְּךָ
m'hayröh yiköray-su,	מְהֵרָה יִכָּרֵתוּ,
umal'chus hörish-öh m'hayröh	וּמַלְכוּת הָרִשְׁעָה מְהֵרָה
s'akayr us'shabayr us'magayr,	תְעַקֵּר וּתְשַׁבֵּר וּתְמַגֵּר,
v' sachni-a bim'hayröh	וְתַכְנִיעַ בִּמְהֵרָה
v'yö-maynu. Böruch atöh	בְיָמֵינוּ: בָּרוּךְ אַתָּה
adonöy, shovayr o-y'vim	יְיָ, שׁוֹבֵר אוֹיְבִים
umach-ni-a zaydim.	וּמַכְנִיעַ זֵדִים:

THE RIGHTEOUS

Al ha-tzadikim v'al ha-chasidim,	עַל הַצַּדִּיקִים וְעַל הַחֲסִידִים,
v'al zik'nay am'chö bays yisrö-ayl,	וְעַל זִקְנֵי עַמְּךָ בֵּית יִשְׂרָאֵל,
v'al p'laytas bays sof'rayhem,	וְעַל פְּלֵיטַת בֵּית סוֹפְרֵיהֶם,
v'al gay-ray ha-tzedek v'ölaynu,	וְעַל גֵּרֵי הַצֶּדֶק וְעָלֵינוּ,
ye-hemu nö racha-mechö adonöy	יֶהֱמוּ נָא רַחֲמֶיךָ יְיָ

32

over us, You alone, O Lord, with kindness and compassion, with righteousness and justice. Blessed are You Lord, *King Who loves righteousness and justice. (*Between Rosh Hashana and Yom Kippur substitute: the King of judgment.)

Against Heretics

וְלַמַּלְשִׁינִים — Let there be no hope for informers, and may all the heretics and all the wicked instantly perish; may all the enemies of Your people be speedily extirpated; and may You swiftly uproot, break, crush and subdue the reign of wickedness speedily in our days. Blessed are You Lord, Who crushes enemies and subdues the wicked.

The Righteous

עַל — May Your mercies be aroused, Lord our God, upon the righteous, upon the pious, upon the elders of Your people, the House of Israel, upon the remnant of their sages, upon the righteous proselytes and upon us. Grant ample reward to all who

INSIGHT

עַל הַצַּדִּיקִים — This is a request for God to bestow His mercy and support upon the righteous and pious amongst the House of Israel, for without their dedicated service the world would not sustain itself.

The righteous are also an example of what it means to fully live a spiritual life. So we request God to 'place our lot amongst them,' as we strive to emulate them.

elo- haynu, v'sayn söchör tov	אֱלֹהֵינוּ, וְתֵן שָׂכָר טוֹב
l'chöl ha-bot'chim b'shim'chö	לְכָל הַבּוֹטְחִים בְּשִׁמְךָ
be-emes, v'sim chel-kaynu	בֶּאֱמֶת, וְשִׂים חֶלְקֵנוּ
imö-hem, ul'olöm lo nay-vosh	עִמָּהֶם, וּלְעוֹלָם לֹא נֵבוֹשׁ
ki v'chö bötöch-nu.	כִּי בְךָ בָּטָחְנוּ:
Böruch atöh adonöy,	בָּרוּךְ אַתָּה יְיָ,
mish-ön umiv-töch la-tzadikim.	מִשְׁעָן וּמִבְטָח לַצַּדִּיקִים:

REBUILDING JERUSALEM

V'li-rushöla-yim ir'chö	וְלִירוּשָׁלַיִם עִירְךָ
b'racha-mim töshuv,	בְּרַחֲמִים תָּשׁוּב,
v'sish-kon b'so-chöh	וְתִשְׁכֹּן בְּתוֹכָהּ
ka-asher dibar-tö, v'chisay dövid	כַּאֲשֶׁר דִּבַּרְתָּ, וְכִסֵּא דָוִד
av-d'chö m'hay-röh b'sochöh	עַבְדְּךָ מְהֵרָה בְּתוֹכָהּ
töchin, uv'nay osöh b'körov	תָּכִין, וּבְנֵה אוֹתָהּ בְּקָרוֹב
b'yömay-nu bin-yan olöm.	בְּיָמֵינוּ בִּנְיַן עוֹלָם:
Böruch atöh adonöy,	בָּרוּךְ אַתָּה יְיָ,
bonay y'rushölö-yim.	בּוֹנֵה יְרוּשָׁלָיִם:

KINGDOM OF DAVID

Es tzemach dövid av-d'chö	אֶת צֶמַח דָּוִד עַבְדְּךָ
m'hay-röh satz-mi-ach,	מְהֵרָה תַצְמִיחַ,
v'kar-no törum bishu-ösechö,	וְקַרְנוֹ תָּרוּם בִּישׁוּעָתֶךָ,
ki l'shu-ös'chö kivi-nu köl ha-yom.	כִּי לִישׁוּעָתְךָ קִוִּינוּ כָּל הַיּוֹם:
Böruch atöh adonöy,	בָּרוּךְ אַתָּה יְיָ,
matz-mi-ach keren y'shu-öh.	מַצְמִיחַ קֶרֶן יְשׁוּעָה:

truly trust in Your Name, and place our lot among them; may we never be disgraced, for we have put our trust in You. Blessed are You Lord, the support and security of the righteous.

REBUILDING JERUSALEM

וְלִירוּשָׁלַיִם — Return in mercy to Jerusalem Your city and dwell therein as You have promised; speedily establish therein the throne of David Your servant, and rebuild it, soon in our days, as an everlasting edifice. Blessed are You Lord, Who rebuilds Jerusalem.

KINGDOM OF DAVID

אֶת — Speedily cause the scion of David Your servant to flourish, and increase his power by Your salvation, for we hope for Your salvation all day. Blessed are You Lord, Who causes the power of salvation to flourish.

INSIGHT

אֶת צֶמַח —The belief in the coming of the *Moshiach* (Messiah) is fundamental to Judaism, and is one of the thirteen principles of faith compiled by Maimonides. Moshiach will usher in the ultimate era of redemption, the ingathering of the exiles, and the rebuilding of the third Temple. In this prayer we request that God bring salvation "speedily in our days", with the awareness that each good deed hastens the Messianic era.

Note the concluding words of the blessing "...for we hope for Your salvation all day." This reminds us that we are to continuously hope and pray for the Messianic era, a period of peace and harmony for all.

ACCEPTANCE OF OUR PRAYER

Sh'ma kolaynu adonöy elo-haynu, שְׁמַע קוֹלֵנוּ יְיָ אֱלֹהֵינוּ,

öv hö-racha-mön, ra-chaym אָב הָרַחֲמָן, רַחֵם

ölaynu, v'kabayl b'racha-mim עָלֵינוּ, וְקַבֵּל בְּרַחֲמִים

uv'rötzon es t'filösaynu, וּבְרָצוֹן אֶת תְּפִלָתֵנוּ,

ki ayl shomay-a t' filos כִּי אֵל שׁוֹמֵעַ תְּפִלּוֹת

v'sacha-nunim ötöh, וְתַחֲנוּנִים אָתָּה,

umil'fö-nechö mal-kaynu וּמִלְפָנֶיךָ מַלְכֵּנוּ

rayköm al tishi-vaynu. Ki atöh רֵיקָם אַל תְּשִׁיבֵנוּ: כִּי אַתָּה

shomay-a t'filas köl peh. Böruch שׁוֹמֵעַ תְּפִלַת כָּל פֶּה: בָּרוּךְ

atöh adonöy, shomay-a t'filöh. אַתָּה יְיָ, שׁוֹמֵעַ תְּפִלָה:

TEMPLE SERVICE

R'tzay adonöy elo-haynu b'am'chö רְצֵה יְיָ אֱלֹהֵינוּ בְּעַמְּךָ

yisrö-ayl v'lis'filösöm sh'ay, יִשְׂרָאֵל וְלִתְפִלָתָם שְׁעֵה,

v'hö-shayv hö-avodöh lid'vir וְהָשֵׁב הָעֲבוֹדָה לִדְבִיר

bay-sechö, v'ishay yisrö-ayl בֵּיתֶךָ, וְאִשֵׁי יִשְׂרָאֵל

us'fi-lösöm b'aha-vöh s'kabayl וּתְפִלָתָם בְּאַהֲבָה תְקַבֵּל

b'rö-tzon, us' hi l'rö-tzon tömid בְּרָצוֹן, וּתְהִי לְרָצוֹן תָּמִיד

avodas yisrö-ayl a-mechö. עֲבוֹדַת יִשְׂרָאֵל עַמֶּךָ:

On Rosh Chodesh, intermediate days of Passover, and Sukkot, add the following:

Elo-haynu vay-lohay avo-saynu אֱלֹהֵינוּ וֵאלֹהֵי אֲבוֹתֵינוּ

ya-aleh v'yövo, v'yagi-a v'yayrö-eh יַעֲלֶה וְיָבֹא, וְיַגִּיעַ וְיֵרָאֶה

v'yay-rö-tzeh, v'yishöma v'yipökayd וְיֵרָצֶה, וְיִשָׁמַע וְיִפָּקֵד

v'yizöchayr, zichro-naynu ufik'do-naynu, וְיִזָּכֵר, זִכְרוֹנֵנוּ וּפִקְדוֹנֵנוּ,

v' zichron avo-saynu, v'zichron וְזִכְרוֹן אֲבוֹתֵינוּ, וְזִכְרוֹן

möshi-ach ben dövid av-dechö, מָשִׁיחַ בֶּן דָּוִד עַבְדֶּךָ,

v'zichron y'rushöla-yim ir köd-shechö, וְזִכְרוֹן יְרוּשָׁלַיִם עִיר קָדְשֶׁךָ,

v' zichron köl am'chö bays yisrö-ayl וְזִכְרוֹן כָּל עַמְּךָ בֵּית יִשְׂרָאֵל

ACCEPTANCE OF OUR PRAYER

שְׁמַע — Hear our voice, Lord our God; merciful Father, have compassion upon us and accept our prayers in mercy and favor, for You are God Who hears prayers and supplications; do not turn us away empty-handed from You, our King. For You hear the prayer of everyone. Blessed are You Lord, Who hears prayer.

TEMPLE SERVICE

רְצֵה — Look with favor, Lord our God, on Your people Israel and pay heed to their prayer; restore the service to Your Sanctuary and accept with love and favor Israel's fire-offerings and prayer; and may the service of Your people Israel always find favor.

On Rosh Chodesh, intermediate days of Passover, and Sukkot, add the following:

אֱלֹהֵינוּ — Our God and God of our fathers, may there ascend, come and reach, be seen, accepted, and heard, recalled and remembered before You, the remembrance and recollection of us, the remembrance of our fathers, the remembrance of Moshiach the son of David Your servant, the remembrance of Jerusalem Your holy city, and the remembrance of all Your people the House of Israel, for deliverance, well-being, grace, kindness,

INSIGHT

שְׁמַע קוֹלֵנוּ — This blessing concludes the formal requests in the Amidah. Here we ask God to accept and fulfill our prayers.

Personal prayers recited during this blessing are especially favorable to God. As such, this moment is used by many to insert requests for family and friends who may be in need of a blessing including those for health, sustenance and happiness.

These personal requests should be uttered before the words *"For You hear the prayer of everyone."*

l'fönechö lif'laytöh l'tovöh, l'chayn
ul'chesed ul'racha-mim ul' cha-yim
tovim ul'shölom b'yom

לְפָנֶיךָ לִפְלֵיטָה לְטוֹבָה, לְחֵן
וּלְחֶסֶד וּלְרַחֲמִים וּלְחַיִּים
טוֹבִים וּלְשָׁלוֹם, בְּיוֹם

On Rosh Chodesh: Rosh ha-chodesh ha-zeh.

בר״ח: רֹאשׁ הַחֹדֶשׁ הַזֶּה.

On Pesach: Chag ha-matzos ha-zeh.

בחה״מ פסח: חַג הַמַּצּוֹת הַזֶּה.

On Sukkot: Chag ha-sukos ha-zeh.

בחה״מ סוכות: חַג הַסֻּכּוֹת הַזֶּה.

Zöch'raynu adonöy elo-haynu bo l'tovöh,
ufök' daynu vo liv'röchöh, v'hoshi-aynu
vo l'cha-yim tovim. Uvid'var y'shu-öh
v'rachamim chus v'chö-naynu v'ra-chaym
ölaynu v'hoshi-aynu ki ay-lechö ay-naynu,
ki ayl melech cha-nun v'rachum ötöh.

זָכְרֵנוּ יְיָ אֱלֹהֵינוּ בּוֹ לְטוֹבָה,
וּפָקְדֵנוּ בוֹ לִבְרָכָה, וְהוֹשִׁיעֵנוּ
בוֹ לְחַיִּים טוֹבִים: וּבִדְבַר יְשׁוּעָה
וְרַחֲמִים חוּס וְחָנֵּנוּ וְרַחֵם
עָלֵינוּ וְהוֹשִׁיעֵנוּ כִּי אֵלֶיךָ עֵינֵינוּ,
כִּי אֵל מֶלֶךְ חַנּוּן וְרַחוּם אָתָּה:

V'se-chezenöh ay-naynu

וְתֶחֱזֶינָה עֵינֵינוּ

b'shuv'chö l'tziyon b'racha-mim.

בְּשׁוּבְךָ לְצִיּוֹן בְּרַחֲמִים:

Böruch atöh adonöy, ha-machazir

בָּרוּךְ אַתָּה יְיָ, הַמַּחֲזִיר

sh'chinöso l'tziyon.

שְׁכִינָתוֹ לְצִיּוֹן:

Bow forward while reciting the first five words below:

THANKSGIVING

Modim anachnu löch,

מוֹדִים אֲנַחְנוּ לָךְ,

shö-atöh hu adonöy elo-haynu

שָׁאַתָּה הוּא יְיָ אֱלֹהֵינוּ

vay-lohay avo-saynu l'olöm

וֵאלֹהֵי אֲבוֹתֵינוּ לְעוֹלָם

vö-ed, tzur cha-yaynu mö-gayn

וָעֶד, צוּר חַיֵּינוּ מָגֵן

yish-aynu, atöh hu l'dor vödor,

יִשְׁעֵנוּ, אַתָּה הוּא לְדוֹר וָדוֹר,

no-deh l'chö un'sapayr

נוֹדֶה לְךָ וּנְסַפֵּר

t'hilö-sechö, al cha-yaynu

תְּהִלָּתֶךָ, עַל חַיֵּינוּ

ha-m'surim b'yödechö,

הַמְּסוּרִים בְּיָדֶךָ,

v'al nish'mosaynu ha-p'kudos

וְעַל נִשְׁמוֹתֵינוּ הַפְּקוּדוֹת

löch, v'al ni-sechö sheb'chöl

לָךְ, וְעַל נִסֶּיךָ שֶׁבְּכָל

yom imönu, v'al nif-l'ösechö

יוֹם עִמָּנוּ, וְעַל נִפְלְאוֹתֶיךָ

mercy, good life and peace, on this day On Rosh Chodesh: Rosh Chodesh. On Passover: the Festival of Matzot. On Sukkot: the Festival of Sukkot. Remember us on this [day], Lord our God, for good; be mindful of us on this [day] for blessing; help us on this [day] for good life. With the promise of deliverance and compassion, spare us and be gracious to us; have mercy upon us and deliver us; for our eyes are directed to You, for You, God, are a gracious and merciful King.

וְתֶחֱזֶינָה — May our eyes behold Your return to Zion in mercy. Blessed are You Lord, Who restores His Divine Presence to Zion.

Bow forward while reciting the words in bold:

THANKSGIVING

מוֹדִים — **We thankfully acknowledge that You are** the Lord our God and God of our fathers forever. You are the strength of our life, the shield of our salvation in every generation. We will give thanks to You and recount Your praise, evening, morning and noon, for our lives which are committed into Your hand, for our souls which are entrusted to You, for Your miracles which are

INSIGHT

יַעֲלֶה וְיָבֹא — On Rosh Chodesh (the first day of each month) and on all the Festivals, this prayer is included in the Amidah and Grace After Meals. We ask God to remember us and Jerusalem and to bring deliverance and peace in our times, because on these special days it is natural to miss the Holy Temple even more.

The prayer opens with eight expressions of ascent, (*Ya-aleh* means Ascend). These expressions refer to the eight stages that our prayers ascend to come before God.

v'tovosechö sheb'chöl ays,	וְטוֹבוֹתֶיךָ שֶׁבְּכָל עֵת,
erev vö-voker v'tzöhö-rö-yim,	עֶרֶב וָבֹקֶר וְצָהֳרָיִם,
ha-tov, ki lo chölu racha-mechö,	הַטּוֹב, כִּי לֹא כָלוּ רַחֲמֶיךָ,
ham'rachaym, ki lo samu	הַמְרַחֵם, כִּי לֹא תַמּוּ
chasö-dechö, ki may-olöm	חֲסָדֶיךָ, כִּי מֵעוֹלָם
kivinu löch.	קִוִּינוּ לָךְ:

During the leader's repetition of the Amidah, recite the portion below while standing. Bow your head while reciting the first five words.

↑
STANDING

Modim anach-nu löch, shö-atöh hu	מוֹדִים אֲנַחְנוּ לָךְ, שָׁאַתָּה הוּא
adonöy elo-haynu vay-lohay avo-saynu,	יְיָ אֱלֹהֵינוּ וֵאלֹהֵי אֲבוֹתֵינוּ,
elohay köl bösör, yo-tz'raynu, yo-tzayr	אֱלֹהֵי כָל בָּשָׂר, יוֹצְרֵנוּ, יוֹצֵר
b'rayshis. B'röchos v'hodö-os l'shim'chö	בְּרֵאשִׁית, בְּרָכוֹת וְהוֹדָאוֹת לְשִׁמְךָ
ha-gödol v'haködosh, al she-heche-yisönu	הַגָּדוֹל וְהַקָּדוֹשׁ, עַל שֶׁהֶחֱיִיתָנוּ
v'kiyam-tönu, kayn t'cha-yaynu	וְקִיַּמְתָּנוּ, כֵּן תְּחַיֵּינוּ
us'ka-y'maynu v'se-esof gölu-yosay-nu	וּתְקַיְּמֵנוּ, וְתֶאֱסֹף גָּלֻיּוֹתֵינוּ
l'chatz'ros köd-shechö, v'nö-shuv ay-lechö	לְחַצְרוֹת קָדְשֶׁךָ, וְנָשׁוּב אֵלֶיךָ
lishmor chukechö, v'la-asos r'tzonechö,	לִשְׁמוֹר חֻקֶּיךָ, וְלַעֲשׂוֹת רְצוֹנֶךָ,
ul'öv-d'chö b' layvöv shölaym, al she-önu	וּלְעָבְדְּךָ בְּלֵבָב שָׁלֵם, עַל שֶׁאָנוּ
modim löch Böruch ayl ha-hodö-os.	מוֹדִים לָךְ, בָּרוּךְ אֵל הַהוֹדָאוֹת:

During the individual Amidah, continue below.

On Chanukah, add the following:

V'al ha-nisim v'al ha-purkön	וְעַל הַנִּסִּים וְעַל הַפֻּרְקָן
v'al ha-g'vuros v'al ha-t'shu-os	וְעַל הַגְּבוּרוֹת וְעַל הַתְּשׁוּעוֹת
v'al ha-niflö-os she-ösisö la-avosaynu	וְעַל הַנִּפְלָאוֹת שֶׁעָשִׂיתָ לַאֲבוֹתֵינוּ
ba-yömim hö-haym biz'man ha-zeh.	בַּיָּמִים הָהֵם בִּזְמַן הַזֶּה:
Bi-may matis-yöhu ben yochö-nön	בִּימֵי מַתִּתְיָהוּ בֶּן יוֹחָנָן
ko-hayn gödol chash- monö-i uvönöv,	כֹּהֵן גָּדוֹל, חַשְׁמוֹנָאִי וּבָנָיו,
k'she- öm'döh mal'chus yövön	כְּשֶׁעָמְדָה מַלְכוּת יָוָן
hö-r'shö-öh al am'chö yisrö-ayl,	הָרְשָׁעָה, עַל עַמְּךָ יִשְׂרָאֵל,

with us daily, and for Your continual wonders and beneficence. You are the Beneficent One, for Your mercies never cease; and the Merciful One, for Your kindnesses never end; for we always place our hope in You.

During the leader's repetition of the Amidah, recite the portion below while standing. Bow your head while reciting the words in bold.

↑
STANDING

מוֹדִים — **We thankfully acknowledge that You are** the Lord our God and God of our fathers, the God of all flesh, our Creator and the Creator of all existence. We offer blessings and thanks to Your great and holy Name, for You have given us life and sustained us; so may You continue to grant us life and sustain us—gather our dispersed to the courtyards of Your Sanctuary and we shall return to You to keep Your laws, to do Your will, and to serve You with a perfect heart—for we thankfully acknowledge You. Blessed is God, Who is worthy of thanks.

During the individual Amidah, continue below.

On Chanukah, add the following:

וְעַל — And [we thank You] for the miracles, for the redemption, for the mighty deeds, for the saving acts, and for the wonders which You have wrought for our ancestors in those days, at this time.

בִּימֵי — In the days of Matisyohu, the son of Yochonon the High Priest, the Hasmonean and his sons, when the wicked Hellenic government rose up against Your people Israel to make them forget Your Torah and violate the decrees of Your Will. But You, in Your abounding mercies, stood by them in the time of their distress. You waged their battles, defended their rights

INSIGHT

וְעַל הַנִּסִּים — On Chanukah we recall and offer thanks for the miraculous events that occurred; namely, salvation from the mighty Greek army by the small band of Maccabees.

l'hash-kichöm torö-sechö ul'ha-aviröm	לְהַשְׁכִּיחָם תּוֹרָתֶךָ וּלְהַעֲבִירָם
may-chukay r'tzo-nechö,	מֵחֻקֵּי רְצוֹנֶךָ,
v'atöh b'racha-mechö hö-rabim ömad-tö	וְאַתָּה בְּרַחֲמֶיךָ הָרַבִּים עָמַדְתָּ
löhem b'ays tzörösöm. Ravtö es rivöm,	לָהֶם בְּעֵת צָרָתָם. רַבְתָּ אֶת רִיבָם,
dantö es dinöm, nökam-tö es nik'mösöm.	דַּנְתָּ אֶת דִּינָם, נָקַמְתָּ אֶת נִקְמָתָם.
Mösartö gi-borim b'yad chalöshim,	מָסַרְתָּ גִבּוֹרִים בְּיַד חַלָּשִׁים,
v'rabim b' yad m'atim, ut'may-im b'yad	וְרַבִּים בְּיַד מְעַטִּים, וּטְמֵאִים בְּיַד
t'horim, ur'shö-im b'yad tzadikim,	טְהוֹרִים, וּרְשָׁעִים בְּיַד צַדִּיקִים,
v'zaydim b'yad os'kay sorö-sechö.	וְזֵדִים בְּיַד עוֹסְקֵי תוֹרָתֶךָ.
Ul' chö ösisö shaym gödol v'ködosh	וּלְךָ עָשִׂיתָ שֵׁם גָּדוֹל וְקָדוֹשׁ
bö-olömechö, ul'am'chö yisrö-ayl ösisö	בָּעוֹלָמֶךָ, וּלְעַמְּךָ יִשְׂרָאֵל עָשִׂיתָ
t'shu-öh g'dolöh ufurkön k'ha-yom	תְּשׁוּעָה גְדוֹלָה וּפֻרְקָן כְּהַיּוֹם
ha-zeh. V'achar kach bö-u vö-nechö	הַזֶּה. וְאַחַר כַּךְ בָּאוּ בָנֶיךָ
lid'vir bay-sechö, ufinu es hay-chölechö,	לִדְבִיר בֵּיתֶךָ, וּפִנּוּ אֶת הֵיכָלֶךָ,
v'tiharu es mik-döshechö, v'hid-liku	וְטִהֲרוּ אֶת מִקְדָּשֶׁךָ, וְהִדְלִיקוּ
nayros b'chatz'ros köd-shechö,	נֵרוֹת בְּחַצְרוֹת קָדְשֶׁךָ,
v'köv'u sh'monas y'may chanuköh aylu	וְקָבְעוּ שְׁמוֹנַת יְמֵי חֲנֻכָּה אֵלוּ
l'hodos ul'halayl l'shim'chö hagödol.	לְהוֹדוֹת וּלְהַלֵּל לְשִׁמְךָ הַגָּדוֹל:

V'al kulöm yis-böraych	וְעַל כֻּלָּם יִתְבָּרַךְ
v'yisromöm v'yisnasay shim'chö	וְיִתְרוֹמָם וְיִתְנַשֵּׂא שִׁמְךָ
malkaynu tömid l'olöm vö-ed.	מַלְכֵּנוּ תָּמִיד לְעוֹלָם וָעֶד:

Between Rosh Hashana and Yom Kippur add:

Uch'sov l'cha-yim tovim	וּכְתוֹב לְחַיִּים טוֹבִים
köl b'nay v'risechö.	כָּל בְּנֵי בְרִיתֶךָ:

At the word "Böruch" bend the knee; at "Atöh" bow forward; and at "Adonöy" straighten up.

V'chöl ha-cha-yim yo-duchö selöh	וְכָל הַחַיִּים יוֹדוּךָ סֶּלָה
viha-l'lu shim'chö ha-gödol l'olöm	וִיהַלְלוּ שִׁמְךָ הַגָּדוֹל לְעוֹלָם
ki tov, hö-ayl y'shu-ösaynu	כִּי טוֹב, הָאֵל יְשׁוּעָתֵנוּ
v'ezrö-saynu selöh, hö-ayl	וְעֶזְרָתֵנוּ סֶלָה, הָאֵל הַטּוֹב:

and avenged the wrong done to them. You delivered the mighty into the hands of the weak, the many into the hands of the few, the impure into the hands of the pure, the wicked into the hands of the righteous, and the wanton sinners into the hands of those who occupy themselves with Your Torah. You made a great and holy name for Yourself in Your world, and effected a great deliverance and redemption for Your people to this very day. Then Your children entered the shrine of Your House, cleansed Your Temple, purified Your Sanctuary, kindled lights in Your holy courtyards, and instituted these eight days of Chanukah to give thanks and raise to Your great name.

וְעַל — And for all these, may Your Name, our King, be continually blessed, exalted and extolled forever and all time.

Between Rosh Hashana and Yom Kippur add:

וּכְתוֹב —— Inscribe all the children of Your Covenant for a good life.

**At the word "Blessed" bend the knee; at "You" bow forward;
and at "Lord" straighten up.**

וְכָל — And all living things shall forever thank You, and praise Your great Name eternally, for You are good. God, You are our everlasting salvation and help, O benevolent God. **Blessed** are

INSIGHT

מוֹדִים — After the opening blessings of praise of God and the intermediate personal supplications, we conclude the Amidah with blessings of thanksgiving. We thank God for giving us the means to communicate with Him through prayer, and for all the miracles He does for us daily, irrespective of whether we are conscious of them or not.

Our sages suggest that we give thanks to God at this juncture even though we may have not yet seen our prayers answered, because we believe that His actions are ultimately for the best.

ha-tov. Böruch atöh adonöy,	בָּרוּךְ אַתָּה יְיָ,
ha- tov shim'chö ul'chö	הַטוֹב שִׁמְךָ וּלְךָ
nö-eh l'hodos.	נָאֶה לְהוֹדוֹת:

PEACE

Sim shölom tovöh uv'röchöh,	שִׂים שָׁלוֹם, טוֹבָה וּבְרָכָה,
cha-yim chay-n vö-chesed	חַיִּים חֵן וָחֶסֶד
v'rachamim, ölaynu v'al köl	וְרַחֲמִים, עָלֵינוּ וְעַל כָּל
yisrö-ayl amechö. Bö-r'chaynu	יִשְׂרָאֵל עַמֶּךָ: בָּרְכֵנוּ
övinu kulönu k' echöd b'or	אָבִינוּ כֻּלָּנוּ כְּאֶחָד, בְּאוֹר
pönechö, ki v'or pönechö,	פָּנֶיךָ, כִּי בְאוֹר פָּנֶיךָ,
nösatö lönu, adonöy el-ohaynu,	נָתַתָּ לָּנוּ יְיָ אֱלֹהֵינוּ
toras cha-yim v'ahavas	תּוֹרַת חַיִּים, וְאַהֲבַת
chesed utz' dököh uv'röchöh	חֶסֶד, וּצְדָקָה וּבְרָכָה
v'rachamim v'cha-yim v'shölom.	וְרַחֲמִים וְחַיִּים וְשָׁלוֹם:
V'tov b'aynechö l'vöraych	וְטוֹב בְּעֵינֶיךָ לְבָרֵךְ
es am'chö yisrö-ayl b'chöl ays	אֶת עַמְּךָ יִשְׂרָאֵל בְּכָל עֵת
uv'chöl shö-öh bish'lomechö.	וּבְכָל שָׁעָה בִּשְׁלוֹמֶךָ:

Between Rosh Hashana and Yom Kippur add:

Uv'sayfer cha-yim b'röchöh v' shölom	וּבְסֵפֶר חַיִּים בְּרָכָה וְשָׁלוֹם
ufar- nösöh tovöh, y'shu-öh v' nechömöh,	וּפַרְנָסָה טוֹבָה יְשׁוּעָה וְנֶחָמָה
ug'zayros tovos, ni-zöchayr v'nikösayv	וּגְזֵרוֹת טוֹבוֹת נִזָּכֵר וְנִכָּתֵב
l'fönechö, anachnu v'chöl am'chö	לְפָנֶיךָ, אֲנַחְנוּ וְכָל עַמְּךָ
bays yisrö-ayl, l'cha-yim tovim ul'shölom.	בֵּית יִשְׂרָאֵל, לְחַיִּים טוֹבִים וּלְשָׁלוֹם:

Böruch atöh adonöy,	בָּרוּךְ אַתָּה יְיָ,
ha-m'vöraych es amo	הַמְבָרֵךְ אֶת עַמּוֹ
yisrö-ayl ba-shölom.	יִשְׂרָאֵל בַּשָּׁלוֹם:

You Lord, Beneficent is Your Name, and to You it is fitting to offer thanks.

PEACE

שִׂים — Bestow peace, goodness and blessing, life, graciousness, kindness and mercy, upon us and upon all Your people Israel. Bless us, our Father, all of us as one, with the light of Your countenance. For by the light of Your countenance You gave us, Lord our God, the Torah of life and lovingkindness, righteousness, blessing, mercy, life and peace. May it be favorable in Your eyes to bless Your people Israel, at all times and at every moment, with Your peace.

Between Rosh Hashana and Yom Kippur add:

וּבְסֵפֶר — And in the Book of Life, blessing, peace and prosperity, deliverance, consolation and favorable decrees, may we and all Your people the House of Israel be remembered and inscribed before You for a happy life and for peace.

בָּרוּךְ — Blessed are You Lord, Who blesses His people Israel with peace.

INSIGHT

שִׂים שָׁלוֹם — This prayer contains the essence of the Priestly Blessing, "Peace, goodness, life, graciousness, kindness and mercy". We all want these blessings in our personal lives and we ask God to bestow them upon us and all of Israel.

The blessing also reminds us of our communal responsibility to each other. Despite the fact that we are scattered around the world, we are one nation and one body.

Yih-yu l'rö-tzon im'ray fi,   יִהְיוּ לְרָצוֹן אִמְרֵי פִי,

v'heg-yon libi l'fönechö,   וְהֶגְיוֹן לִבִּי לְפָנֶיךָ,

adonöy tzuri v'go- ali.   יְיָ צוּרִי וְגוֹאֲלִי:

(The leader's repetition of the Amidah concludes here)

Elohai, n'tzor l'shoni may-rö,   אֱלֹהַי, נְצוֹר לְשׁוֹנִי מֵרָע,

us'fösai midabayr mirmöh.   וּשְׂפָתַי מִדַּבֵּר מִרְמָה:

V'lim'kal'lai, nafshi sidom,   וְלִמְקַלְלַי, נַפְשִׁי תִדּוֹם,

v'nafshi ke-öför la-kol   וְנַפְשִׁי כֶּעָפָר לַכֹּל תִּהְיֶה:

tih-yeh.P'sach libi b'sorösechö,   פְּתַח לִבִּי בְּתוֹרָתֶךָ,

uv'mitzvosechö tirdof nafshi,   וּבְמִצְוֹתֶיךָ תִּרְדּוֹף נַפְשִׁי,

v'chöl ha-chosh'vim ölai   וְכָל הַחוֹשְׁבִים עָלַי

rö-öh, m'hayröh hö-fayr atzösöm   רָעָה, מְהֵרָה הָפֵר עֲצָתָם

v'kalkayl ma-chashavtöm.   וְקַלְקֵל מַחֲשַׁבְתָּם:

Yih-yu k'motz lif'nay ru-ach   יִהְיוּ כְּמוֹץ לִפְנֵי רוּחַ

umal-ach adonöy do-cheh.   וּמַלְאַךְ יְיָ דּוֹחֶה:

L'ma-an yay-chöl'tzun y'didechö,   לְמַעַן יֵחָלְצוּן יְדִידֶיךָ,

hoshi-öh y'min'chö va-anayni.   הוֹשִׁיעָה יְמִינְךָ וַעֲנֵנִי:

Asay l'ma-an sh'mechö,   עֲשֵׂה לְמַעַן שְׁמֶךָ,

asay l'ma-an y'minechö,   עֲשֵׂה לְמַעַן יְמִינֶךָ,

asay l'ma-an torösechö,   עֲשֵׂה לְמַעַן תּוֹרָתֶךָ,

asay l'ma-an k'dusho-sechö.   עֲשֵׂה לְמַעַן קְדֻשָּׁתֶךָ:

Yih-yu l'rö-tzon im'ray fi,   יִהְיוּ לְרָצוֹן אִמְרֵי פִי,

v'heg-yon libi l'fönechö,   וְהֶגְיוֹן לִבִּי לְפָנֶיךָ,

adonöy tzuri v'go-ali.   יְיָ צוּרִי וְגוֹאֲלִי:

יִהְיוּ — May the words of my mouth and the meditation of my heart be acceptable before You, Lord, my Strength and my Redeemer.

(The leader's repetition of the Amidah concludes here)

אֱלֹהַי — My God, guard my tongue from evil and my lips from speaking deceitfully. Let my soul be silent to those who curse me; let my soul be as dust to all. Open my heart to Your Torah, and let my soul eagerly pursue Your commandments. As for all those who plot evil against me, hasten to annul their counsel and frustrate their design. Let them be as chaff before the wind; let the angel of the Lord thrust them away. That Your beloved ones may be delivered, help with Your right hand and answer me. Do it for the sake of Your Name; do it for the sake of Your right hand; do it for the sake of Your Torah; do it for the sake of Your holiness. May the words of my mouth and the meditation of my heart be acceptable before You, Lord, my Strength and my Redeemer.

INSIGHT

אֱלֹהַי — This prayer was composed by the Sage Mar the son of Ravina, who used to conclude his prayer with this petition.

The Torah places a great emphasis on creating harmony between people. Therefore it is critical that we constantly train ourselves and pray to God to *"guard my tongue from evil and my lips from speaking with deceit."* However, it is insufficient to only abstain from evil, we must also strive to do good and add light through the lessons of the Torah and therefore we beseech God to *"open my heart to Your Torah."*

Take three steps back and say the following, while bowing the head to the left, straight ahead, right, straight ahead, and bow down (as indicated):

< O-seh *sholom (*Between Rosh Hashana and Yom Kippur: ha- sholom) bim' romöv, hu > ya-aseh shölom ölaynu v'al köl yisrö-ayl, °v'im'ru ömayn.°

‹עֹשֶׂה שָׁלוֹם (בעשי״ת: הַשָּׁלוֹם) בִּמְרוֹמָיו, הוּא › יַעֲשֶׂה שָׁלוֹם עָלֵינוּ וְעַל כָּל יִשְׂרָאֵל, °וְאִמְרוּ אָמֵן:°

Y'hi rö-tzon mil'fö-nechö, adonöy elo-haynu vay-lohay avo-saynu, she-yibö- neh bays ha-mikdösh bim' hayröh v'yö-maynu, v'sayn chel-kaynu b'sorö-sechö.

יְהִי רָצוֹן מִלְּפָנֶיךָ, יְיָ אֱלֹהֵינוּ וֵאלֹהֵי אֲבוֹתֵינוּ, שֶׁיִּבָּנֶה בֵּית הַמִּקְדָּשׁ בִּמְהֵרָה בְיָמֵינוּ, וְתֵן חֶלְקֵנוּ בְּתוֹרָתֶךָ:

Take three steps forward. This concludes the Amidah.

The leader repeats the Amidah aloud, including all the additions marked for the leader's repetition, followed by a "Whole-Kaddish" (below).

WHOLE KADDISH
The leader recites the Kaddish below.

↑ **STANDING**

Yis-gadal v'yis-kadash °sh'may rabö°.

יִתְגַּדַּל וְיִתְקַדַּשׁ °שְׁמֵהּ רַבָּא°:

(Cong.: Ömayn.)

אמן

B'öl'mö di v'rö chir'u-say v'yam-lich mal'chusay,
Nussach Sfard: v'yatz-mach pur-könay °vikö-rayv m'shi-chay°.

בְּעָלְמָא דִּי בְרָא כִרְעוּתֵהּ וְיַמְלִיךְ מַלְכוּתֵהּ,
נוסח ספרד: וְיַצְמַח פּוּרְקָנֵהּ °וִיקָרֵב מְשִׁיחֵהּ°:

(Cong.: Ömayn.)

אמן

B'cha-yay-chon uv'yomay-chon uv'cha-yay d'chöl bays yisrö-ayl, ba-agölö uviz'man köriv °v'im'ru ömayn°.

בְּחַיֵּיכוֹן וּבְיוֹמֵיכוֹן וּבְחַיֵּי דְכָל בֵּית יִשְׂרָאֵל, בַּעֲגָלָא וּבִזְמַן קָרִיב °וְאִמְרוּ אָמֵן°:

(Cong.: Ömayn. Y'hay sh'may rabö m'vörach l'ölam ul'öl'may öl'ma-yö. Yisböraych)

אמן. יְהֵא שְׁמֵהּ רַבָּא מְבָרַךְ לְעָלַם וּלְעָלְמֵי עָלְמַיָּא: יִתְבָּרַךְ)

48

Take three steps back and say the following, while bowing the head to the left, straight ahead, right, straight ahead, and bow down (as indicated):

עֹשֶׂה — <He Who makes peace (Between Rosh Hashana and Yom Kippur substitute: the peace) in His heavens, may He > make peace for us and for all Israel; °and say: Amen°.

יְהִי — May it be Your will, Lord our God and God of our fathers, that the *Beit Hamikdash* (Holy Temple) be speedily rebuilt in our days, and grant us our portion in Your Torah.

Take three steps forward. This concludes the Amidah.

The leader repeats the Amidah aloud, including all the additions marked for the leader's repetition, followed by a "Whole-Kaddish" (below).

STANDING

WHOLE KADDISH
The leader recites the Kaddish below

יִתְגַּדֵּל — Exalted and hallowed be His great Name. (Cong.: Amen)

בְּעָלְמָא — Throughout the world which He has created according to His Will. May He establish His kingship, (Nussach Sfard: bring forth His redemption and hasten the coming of His Moshiach. (Cong.: Amen))

בְּחַיֵּיכוֹן — In your lifetime and in your days and in the lifetime of the entire House of Israel, speedily and soon, and say, Amen. (Cong.: Amen. May His great Name be blessed forever and to all eternity. Blessed)

יְהֵא — May His great Name be blessed forever and to all eternity. Blessed and praised, glorified, exalted and extolled, honored, adored and lauded be the Name of the Holy One, blessed be He. (Cong.: Amen).

לְעֵלָּא — Beyond all the blessings, hymns, praises and consolations that are uttered in the world; and say, Amen. (Cong.: Amen)

תִּתְקַבֵּל — May the prayers and supplications of the entire House of Israel be accepted before their Father in heaven; and say, Amen. (Cong: Amen.)

°Y'hay sh'may rabö m'vörach   יִהֵא שְׁמֵהּ רַבָּא מְבָרַךְ°

l'ölam ul'öl'may öl'ma-yö.   לְעָלַם וּלְעָלְמֵי עָלְמַיָּא:

Yis-böraych° °v'yish-tabach, v'yispö-ayr,   יִתְבָּרַךְ° °וְיִשְׁתַּבַּח, וְיִתְפָּאַר,

v'yis-romöm, v'yis-nasay,   וְיִתְרוֹמַם, וְיִתְנַשֵּׂא,

v'yis-hadör, v'yis-aleh, v'yis-halöl°, °sh'may   וְיִתְהַדָּר, וְיִתְעַלֶּה, וְיִתְהַלָּל°,

d'kud-shö b'rich hu°.   שְׁמֵהּ דְּקֻדְשָׁא בְּרִיךְ הוּא°:

(Cong.: Ömayn.)   אמן

L'aylö min köl bir'chösö v'shi-rösö,   לְעֵלָּא מִן כָּל בִּרְכָתָא וְשִׁירָתָא,

tush-b'chösö v'neche-mösö,   תֻּשְׁבְּחָתָא וְנֶחֱמָתָא,

da-amirön b'öl'mö,   דַּאֲמִירָן בְּעָלְמָא,

°v'im'ru ömayn°.   °וְאִמְרוּ אָמֵן°:

(Cong.: Ömayn.)   אמן

Tiskabayl tz'los-hon uvö-us-hon d'chöl   תִּתְקַבֵּל צְלוֹתְהוֹן וּבָעוּתְהוֹן דְּכָל

bays yisrö-ayl, ködöm avu-hon   בֵּית יִשְׂרָאֵל, קֳדָם אֲבוּהוֹן

di vish'ma-yö, °v'im'ru ömayn.°   דִּי בִשְׁמַיָּא, °וְאִמְרוּ אָמֵן°:

(Cong: Ömayn)   אמן

Y'hay sh'lömö rabö min sh'ma-yö,   יְהֵא שְׁלָמָא רַבָּא מִן שְׁמַיָּא

v'cha-yim tovim ölaynu v'al köl yisrö-ayl   וְחַיִּים טוֹבִים עָלֵינוּ וְעַל כָּל יִשְׂרָאֵל

°v'im'ru ömayn.°   °וְאִמְרוּ אָמֵן°:

(Cong: Ömayn)   אמן

**The leader takes three steps back and says the following,
while bowing the head to the right, straight ahead, left, straight ahead,
and bow down (as indicated):**

> O-seh *shölom (*Between Rosh Hashana and   > עֹשֶׂה שָׁלוֹם (בעשי״ת:

Yom Kippur: ha- shölom) bim' romöv, ^ hu   הַשָּׁלוֹם) בִּמְרוֹמָיו,^ הוּא > יַעֲשֶׂה שָׁלוֹם

< ya-aseh shölom ölaynu v'al köl yisrö-ayl,   עָלֵינוּ וְעַל כָּל יִשְׂרָאֵל,

°v'im'ru ömayn.°   °וְאִמְרוּ אָמֵן°:

Take three steps forward.

יְהֵא May there be abundant peace from heaven, and a good life for us and for all Israel; and say, Amen. (Cong: Amen.)

עֹשֶׂה He Who makes peace (Between Rosh Hashana and Yom Kippur say: the peace) in His heavens, may He make peace for us and for all Israel; and say, Amen. (Cong: Amen.)

Continue on the following page

INSIGHT

יִתְגַּדֵּל — The Kaddish is a deeply meaningful prayer that in essence is a prayer of praise for God.

Originally the Kaddish was authored as a prayer following study in the *Bet Midrash* (study hall). However it soon moved from the study hall to the synagogue where it became an integral part of the prayer service.

It was written in Aramaic, the common language in Talmudic times. The word *Kaddish* means holy, and its opening words, "*Yis-gadal v'yis-kadash*" were inspired by the prophet Ezekiel (Ezekiel 38:23), where the prophet envisions a time when God will be glorified and sanctified in the eyes of the nation.

The Kaddish recited here is known as the 'Whole Kaddish' and is said at the conclusion of the major part of the service, in this instance the conclusion of the Amidah.

In the 'Whole Kaddish' we include the request, "*Tiskabayl*" let it be accepted, where we ask God to accept all the prayers that we just recited.

Continue with "*Ōlaynu*" on the following page.

From the first day of Rosh Chodesh Elul, through Hoshana Rabbah, it is customary to recite Psalm 27 below. *Nussach Ashkenaz* recites this Psalm after the *Ōlaynu* of the evening service.

PSALM 27

L'dövid, adonöy ori v'yish-i mimi irö,	לְדָוִד, יְיָ אוֹרִי וְיִשְׁעִי מִמִּי אִירָא,
adonöy mö-oz cha-yai mimi efchöd.	יְיָ מָעוֹז חַיַּי מִמִּי אֶפְחָד:
Bik'rov ölai m'ray-im le-echol es b'söri,	בִּקְרֹב עָלַי מְרֵעִים לֶאֱכֹל אֶת בְּשָׂרִי,
tzörai v'oy'vai li, haymöh kösh'lu	צָרַי וְאֹיְבַי לִי, הֵמָּה כָשְׁלוּ
v'nöfölu. Im tacha-neh ölai macha-neh lo	וְנָפָלוּ: אִם תַּחֲנֶה עָלַי מַחֲנֶה לֹא
yirö libi, im tökum ölai milchömöh,	יִירָא לִבִּי, אִם תָּקוּם עָלַי מִלְחָמָה,
b'zos ani vo-tayach. Achas shö-alti	בְּזֹאת אֲנִי בוֹטֵחַ: אַחַת שָׁאַלְתִּי
may-ays adonöy osöh avakaysh,	מֵאֵת יְיָ, אוֹתָהּ אֲבַקֵּשׁ,
shivti b'vais adonöy köl y'may cha-yai,	שִׁבְתִּי בְּבֵית יְיָ כָּל יְמֵי חַיַּי,
la-chazos b'no-am adonöy ul'vakayr	לַחֲזוֹת בְּנֹעַם יְיָ וּלְבַקֵּר
b'haychölo. Ki yitzp'nayni b'suko	בְּהֵיכָלוֹ: כִּי יִצְפְּנֵנִי בְּסֻכֹּה
b'yom rö-öh yasti-rayni b'sayser öhölo,	בְּיוֹם רָעָה, יַסְתִּירֵנִי בְּסֵתֶר אָהֳלוֹ,
b'tzur y'romi-mayni. V'atöh yörum	בְּצוּר יְרוֹמְמֵנִי: וְעַתָּה יָרוּם
roshi al oy-vai s'vi-voisai,	רֹאשִׁי עַל אֹיְבַי סְבִיבוֹתַי,
v'ezb'chöh v'öhöloy ziv'chai s'ruöh,	וְאֶזְבְּחָה בְאָהֳלוֹ זִבְחֵי תְרוּעָה,
öshirö va-azam'röh la-donöy. Sh'ma adonöy	אָשִׁירָה וַאֲזַמְּרָה לַיְיָ: שְׁמַע יְיָ
koli ekröh, v'chö-nayni va-anayni.	קוֹלִי אֶקְרָא, וְחָנֵּנִי וַעֲנֵנִי:
L'chö ömar libi bak'shu fönöy	לְךָ אָמַר לִבִּי בַּקְּשׁוּ פָנָי,
es pö-nechö adonöy ava-kaysh.	אֶת פָּנֶיךָ יְיָ אֲבַקֵּשׁ:
Al tas-tayr pönechö mi-meni,	אַל תַּסְתֵּר פָּנֶיךָ מִמֶּנִּי,
al tat b'af avdeschö ez'rösi hö-yiso,	אַל תַּט בְּאַף עַבְדֶּךָ, עֶזְרָתִי הָיִיתָ,
al tit'shayni v'al ta-azvayni elohai yish-i.	אַל תִּטְּשֵׁנִי וְאַל תַּעַזְבֵנִי אֱלֹהֵי יִשְׁעִי:
Ki övi v'imi özövuni, vadonöy ya-as'fayni.	כִּי אָבִי וְאִמִּי עֲזָבוּנִי, וַיְיָ יַאַסְפֵנִי:
Horayni adonöy darkechö un'chayni	הוֹרֵנִי יְיָ דַּרְכֶּךָ, וּנְחֵנִי
b'orach mishor, l'ma-an sho-r'röy.	בְּאֹרַח מִישׁוֹר, לְמַעַן שׁוֹרְרָי:
Al tit'nayni b'nefesh tzöröy, ki kömu	אַל תִּתְּנֵנִי בְּנֶפֶשׁ צָרָי, כִּי קָמוּ
vi ayday sheker vi-faych chömös.	בִי עֵדֵי שֶׁקֶר וִיפֵחַ חָמָס:
Lulay he-emanti liros b'tuv adonöy	לוּלֵא הֶאֱמַנְתִּי לִרְאוֹת בְּטוּב יְיָ
b'eretz chaim. Kavay el adonöy chazak	בְּאֶרֶץ חַיִּים: קַוֵּה אֶל יְיָ, חֲזַק
v'ya-amaytz libechö v'kavay el adonöy.	וְיַאֲמֵץ לִבֶּךָ, וְקַוֵּה אֶל יְיָ:

Continue with "Ölaynu" on the following page.

From the first day of Rosh Chodesh Elul, through Hoshana Rabbah, it is customary to recite Psalm 27 below. *Nussach Ashkenaz* **recites this Psalm after the** *Ölaynu* **of the evening service.**

PSALM 27

לְדָוִד By David. The Lord is my light and my salvation — whom shall I fear? The Lord is the strength of my life — whom shall I dread? When evildoers approached me to devour my flesh, my oppressors and my foes, they stumbled and fell. If an army were to beleaguer me, my heart would not fear; if war were to arise against me, in this I trust [ed. that the Lord is my light and salvation]. One thing I have asked of the Lord, this I seek, that I may dwell in the House of the Lord all the days of my life, to behold the pleasantness of the Lord, and to visit in His Sanctuary. For He will hide me in His tabernacle on a day of adversity; He will conceal me in the hidden places of His tent; He will lift me upon a rock. And then my head will be raised above my enemies around me, and I will offer in His tabernacle sacrifices of jubilation; I will sing and chant to the Lord. Lord, hear my voice as I call; be gracious to me and answer me. In Your behalf my heart says, "Seek My countenance;" Your countenance, Lord, I seek. Do not conceal Your countenance from me; do not cast aside Your servant in wrath; You have been my help; do not abandon me nor forsake me, God of my deliverance. Though my father and mother have forsaken me, the Lord has taken me in. Lord, teach me Your way and lead me in the path of righteousness because of my watchful enemies. Do not give me over to the will of my oppressors, for there have risen against me false witnesses and they speak evil. [They would have crushed me] had I not believed that I would see the goodness of the Lord in the land of the living. Hope in the Lord, be strong and let your heart be valiant, and hope in the Lord.

INSIGHT

לְדָוִד — It is customary to recite this Psalm from the beginning of Elul to the end of Sukkot as it reflects ideas of the High Holidays. The midrash explains that the verse *"The Lord is my light,"* refers to Rosh Hashana; *"and my salvation,"* to Yom Kippur; and *"For He will hide me in His tabernacle,"* to Sukkot.

↑ STANDING

Ölaynu l'shabay-ach la-adon	עָלֵינוּ לְשַׁבֵּחַ לַאֲדוֹן
ha-kol, lösays g'dulöh l'yo-tzayr	הַכֹּל, לָתֵת גְּדֻלָּה לְיוֹצֵר
b'rayshis, shelo ösönu k'go-yay	בְּרֵאשִׁית, שֶׁלֹּא עָשָׂנוּ כְּגוֹיֵי
hö-arö-tzos, v'lo sömönu	הָאֲרָצוֹת, וְלֹא שָׂמָנוּ
k'mish-p'chos hö-adömöh,	כְּמִשְׁפְּחוֹת הָאֲדָמָה,
shelo söm chel-kaynu köhem,	שֶׁלֹּא שָׂם חֶלְקֵנוּ כָּהֶם,
v'gorö-laynu k'chöl ha-monöm	וְגֹרָלֵנוּ כְּכָל הֲמוֹנָם
she-haym mish-tachavim l'hevel	שֶׁהֵם מִשְׁתַּחֲוִים לְהֶבֶל
v'lörik. Va-anachnu kor'im	וְלָרִיק. וַאֲנַחְנוּ כּוֹרְעִים
umish-tachavim umodim,	וּמִשְׁתַּחֲוִים וּמוֹדִים,
lif'nay melech, mal'chay	לִפְנֵי מֶלֶךְ, מַלְכֵי
ha-m'löchim, ha-ködosh	הַמְּלָכִים, הַקָּדוֹשׁ
böruch hu. She-hu noteh	בָּרוּךְ הוּא. שֶׁהוּא נוֹטֶה
shöma-yim v'yosayd ö-retz,	שָׁמַיִם וְיוֹסֵד אָרֶץ,
umo-shav y'köro ba-shöma-yim	וּמוֹשַׁב יְקָרוֹ בַּשָּׁמַיִם
mima-al, ush'chinas uzo b'göv'hay	מִמַּעַל, וּשְׁכִינַת עֻזּוֹ בְּגָבְהֵי
m'romim, hu elo-haynu ayn	מְרוֹמִים, הוּא אֱלֹהֵינוּ אֵין
od. Emes mal-kaynu, efes zulöso,	עוֹד: אֱמֶת מַלְכֵּנוּ, אֶפֶס זוּלָתוֹ,
kakösuv b'soröso: V'yöda-tö	כַּכָּתוּב בְּתוֹרָתוֹ: וְיָדַעְתָּ
ha-yom va-hashay-vosö el	הַיּוֹם וַהֲשֵׁבֹתָ אֶל
l'vövechö, ki adonöy hu	לְבָבֶךָ, כִּי יְיָ הוּא
hö-elohim ba-shöma-yim	הָאֱלֹהִים בַּשָּׁמַיִם
mima-al, v'al hö-öretz	מִמַּעַל, וְעַל הָאָרֶץ
mi-töchas, ayn od.	מִתָּחַת, אֵין עוֹד:
V'al kayn n'ka-veh l'chö	וְעַל כֵּן נְקַוֶּה לְךָ
adonöy elo-haynu, lir-os	יְיָ אֱלֹהֵינוּ, לִרְאוֹת

STANDING

עָלֵינוּ — It is incumbent upon us to praise the Master of all things, to exalt the Creator of all existence, that He has not made us like the nations of the world, nor caused us to be like the families of the earth; that He has not assigned us a portion like theirs, nor a lot like that of all their multitudes, for they bow to vanity and nothingness. But we bend the knee, bow down, and offer praise before the supreme King of kings, the Holy One, blessed be He, Who stretches forth the heavens and establishes the earth, the seat of Whose glory is in the heavens above and the abode of Whose majesty is in the loftiest heights. He is our God; there is none else. Truly, He is our King; there is nothing besides Him, as it is written in His Torah: Know this day and take unto your heart that the Lord is God; in the heavens above and upon the earth below there is nothing else.

וְעַל — And therefore we hope to You, Lord our God, that we may speedily behold the splendor of Your might, to banish idola-

---

INSIGHT

עָלֵינוּ — Authored by Joshua the son of Nun, *Olaynu* is considered to be one of the loftiest prayers in our liturgy. It articulates the Jewish people's unique acceptance of God as the One and Only — the Creator and Master of the Universe.

Because it refers to God as the King of Kings, Olaynu was initially only recited on Rosh Hashanah as part of the 'Kingship section' of the Mussaf Amidah. During the thirteenth century it became the closing prayer of every daily service (with the exception of Musaf and Mincha of Yom Kippur). This is possibly because Olaynu, like *Shema Yisrael*, was the final sanctification of God chanted by martyrs during the Crusades.

m'hayröh b'sif-eres uzechö,	מְהֵרָה בְּתִפְאֶרֶת עֻזֶּךָ,
l'ha-avir gilulim min hö-öretz	לְהַעֲבִיר גִּלּוּלִים מִן הָאָרֶץ
v'hö-elilim köros yiköray-sun,	וְהָאֱלִילִים כָּרוֹת יִכָּרֵתוּן,
l'sakayn olöm b'mal'chus	לְתַקֵּן עוֹלָם בְּמַלְכוּת
shadai, v'chöl b'nay vösör	שַׁדַּי, וְכָל בְּנֵי בָשָׂר
yik-r'u vish'mechö, l'hafnos	יִקְרְאוּ בִשְׁמֶךָ, לְהַפְנוֹת
ay-lechö köl rish'ay öretz.	אֵלֶיךָ כָּל רִשְׁעֵי אָרֶץ:
Yakiru v'yay-d'u köl yosh'vay	יַכִּירוּ וְיֵדְעוּ כָּל יוֹשְׁבֵי
sayvayl ki l'chö tichra köl	תֵבֵל, כִּי לְךָ תִּכְרַע כָּל
berech, ti-shöva köl löshon.	בֶּרֶךְ, תִּשָּׁבַע כָּל לָשׁוֹן.
L'fönechö adonöy elo-haynu	לְפָנֶיךָ יְיָ אֱלֹהֵינוּ
yich-r'u v'yipolu, v'lich'vod	יִכְרְעוּ וְיִפּוֹלוּ, וְלִכְבוֹד
shim'chö y'kör yi-taynu,	שִׁמְךָ יְקָר יִתֵּנוּ,
vi-kab'lu chulöm alay-hem	וִיקַבְּלוּ כֻלָּם עֲלֵיהֶם
es ol mal'chu-sechö, v'simloch	אֶת עוֹל מַלְכוּתֶךָ, וְתִמְלוֹךְ
alay-hem m'hayröh l'olöm	עֲלֵיהֶם מְהֵרָה לְעוֹלָם
vö-ed, ki ha-mal'chus shel'chö hi,	וָעֶד, כִּי הַמַּלְכוּת שֶׁלְךָ הִיא,
ul'ol'may ad tim-loch b'chövod,	וּלְעוֹלְמֵי עַד תִּמְלוֹךְ בְּכָבוֹד,
ka-kösuv b'sorö-sechö,	כַּכָּתוּב בְּתוֹרָתֶךָ:
adonöy yim-loch l'olöm vö-ed.	יְיָ יִמְלֹךְ לְעֹלָם וָעֶד.
V'ne-emar: v'hö-yöh adonöy	וְנֶאֱמַר: וְהָיָה יְיָ
l'melech al köl hö-öretz,	לְמֶלֶךְ עַל כָּל הָאָרֶץ,
ba-yom hahu yih-yeh adonöy	בַּיּוֹם הַהוּא יִהְיֶה יְיָ
echöd ush'mo echöd.	אֶחָד וּשְׁמוֹ אֶחָד:

try from the earth — and false gods will be utterly destroyed; to perfect the world under the sovereignty of the Almighty. All mankind shall invoke Your Name, to turn to You all the wicked of the earth. Then all the inhabitants of the world will recognize and know that every knee should bend to You, every tongue should swear [by Your Name]. Before You, Lord our God, they will bow and prostrate themselves, and give honor to the glory of Your Name; and they will all take upon themselves the yoke of Your kingdom. May You soon reign over them forever and ever, for kingship is Yours, and to all eternity You will reign in glory, as it is written in Your Torah: The Lord will reign forever and ever. And it is said: The Lord shall be King over the entire earth; on that day the Lord shall be One and His Name One.

INSIGHT

וְעַל כֵּן — In this prayer we express our fervent hope for that Great Day, when all idolatry and wickedness will be abolished and all humanity acknowledges the sovereignty of God.

Then, even the wicked will submit to God's rule, and God in return, will reign upon all the earth. Then, *"the Lord shall be One and His Name One"* will be made truly manifest.

At present many people accept God's rule in theory only. They do not realize or feel deeply that God directly rules the world and the affairs of humanity. So we pray for the day when this recognition will be complete.

MOURNER'S KADDISH
Mourners recite the Kaddish below

Yis-gadal v'yis-kadash °sh'may rabö°. :יִתְגַּדַּל וְיִתְקַדַּשׁ °שְׁמֵהּ רַבָּא°

(Cong.: Ömayn.) אמן

B'öl'mö di v'rö chir'u-say בְּעָלְמָא דִּי בְרָא כִרְעוּתֵהּ

v'yam-lich mal'chusay, וְיַמְלִיךְ מַלְכוּתֵהּ,

Nussach Sfard: v'yatz-mach pur-könay נוסח ספרד: וְיַצְמַח פּוּרְקָנֵהּ

°vikö-rayv m'shi-chay°. :°וִיקָרֵב מְשִׁיחֵהּ°

(Cong.: Ömayn.) אמן

B'cha-yay-chon uv'yomay-chon uv'cha-yay בְּחַיֵּיכוֹן וּבְיוֹמֵיכוֹן וּבְחַיֵּי

d'chöl bays yisrö-ayl, ba-agölö uviz'man דְכָל בֵּית יִשְׂרָאֵל, בַּעֲגָלָא וּבִזְמַן

köriv °v'im'ru ömayn°. :קָרִיב °וְאִמְרוּ אָמֵן°

(Cong.: Ömayn. Y'hay sh'may rabö m'vörach אמן. יְהֵא שְׁמֵהּ רַבָּא מְבָרַךְ

l'ölam ul'öl'may öl'ma-yö. :לְעָלַם וּלְעָלְמֵי עָלְמַיָּא

Yisböraych) :יִתְבָּרֵךְ

°Y'hay sh'may rabö m'vörach °יְהֵא שְׁמֵהּ רַבָּא מְבָרַךְ

l'ölam ul'öl'may öl'ma-yö: לְעָלַם וּלְעָלְמֵי עָלְמַיָּא:

Yis-böraych° °v'yish-tabach, v'yispö-ayr, יִתְבָּרֵךְ° °וְיִשְׁתַּבַּח, וְיִתְפָּאַר,

v'yis-romöm, v'yis-nasay, וְיִתְרוֹמַם, וְיִתְנַשֵּׂא,

v'yis-hadör, v'yis-aleh, v'yis-halöl°, וְיִתְהַדָּר, וְיִתְעַלֶּה, וְיִתְהַלָּל°,

°sh'may d'kud-shö b'rich hu°. :°שְׁמֵהּ דְּקֻדְשָׁא בְּרִיךְ הוּא°

(Cong.: Ömayn.) אמן

L'aylö min köl bir'chösö v'shi-rösö, לְעֵלָּא מִן כָּל בִּרְכָתָא וְשִׁירָתָא,

tush-b'chösö v'neche-mösö, תֻּשְׁבְּחָתָא וְנֶחֱמָתָא,

da-amirön b'öl'mö, דַּאֲמִירָן בְּעָלְמָא,

°v'im'ru ömayn°. :°וְאִמְרוּ אָמֵן°

(Cong.: Ömayn.) אמן

Y'hay sh'lömö rabö min sh'ma-yö, יְהֵא שְׁלָמָא רַבָּא מִן שְׁמַיָּא

v'cha-yim tovim ölaynu v'al köl וְחַיִּים טוֹבִים עָלֵינוּ וְעַל כָּל

yisrö-ayl °v'im'ru ömayn.° :יִשְׂרָאֵל °וְאִמְרוּ אָמֵן°

(Cong: Ömayn) אמן

MOURNER'S KADDISH
Mourners recite the Kaddish below

יִתְגַּדֵּל — Exalted and hallowed be His great Name. (Cong.: Amen)

בְּעָלְמָא — Throughout the world which He has created according to His Will. May He establish His kingship, (Nussach Sfard: bring forth His redemption and hasten the coming of His Moshiach. (Cong.: Amen))

בְּחַיֵּיכוֹן — In your lifetime and in your days and in the lifetime of the entire House of Israel, speedily and soon, and say, Amen. (Cong.: Amen. May His great Name be blessed forever and to all eternity. Blessed)

יְהֵא — May His great Name be blessed forever and to all eternity. Blessed and praised, glorified, exalted and extolled, honored, adored and lauded be the Name of the Holy One, blessed be He. (Cong.: Amen).

לְעֵלָּא — Beyond all the blessings, hymns, praises and consolations that are uttered in the world; and say, Amen. (Cong.: Amen)

יְהֵא — May there be abundant peace from heaven, and a good life for us and for all Israel; and say, Amen. (Cong: Amen.)

INSIGHT

יִתְגַּדֵּל — Remarkably, the Mourner's Kaddish does not mention death nor make any reference to the deceased. It is directed, instead, at the living. The Kaddish affirms God's justice and states that God is the Creator of the world and is it's Ruler. Kaddish also alludes to the era of Moshiach, when all illness and suffering will cease, and requests that this time be ushered in during our lifetime. Further, it praises God's Name and describes His Glory.

According to the Talmud, parents are judged by the deeds of their children. If one's children follow in God's ways, then the lives of the parents attain additional sanctity. Similarly, if reciting Kaddish serves as a catalyst for personal spiritual growth, this adds sanctity to the life the parent lived, elevating their soul in Heaven.

The one reciting Kaddish takes three steps back and says the following,
while bowing the head to the right, straight ahead, left, straight ahead,
and bow down (as indicated):

> O-seh *shölom (*Between Rosh Hashana and   עֹשֶׂה שָׁלוֹם (בעשי״ת: <
Yom Kippur: ha- shölom) bim' romöv, ^ hu   הַשָּׁלוֹם) בִּמְרוֹמָיו,^ הוּא < יַעֲשֶׂה שָׁלוֹם
< ya-aseh shölom ölaynu v'al köl yisrö-ayl,   עָלֵינוּ וְעַל כָּל יִשְׂרָאֵל,
°v'im'ru ömayn.°   °וְאִמְרוּ אָמֵן:°

The leader takes three steps forward

Al tirö mi-pachad pis-om,   אַל תִּירָא מִפַּחַד פִּתְאֹם,
umi-sho-as r'shö-im ki sövo.   וּמִשֹּׁאַת רְשָׁעִים כִּי תָבֹא:
Utzu ay-tzöh v'suför,   עֻצוּ עֵצָה וְתֻפָר,
dab'ru dövör v'lo yökum,   דַּבְּרוּ דָבָר וְלֹא יָקוּם,
ki imönu ayl. V'ad zik-nöh   כִּי עִמָּנוּ אֵל: וְעַד זִקְנָה
ani hu, v'ad sayvöh ani   אֲנִי הוּא, וְעַד שֵׂיבָה אֲנִי
esbol, ani ösisi va-ani   אֶסְבֹּל, אֲנִי עָשִׂיתִי וַאֲנִי
esö, va-ani esbol va-ama-layt.   אֶשָּׂא, וַאֲנִי אֶסְבֹּל וַאֲמַלֵּט:

Ach tzadikim yodu lish'mechö   אַךְ צַדִּיקִים יוֹדוּ לִשְׁמֶךָ
yay-sh'vu y'shörim es pö-nechö.   יֵשְׁבוּ יְשָׁרִים אֶת פָּנֶיךָ:

MOURNER'S KADDISH D'RABBANAN
**Mourners recite the Kaddish below after reciting a section of mishna
(traditionally, chapter seven of tractate Mikvaot)**

Yis-gadal v'yis-kadash °sh'may rabö°.   יִתְגַּדַּל וְיִתְקַדַּשׁ °שְׁמֵהּ רַבָּא:°
(Cong.: Ömayn.)   אמן

B'öl'mö di v'rö chir'u-say   בְּעָלְמָא דִּי בְרָא כִרְעוּתֵהּ
v'yam-lich mal'chusay,   וְיַמְלִיךְ מַלְכוּתֵהּ,
Nussach Sfard: v'yatz-mach pur-könay   נוסח ספרד: וְיַצְמַח פּוּרְקָנֵהּ
°vikö-rayv m'shi-chay°.   °וִיקָרֵב מְשִׁיחֵהּ:°
(Cong.: Ömayn.)   אמן

עֹשֶׂה — He Who makes peace (Between Rosh Hashana and Yom Kippur say: the peace) in His heavens, may He make peace for us and for all Israel; and say, Amen. (Cong: Amen.)

אַל — Do not fear sudden terror, nor the destruction of the wicked when it comes. Contrive a scheme, but it will be foiled; conspire a plot, but it will not materialize, for God is with us. To your old age I am [with you]; to your hoary years I will sustain you; I have made you, and I will carry you; I will sustain you and deliver you.

אַךְ — Indeed, the righteous will extol Your Name; the upright will dwell in Your presence.

INSIGHT

אַל תִּירָא — The service concludes with verses from Proverbs and Isaiah emphasizing that no matter how long our exile may be, or what fears and anxieties beset us, God will always 'carry' us; He will surely deliver and sustain us.

MOURNER'S KADDISH D'RABBANAN
Mourners recite the Kaddish below after reciting a section of mishna (traditionally, chapter seven of tractate Mikvaot)

יִתְגַּדַּל — Exalted and hallowed be His great Name. (Cong.: Amen)

בְּעָלְמָא — Throughout the world which He has created according to His Will. May He establish His kingship, (Nussach Sfard: bring forth His redemption and hasten the coming of His Moshiach. (Cong.: Amen))

B'cha-yay-chon uv'yomay-chon uv'cha-yay
d'chöl bays yisrö-ayl, ba-agölö uviz'man
köriv °v'im'ru ömayn°.
(Cong.: Ömayn. Y'hay sh'may rabö
m'vörach l'ölam ul'öl'may
öl'ma-yö. Yisböraych)

בְּחַיֵּיכוֹן וּבְיוֹמֵיכוֹן וּבְחַיֵּי
דְכָל בֵּית יִשְׂרָאֵל, בַּעֲגָלָא וּבִזְמַן
קָרִיב °וְאִמְרוּ אָמֵן°:
אמן. יְהֵא שְׁמֵהּ רַבָּא מְבָרַךְ
לְעָלַם וּלְעָלְמֵי עָלְמַיָּא:
יִתְבָּרַךְ

°Y'hay sh'may rabö m'vörach
l'ölam ul'öl'may öl'ma-yö.
Yis-böraych° °v'yish-tabach, v'yispö-ayr,
v'yis-romöm, v'yis-nasay,
v'yis-hadör, v'yis-aleh, v'yis-halöl°, °sh'may
d'kud-shö b'rich hu°.
(Cong.: Ömayn.)

°יְהֵא שְׁמֵהּ רַבָּא מְבָרַךְ
לְעָלַם וּלְעָלְמֵי עָלְמַיָּא:
יִתְבָּרַךְ° °וְיִשְׁתַּבַּח, וְיִתְפָּאַר,
וְיִתְרוֹמַם, וְיִתְנַשֵּׂא,
וְיִתְהַדָּר, וְיִתְעַלֶּה, וְיִתְהַלָּל°,
°שְׁמֵהּ דְּקֻדְשָׁא בְּרִיךְ הוּא°:
אמן

L'aylö min köl bir'chösö v'shi-rösö,
tush-b'chösö v'neche-mösö,
da-amirön b'öl'mö,
°v'im'ru ömayn°.
(Cong.: Ömayn.)

לְעֵלָּא מִן כָּל בִּרְכָתָא וְשִׁירָתָא,
תֻּשְׁבְּחָתָא וְנֶחֱמָתָא,
דַּאֲמִירָן בְּעָלְמָא,
°וְאִמְרוּ אָמֵן°:
אמן

Al yisrö-ayl v'al rabö-nön,
v'al tal-miday-hon, v'al köl tal-miday
sal-miday-hon, v'al köl mön d'ös'kin
b'oray'sö, di v'asrö hö-dayn, v'di v'chöl
asar v'asar, y'hay l'hon ul'chon
sh'lömö rabö, chinö v'chisdö
v'rachamin v'cha-yin ari-chin,
um'zonö r'vichö ufur-könö,
min ködöm avu-hon d'vish'ma-yö,
°v'im'ru ömayn°.
(Cong: Ömayn)

עַל יִשְׂרָאֵל וְעַל רַבָּנָן,
וְעַל תַּלְמִידֵיהוֹן וְעַל כָּל תַּלְמִידֵי
תַלְמִידֵיהוֹן, וְעַל כָּל מָאן דְּעָסְקִין
בְּאוֹרַיְתָא, דִּי בְאַתְרָא הָדֵין וְדִי בְכָל
אֲתַר וַאֲתַר, יְהֵא לְהוֹן וּלְכוֹן
שְׁלָמָא רַבָּא חִנָּא וְחִסְדָּא
וְרַחֲמִין וְחַיִּין אֲרִיכִין,
וּמְזוֹנָא רְוִיחָא וּפוּרְקָנָא,
מִן קֳדָם אֲבוּהוֹן דְּבִשְׁמַיָּא,
°וְאִמְרוּ אָמֵן°:
אמן

Y'hay sh'lömö rabö min sh'ma-yö,
v'cha-yim tovim ölaynu v'al köl
yisrö-ayl °v'im'ru ömayn.°
(Cong: Ömayn)

יְהֵא שְׁלָמָא רַבָּא מִן שְׁמַיָּא
וְחַיִּים טוֹבִים עָלֵינוּ וְעַל כָּל
יִשְׂרָאֵל °וְאִמְרוּ אָמֵן°:
אמן

בְּחַיֵּיכוֹן — In your lifetime and in your days and in the lifetime of the entire House of Israel, speedily and soon, and say, Amen. (Cong.: Amen. May His great Name be blessed forever and to all eternity. Blessed)

יְהֵא — May His great Name be blessed forever and to all eternity. Blessed and praised, glorified, exalted and extolled, honored, adored and lauded be the Name of the Holy One, blessed be He. (Cong.: Amen).

לְעֵלָּא — Beyond all the blessings, hymns, praises and consolations that are uttered in the world; and say, Amen. (Cong.: Amen)

עַל — May Upon Israel, and upon our sages, and upon their disciples, and upon all the disciples of their disciples, and upon all those who occupy themselves with the Torah, here or in any other place, upon them and upon you, may there be abundant peace, grace, kindness, compassion, long life, ample sustenance and deliverance, from their Father in heaven; and say, Amen. (Cong: Amen.)

יְהֵא — May there be abundant peace from heaven, and a good life for us and for all Israel; and say, Amen. (Cong: Amen.)

DID YOU KNOW?

The Mourner's Kaddish can only be recited in the presence of a Minyan (quorum of ten Jewish males over age thirteen) during a prayer service, or after reciting Psalms or *Mishnayot*. It is normally recited at specific points during each of the three daily services.

Our tradition teaches that a son who recites Kaddish for his father or mother saves them from certain judgment. One should therefore, do the utmost to recite Kaddish at every opportunity during the first 11 months from the passing, and on each Yahrtzeit (the anniversary of the day of the passing) thereafter.

Women may undertake to do a specific Mitzvah in honor and memory of the loved one. Our sages state that for women, this brings the same merit to the soul as does the recitation of Kaddish by men.

Many mourners make a point of leading the weekday prayer services in their synagogue for the entire 11 months, for then one can recite all the different forms of Kaddish throughout the services. This adds more and more holiness to the soul of the departed. By leading the services, one also joins the merit of all those praying and praising God to the soul of their dear departed.

The one reciting Kaddish takes three steps back and says the following, while bowing the head to the right, straight ahead, left, straight ahead, and bow down (as indicated):

> O-seh *shölom (*Between Rosh Hashana and
Yom Kippur: ha- shölom) bim' romöv, ^ hu
< ya-aseh shölom ölaynu v'al köl yisrö-ayl,
°v'im'ru ömayn.°

‹ עֹשֶׂה שָׁלוֹם (בעשי״ת) :
הַשָּׁלוֹם) בִּמְרוֹמָיו,^ הוּא ‹ יַעֲשֶׂה שָׁלוֹם
עָלֵֽינוּ וְעַל כָּל יִשְׂרָאֵל,
°וְאִמְרוּ אָמֵן:°

The leader takes three steps forward

THIS CONCLUDES THE MINCHA SERVICE

עֹשֶׂה — He Who makes peace (Between Rosh Hashana and Yom Kippur say: the peace) in His heavens, may He make peace for us and for all Israel; and say, Amen. (Cong: Amen.)

THIS CONCLUDES THE MINCHA SERVICE

Shabbat & Festival Candle Lighting

About Shabbat and Festival Candle Lighting

Lighting Shabbat and Jewish holiday candles is an ancient Jewish tradition which Jewish women observe in welcoming the "Shabbat Queen" and Jewish festivals, and is traditionally the responsibility of every Jewish wife and mother.

It is this mitzvah that rekindles the Divine spark in every Jewish person. Married women customarily kindle two candles, adding an additional candle for each member of their household. As soon as one's daughter is old enough to recite the blessing (approximately 3 years old), it's a beautiful custom for her to kindle her own Shabbat/Festival candle as well (of course with the help of an adult before lighting her own candle(s).

It is customary to place a few coins in a charity box prior to lighting the candles (except when lighting on the second night of a Festival or when the Festival starts on Saturday night, when the handling of money is forbidden). Children should light prior to their mother, in case they need assistance.

The candles are lit not later than 18 minutes before sunset on Friday or on the first Festival evening, and—using a flame source that was kindled before the onset of the Festival or Shabbat—45 minutes after sunset on the second night of a Festival, and when a Festival starts on Saturday night. The time of lighting is considered especially propitious for praying for health and happiness.

BLESSINGS FOR CANDLE LIGHTING
1. At the set time (see local Jewish calendar), light the candles.
2. Draw your hands three times around the candles and toward your face.
3. Cover your eyes with your hands, and recite the blessing.

On Friday Evening

Böruch atöh adonöy,	בָּרוּךְ אַתָּה יְיָ,
elohaynu melech hö-olöm,	אֱלֹהֵינוּ מֶלֶךְ הָעוֹלָם,
asher kid'shönu b'mitzvosöv,	אֲשֶׁר קִדְּשָׁנוּ בְּמִצְוֹתָיו,
v'tzivönu l'hadlik nayr	וְצִוָּנוּ לְהַדְלִיק נֵר
shel shabös kodesh.	שֶׁל שַׁבָּת קֹדֶשׁ:

בָּרוּךְ Blessed are You, Lord our God, King of the universe, who has sanctified us with His commandments, and commanded us to kindle the light of the holy Shabbat.

On the Eve of Passover, Shavuot and Sukkot

Böruch atöh adonöy,	בָּרוּךְ אַתָּה יְיָ,
elohaynu melech hö-olöm,	אֱלֹהֵינוּ מֶלֶךְ הָעוֹלָם,
asher kid'shönu b'mitzvosöv,	אֲשֶׁר קִדְּשָׁנוּ בְּמִצְוֹתָיו,
v'tzivönu l'hadlik nayr	וְצִוָּנוּ לְהַדְלִיק נֵר
shel yom tov.	שֶׁל יוֹם טוֹב:

בָּרוּךְ Blessed are You, Lord our God, King of the universe, who has sanctified us with His commandments, and commanded us to kindle the Yom Tov light.

Except on the last two nights of Passover, continue with:

Böruch atöh adonöy,	בָּרוּךְ אַתָּה יְיָ,
elohaynu melech hö-olöm,	אֱלֹהֵינוּ מֶלֶךְ הָעוֹלָם,
shehecheyönu v'kiy'mönu	שֶׁהֶחֱיָנוּ וְקִיְּמָנוּ
v'higi-önu liz'man ha-zeh.	וְהִגִּיעָנוּ לִזְמַן הַזֶּה:

בָּרוּךְ Blessed are You, Lord our God, King of the universe, who has granted us life, sustained us and enabled us to reach this occasion.

On the Eve of Passover, Shavuot and Sukkot that fall on Friday Evening

Böruch atöh adonöy,	בָּרוּךְ אַתָּה יְיָ,
elohaynu melech hö-olöm,	אֱלֹהֵינוּ מֶלֶךְ הָעוֹלָם,
asher kid'shönu b'mitzvosöv,	אֲשֶׁר קִדְּשָׁנוּ בְּמִצְוֹתָיו,
v'tzivönu l'hadlik nayr	וְצִוָּנוּ לְהַדְלִיק נֵר
shel shabös v'shel yom tov.	שֶׁל שַׁבָּת וְשֶׁל יוֹם טוֹב:

בָּרוּךְ Blessed are You, Lord our God, King of the universe, who has sanctified us with His commandments, and commanded us to kindle the Shabbat and Yom Tov light.

Except on the last two nights of Passover, continue with:

Böruch atöh adonöy,   בָּרוּךְ אַתָּה יְיָ,

elohaynu melech hö-olöm,   אֱלֹהֵינוּ מֶלֶךְ הָעוֹלָם,

shehecheyönu v'kiy'mönu   שֶׁהֶחֱיָנוּ וְקִיְּמָנוּ

v'higi-önu liz'man ha-zeh.   וְהִגִּיעָנוּ לִזְמַן הַזֶּה:

בָּרוּךְ Blessed are You, Lord our God, King of the universe, who has granted us life, sustained us and enabled us to reach this occasion.

DID YOU KNOW?

Q: What is the significance of the Shabbat and Festival candle lighting?

A: The Shabbat candles are lit to imbue the home with the spiritual light of the Shabbat as well as provide physical festive light.

Q: It is past 18 minutes to sunset on Friday afternoon, what should I do?

A: If it is still before sunset, you should light the candles, but if it is past sunset, you should not light the candles. (Check your local Jewish calendar for the proper candle lighting times.)

Q: Why are the hands drawn around the candles and toward the face?

A: Since usually a verbal blessing must be made before the actual performance of the Mitzvah, which in this case, is the kindling of the candles, the woman therefore 'conceals' the lit candles with her hands so the candles cannot be seen, she then says the blessings and then 'reveals' the lit candles by removing her hands.

Q: Can men light the Shabbat candles?

A: If there are no women in the household who are lighting the candles then men should light the candles (following the same procedure, except that men do not draw their hands around the candles and toward the face).

Yedid Nefesh

Yedid Nefesh

Y'did nefesh öv höra-chamön,	יְדִיד נֶפֶשׁ אָב הָרַחֲמָן,
m'shoch av-d'chö el r'tzonechö,	מְשׁוֹךְ עַבְדְּךָ אֶל רְצוֹנֶךָ,
yörutz av-d'chö k'mo ayöl,	יָרוּץ עַבְדְּךָ כְּמוֹ אַיָּל,
yishta-chaveh el mul ha-dörechö,	יִשְׁתַּחֲוֶה אֶל מוּל הַדָרֶךָ,
ye-erav lo y'dido-sechö,	יֶעֱרַב לוֹ יְדִידוֹתֶיךָ,
mi-nofes tzuf v'chöl tö-am.	מִנוֹפֶת צוּף וְכָל טָעַם:
Hödur nö-eh ziv hö-olöm,	הָדוּר נָאֶה זִיו הָעוֹלָם,
nafshi cholas ahavö-sechö,	נַפְשִׁי חוֹלַת אַהֲבָתֶךָ,
önö ayl nö r'fö nö löh,	אָנָא אֵל נָא רְפָא נָא לָה,
b'har-os löh no-am zivechö,	בְּהַרְאוֹת לָה נוֹעַם זִיוֶךָ,
öz tis-chazayk v'sis-rapay,	אָז תִּתְחַזֵּק וְתִתְרַפֵּא,
v'hö-y'söh löh sim-chas olöm.	וְהָיְתָה לָה שִׂמְחַת עוֹלָם:
Vösik ye-hemu racha-mechö,	וָתִיק יֶהֱמוּ רַחֲמֶיךָ,
v'chusö nö al bayn ahu-vechö,	וְחוּסָה נָא עַל בֵּן אֲהוּבֶךָ,
ki zeh kamöh nich-sof nich-safti	כִּי זֶה כַּמָּה נִכְסוֹף נִכְסַפְתִּי
lir-os b'sif-eres uzechö, ay-leh	לִרְאוֹת בְּתִפְאֶרֶת עֻזֶּךָ, אֵלֶּה
chö-m'döh libi v'chusöh nö	חָמְדָה לִבִּי וְחוּסָה נָא
v'al tis-alöm.	וְאַל תִּתְעַלָּם:
Higö-leh nö uf'ros chavivi	הִגָּלֵה נָא וּפְרוֹס חֲבִיבִי
ölai es sukas sh'lomechö,	עָלַי אֶת סֻכַּת שְׁלוֹמֶךָ,
tö-ir eretz mik'vodechö,	תָּאִיר אֶרֶץ מִכְּבוֹדֶךָ,
nögilöh v'nis-m'chöh böch,	נָגִילָה וְנִשְׂמְחָה בָּךְ,
ma-hayr öhuv ki vö mo-ayd,	מַהֵר אָהוּב כִּי בָא מוֹעֵד,
v'chönaynu kimay olöm.	וְחָנֵּנוּ כִּימֵי עוֹלָם:

Yedid Nefesh

MAY BE SEATED

**It is customary in some communities to recite or sing
the following before *Kabbalat Shabbat* services.**

יְדִיד — Beloved of [my] soul, merciful Father, draw Your servant to Your will. [Then] Your servant will run as swiftly as a deer; he will bow before Your splendor; Your acts of affection will be sweeter than honeycomb and every pleasant taste. Glorious, resplendent One, Light of the world, my soul is lovesick for You; I beseech You, O God, pray heal it by showing it the sweetness of Your splendor. Then it will be strengthened and healed and will experience everlasting joy. O pious One, may Your mercy be aroused and have compassion upon Your beloved child. For it is long that I have been yearning to behold the glory of Your majesty. These my heart desires, so have pity and do not conceal Yourself. Reveal Yourself, my Beloved, and spread over me the shelter of Your peace. Let the earth be illuminated by Your glory; we will rejoice and exult in You. Hasten, Beloved, for the time has come; and be gracious unto us as in days of yore.

DID YOU KNOW?

This beautiful poem was originally written by the sixteenth century kabbalist, Rabbi Elazar Azikri from Tsfat, the author of Sefer Charedim.

The author expresses his intense love for God, which is heightened as we enter the spiritually charged day of the Holy Shabbat. The first letters of each of the four verses make up the essential name of God.

Kabbalat Shabbat
Welcoming the Shabbat

THE KABBALAT SHABBAT

The Kabbalat Shabbat ('welcoming the Shabbat') begins with six Psalms: 95 – 99 and 29. In ancient days, the Shabbat was welcomed in a special and joyous way, just before sunset on Friday. From the Talmud we learn, for example, that sages used to put on their best clothes and say, *"Come, let us go forth and welcome the Shabbat Queen."*

The Friday evening service begins here.
Some have the custom to first recite the *Yedid Nefesh* **(page 71).**
When a Festival or Chol HaMoed falls on Shabbat, omit the following and begin with *Mizmor L'Dovid* **(page 86).**

MAY BE SEATED

L'chu n'ran'nöh la-donöy,	לְכוּ נְרַנְּנָה לַיָי,
nöri-öh l'tzur yish-aynu	נָרִיעָה לְצוּר יִשְׁעֵנוּ:
N'kad'möh fönöv b'sodöh,	נְקַדְּמָה פָנָיו בְּתוֹדָה,
biz'miros nöri-a lo.	בִּזְמִרוֹת נָרִיעַ לוֹ:
Ki ayl gödol adonöy,	כִּי אֵל גָּדוֹל יְיָ,
umelech gödol al köl elohim.	וּמֶלֶךְ גָּדוֹל עַל כָּל אֱלֹהִים:
Asher b'yödo mech-k'ray öretz,	אֲשֶׁר בְּיָדוֹ מֶחְקְרֵי
v'so-afos hörim lo.	אָרֶץ, וְתוֹעֲפוֹת הָרִים לוֹ:
Asher lo ha-yöm v'hu ösöhu,	אֲשֶׁר לוֹ הַיָּם וְהוּא עָשָׂהוּ,
v'yabeshes yödöv yö-tzöru.	וְיַבֶּשֶׁת יָדָיו יָצָרוּ:
Bo-u nish-tachaveh v'nichrö-öh,	בֹּאוּ נִשְׁתַּחֲוֶה וְנִכְרָעָה,
niv-r'chöh lif'nay adonöy osaynu.	נִבְרְכָה לִפְנֵי יְיָ עֹשֵׂנוּ:
Ki hu elohaynu va-anachnu	כִּי הוּא אֱלֹהֵינוּ וַאֲנַחְנוּ
am mar-iso v'tzon yödo,	עַם מַרְעִיתוֹ וְצֹאן יָדוֹ,
ha-yom im b'kolo sishmö-u.	הַיּוֹם אִם בְּקֹלוֹ תִשְׁמָעוּ:
Al tak-shu l'vav'chem kim'rivöh,	אַל תַּקְשׁוּ לְבַבְכֶם כִּמְרִיבָה,
k'yom masö ba-midbör.	כְּיוֹם מַסָּה בַּמִּדְבָּר:

The Friday evening service begins here.
Some have the custom to first recite the *Yedid Nefesh* (page 71).
When a Festival or Chol HaMoed falls on Shabbat, omit the following and
begin with *Mizmor L'Dovid* (page 86).

INSIGHT

לְכוּ — In this opening Psalm of the service, our sages teach that Adam's first word after creation on Friday eve were *"Come let us prostrate ourselves and bow down; let us bend the knee before the Lord our Maker."* Adam called to every living creature to acknowledge the Creator and submit to His will.

The Psalm also notes the special relationship between God and the Jewish people; looking after us as a shepherd tends to his flock. It concludes with the miraculous exodus from Egypt, where God showed His personal concern for our people.

לְכוּ — Come, let us sing to the Lord; let us raise our voices in jubilation to the Rock of our deliverance. Let us approach Him with thanksgiving; let us raise our voices to Him in song. For the Lord is a great God, and a great King over all supernal beings; in His hands are the depths of the earth, and the heights of the mountains are His. Indeed, the sea is His, for He made it; His hands formed the dry land. Come, let us prostrate ourselves and bow down; let us bend the knee before the Lord our Maker. For He is our God, and we are the people that He tends, the flock under His [guiding] hand — even this very day, if you would but hearken to His voice! Do not harden your heart as at Merivah, as on the day at Massah in the wilderness, where your fathers

Asher nisuni avo-saychem, אֲשֶׁר נִסּוּנִי אֲבוֹתֵיכֶם,

b'chönuni, gam rö-u fö-öli. בְּחָנוּנִי, גַּם רָאוּ פָעֳלִי:

Arbö-im shönöh ökut b'dor, אַרְבָּעִים שָׁנָה אָקוּט בְּדוֹר,

vö-omar am to-ay layvöv haym וָאֹמַר עַם תֹּעֵי לֵבָב הֵם

v'haym lo yöd'u d'röchöy. וְהֵם לֹא יָדְעוּ דְרָכָי:

Asher nishba-ti v'api, אֲשֶׁר נִשְׁבַּעְתִּי בְאַפִּי,

im y'vo-un el m'nuchösi. אִם יְבֹאוּן אֶל מְנוּחָתִי:

Shiru la-donöy shir chödösh, שִׁירוּ לַיָי שִׁיר חָדָשׁ,

shiru la-donöy köl hö-öretz. שִׁירוּ לַיָי כָּל הָאָרֶץ:

Shiru ladonöy bö-r'chu sh'mo, שִׁירוּ לַיָי בָּרְכוּ שְׁמוֹ,

bas'ru mi-yom l'yom y'shu-öso. בַּשְּׂרוּ מִיּוֹם לְיוֹם יְשׁוּעָתוֹ:

Sap'ru vago-yim k'vodo, סַפְּרוּ בַגּוֹיִם כְּבוֹדוֹ,

b'chöl hö-amim nif-l'osöv. בְּכָל הָעַמִּים נִפְלְאוֹתָיו:

Ki gödol adonöy um'hulöl m'od, כִּי גָדוֹל יְיָ וּמְהֻלָּל מְאֹד,

norö hu al köl elohim. נוֹרָא הוּא עַל כָּל אֱלֹהִים:

Ki köl elohay hö-amim elilim, כִּי כָּל אֱלֹהֵי הָעַמִּים אֱלִילִים,

vadonöy shöma-yim ösöh. וַיְיָ שָׁמַיִם עָשָׂה:

Hod v'hödör l'fönöv, הוֹד וְהָדָר לְפָנָיו,

oz v'sif-eres b'mik-dösho. עֹז וְתִפְאֶרֶת בְּמִקְדָּשׁוֹ:

Hövu ladonöy mish-p'chos amim, הָבוּ לַיָי מִשְׁפְּחוֹת עַמִּים,

hövu ladonöy kövod vö-oz. הָבוּ לַיָי כָּבוֹד וָעֹז:

Hövu la-donöy k'vod sh'mo, הָבוּ לַיָי כְּבוֹד שְׁמוֹ,

s'u min-chöh uvo-u l'chatz'rosöv. שְׂאוּ מִנְחָה וּבֹאוּ לְחַצְרוֹתָיו:

Hish-tachavu ladonöy b'had'ras הִשְׁתַּחֲווּ לַיָי בְּהַדְרַת

kodesh, chilu mipönöv קֹדֶשׁ, חִילוּ מִפָּנָיו

köl hö-öretz. Im'ru vago-yim כָּל הָאָרֶץ: אִמְרוּ בַגּוֹיִם

tested Me; they tried Me, though they had seen My deeds. For forty years I quarreled with that generation; and I said, they are a people of erring hearts, they do not know My ways. So I vowed in My anger that they shall not enter My resting place.

INSIGHT

שִׁירוּ — The following Psalm begins with a call to sing God's praises. It speaks of the Messianic Era, when the extraordinary salvation will require a new kind of praise and God's glory will be recognized by the nations of the world. So too, the whole of nature will join in a chorus of praises to God.

שִׁירוּ — Sing to the Lord a new song; sing to the Lord, all the earth. Sing to the Lord, bless His Name; proclaim His deliverance from day to day. Recount His glory among the nations, His wonders among all the peoples. For the Lord is great and highly praised; He is awesome above all gods. For all the gods of the nations are naught, but the Lord made the heavens. Majesty and splendor are before Him, might and beauty in His Sanctuary. Render to the Lord, O families of nations, render to the Lord honor and might. Render to the Lord the honor due to His Name; bring an offering and come to His courtyards. Bow down to the Lord in resplendent holiness; tremble before Him, all the earth. Proclaim among the nations: "The Lord reigns"; indeed,

adonöy mölöch, af tikon	יְיָ מָלָךְ, אַף תִּכּוֹן
tayvayl bal timot, yödin	תֵּבֵל בַּל תִּמּוֹט, יָדִין
amim b'may-shörim.	עַמִּים בְּמֵישָׁרִים:
Yis-m'chu ha-shöma-yim	יִשְׂמְחוּ הַשָּׁמַיִם
v'sögayl hö-öretz, yir-am ha-yöm	וְתָגֵל הָאָרֶץ, יִרְעַם הַיָּם
um'lo-o. Ya-aloz södai v'chöl	וּמְלֹאוֹ: יַעֲלֹז שָׂדַי וְכָל
asher bo, öz y'ran'nu köl atzay	אֲשֶׁר בּוֹ, אָז יְרַנְּנוּ כָּל עֲצֵי
yö-ar. Lif'nay adonöy ki vö,	יָעַר: לִפְנֵי יְיָ כִּי בָא,
ki vö lishpot hö-öretz,	כִּי בָא לִשְׁפֹּט הָאָרֶץ,
yishpot tayvayl b'tzedek,	יִשְׁפֹּט תֵּבֵל בְּצֶדֶק,
v'amim be-emunöso.	וְעַמִּים בֶּאֱמוּנָתוֹ:

Adonöy mölöch	יְיָ מָלָךְ
tö-gayl hö-öretz,	תָּגֵל הָאָרֶץ,
yis-m'chu i-yim rabim.	יִשְׂמְחוּ אִיִּים רַבִּים:
Önön va-aröfel s'vivöv,	עָנָן וַעֲרָפֶל סְבִיבָיו,
tzedek umish-pöt m'chon	צֶדֶק וּמִשְׁפָּט מְכוֹן
kis'o. Aysh l'fönöv tay-laych.	כִּסְאוֹ: אֵשׁ לְפָנָיו תֵּלֵךְ,
us'la-hayt söviv tzöröv.	וּתְלַהֵט סָבִיב צָרָיו:
Hay-iru v'rököv tayvayl,	הֵאִירוּ בְרָקָיו תֵּבֵל,
rö-asöh va-töchel hö-öretz.	רָאֲתָה וַתָּחֵל הָאָרֶץ:
Hörim ka-donag nö-masu	הָרִים כַּדּוֹנַג נָמַסּוּ
milif'nay adonöy, mi-lif'nay	מִלִּפְנֵי יְיָ, מִלִּפְנֵי
adon köl hö-öretz.	אֲדוֹן כָּל הָאָרֶץ:
Higidu ha-shöma-yim tzidko,	הִגִּידוּ הַשָּׁמַיִם צִדְקוֹ,
v'rö-u chöl hö-amim k'vodo.	וְרָאוּ כָל הָעַמִּים כְּבוֹדוֹ:
Yay-voshu köl ov'day fesel	יֵבֹשׁוּ כָּל עֹבְדֵי פֶסֶל
ha-mis-hal'lim bö-elilim,	הַמִּתְהַלְלִים בָּאֱלִילִים,

the world is firmly established that it shall not falter; He will judge the people with righteousness. The heavens will rejoice, the earth will exult; the sea and its fullness will roar. The fields and everything therein will jubilate; then all the trees of the forest will sing. Before the Lord [they shall rejoice] for He has come, for He has come to judge the earth; He will judge the world with justice, and the nations with His truth.

INSIGHT

יְיָ מֶלָךְ — The following Psalm continues the theme of the Messianic Era. It will be an occasion for tremendous rejoicing, for the world will enter the era of fulfillment and perfection. God's reign on earth will be clearly recognized by all.

The words *"Light is sown for the righteous,"* are a metaphor for good deeds and the enhancement of Judaic values which are likened to the sowing of seeds.

These acts of light are infinite in nature and therefore the effects are enduring and benefit us and the world for all time.

יְיָ — When the Lord will reveal His kingship, the earth will exult; the multitudes of islands will rejoice. Clouds and dense darkness will surround Him; justice and mercy will be the foundation of His throne. Fire will go before Him and consume His foes all around. His lightnings will illuminate the world; the earth will see and tremble. The mountains will melt like wax before the Lord, before the Master of all the earth. The heavens will declare His justice, and all the nations will behold His glory. All who worship graven images, who take pride in idols, will be ashamed; all idol worshippers will prostrate themselves before Him. Zion will

hish-tachavu lo köl elohim. הִשְׁתַּחֲווּ לוֹ כָּל אֱלֹהִים:

Shöm'öh va-tismach tziyon, שָׁמְעָה וַתִּשְׂמַח צִיּוֹן,

vatö-gaylnö b'nos y'hudöh, וַתָּגֵלְנָה בְּנוֹת יְהוּדָה,

l'ma-an mishpötechö adonöy. לְמַעַן מִשְׁפָּטֶיךָ יְיָ:

Ki atöh adonöy elyon כִּי אַתָּה יְיָ עֶלְיוֹן

al köl hö-öretz, m'od עַל כָּל הָאָרֶץ, מְאֹד

na-alaysö al köl elohim. נַעֲלֵיתָ עַל כָּל אֱלֹהִים:

O-havay adonöy si-n'u rö, אֹהֲבֵי יְיָ שִׂנְאוּ רָע,

sho-mayr naf'shos cha-sidöv, שֹׁמֵר נַפְשׁוֹת חֲסִידָיו,

mi-yad r'shö-im ya-tzilaym. מִיַּד רְשָׁעִים יַצִּילֵם:

Or zöru-a la-tzadik, אוֹר זָרֻעַ לַצַּדִּיק,

ul'yish'ray layv sim-chöh. וּלְיִשְׁרֵי לֵב שִׂמְחָה:

Sim'chu tzadikim ba-donöy, שִׂמְחוּ צַדִּיקִים בַּיְיָ,

v'hodu l'zaycher köd-sho. וְהוֹדוּ לְזֵכֶר קָדְשׁוֹ:

Mizmor, shiru ladonöy מִזְמוֹר, שִׁירוּ לַיְיָ

shir chödösh, ki niflö-os ösöh, שִׁיר חָדָשׁ, כִּי נִפְלָאוֹת עָשָׂה,

hoshi-öh lo y'mino uz'roa köd-sho. הוֹשִׁיעָה לּוֹ יְמִינוֹ וּזְרוֹעַ קָדְשׁוֹ:

Hodi-a adonöy y'shu-öso, l'aynay הוֹדִיעַ יְיָ יְשׁוּעָתוֹ, לְעֵינֵי

ha-go-yim gilöh tzid'koso. הַגּוֹיִם גִּלָּה צִדְקָתוֹ:

Zöchar chasdo ve-emunöso l'vays זָכַר חַסְדּוֹ וֶאֱמוּנָתוֹ לְבֵית

yisrö-ayl, rö-u chöl af'say öretz, יִשְׂרָאֵל, רָאוּ כָל אַפְסֵי אָרֶץ,

ays y'shu-as elohaynu. אֵת יְשׁוּעַת אֱלֹהֵינוּ:

Höri-u ladonöy köl hö-öretz, הָרִיעוּ לַיְיָ כָּל הָאָרֶץ,

pitz'chu v'ran'nu v'zamayru. פִּצְחוּ וְרַנְּנוּ וְזַמֵּרוּ:

Zam'ru ladonöy b'chi-nor, זַמְּרוּ לַיְיָ בְּכִנּוֹר,

b'chi-nor v'kol zimröh. בְּכִנּוֹר וְקוֹל זִמְרָה:

Ba-chatzo-tz'ros v'kol shoför, בַּחֲצֹצְרוֹת וְקוֹל שׁוֹפָר,

hear and rejoice, the towns of Judah will exult, because of Your judgments, O Lord. For You, Lord, transcend all the earth; You are exceedingly exalted above all the supernal beings. You who love the Lord, hate evil; He watches over the souls of His pious ones, He saves them from the hand of the wicked. Light is sown for the righteous, and joy for the upright in heart. Rejoice in the Lord, you righteous, and extol His holy Name.

INSIGHT

מִזְמוֹר — During the long and dark exiles, we have always been confident that the Lord will 'reveal His justice' and deliver us.

The Psalm focuses on the Messianic Era when God will reveal His might and glory and we will praise His wondrous acts.

מִזְמוֹר — A Psalm. Sing to the Lord a new song, for He has performed wonders; His right hand and holy arm have wrought deliverance for Him. The Lord has made known His salvation; He has revealed His justice before the eyes of the nations. He has remembered His loving-kindness and faithfulness to the House of Israel; all, from the farthest corners of the earth, witnessed the deliverance by our God. Raise your voices in jubilation to the Lord, all the earth; burst into joyous song and chanting. Sing to the Lord with a harp, with a harp and the sound of song. With trumpets and the sound of the shofar, jubilate before the King,

hö-ri-u lif'nay ha-melech adonöy.	הָרִיעוּ לִפְנֵי הַמֶּלֶךְ יְיָ:
Yir-am ha-yöm um'lo-o,	יִרְעַם הַיָּם וּמְלֹאוֹ,
tay-vayl v'yosh'vay vöh.	תֵּבֵל וְיֹשְׁבֵי בָהּ:
N'höros yimcha-u chöf,	נְהָרוֹת יִמְחֲאוּ כָף,
yachad hörim y'ranaynu.	יַחַד הָרִים יְרַנֵּנוּ:
Lif'nay adonöy ki vö	לִפְנֵי יְיָ כִּי בָא
lish-pot hö-öretz,	לִשְׁפֹּט הָאָרֶץ,
yish-pot tay-vayl b'tzedek,	יִשְׁפֹּט תֵּבֵל בְּצֶדֶק,
v'amim b'may-shörim.	וְעַמִּים בְּמֵישָׁרִים:

Adonöy mölöch yir-g'zu amim,	יְיָ מָלָךְ יִרְגְּזוּ עַמִּים,
yo-shayv k'ruvim tönut hö-öretz.	יֹשֵׁב כְּרוּבִים תָּנוּט הָאָרֶץ:
Adonöy b'tziyon gödol,	יְיָ בְּצִיּוֹן גָּדוֹל,
v'röm hu al köl hö-amim.	וְרָם הוּא עַל כָּל הָעַמִּים:
Yodu shim'cho gödol v'norö,	יוֹדוּ שִׁמְךָ גָּדוֹל וְנוֹרָא,
ködosh hu. V'oz melech mish-pöt	קָדוֹשׁ הוּא: וְעֹז מֶלֶךְ מִשְׁפָּט
öhayv, atöh ko-nantö may-shörim,	אָהֵב, אַתָּה כּוֹנַנְתָּ מֵישָׁרִים,
mish-pöt utz'dököh b'ya-akov atöh	מִשְׁפָּט וּצְדָקָה בְּיַעֲקֹב אַתָּה
ösisö. Rom'mu adonöy elohaynu	עָשִׂיתָ: רוֹמְמוּ יְיָ אֱלֹהֵינוּ
v'hishta-chavu la-hadom rag-löv,	וְהִשְׁתַּחֲווּ לַהֲדֹם רַגְלָיו,
ködosh hu. Mosheh V'aharon	קָדוֹשׁ הוּא: מֹשֶׁה וְאַהֲרֹן
b'cho-hanöv ush'mu-ayl b'kor'ay	בְּכֹהֲנָיו וּשְׁמוּאֵל בְּקֹרְאֵי
sh'mo, kor-im el adonöy v'hu	שְׁמוֹ, קֹרְאִים אֶל יְיָ וְהוּא
ya-anaym. B'amud önön y'dabayr	יַעֲנֵם: בְּעַמּוּד עָנָן יְדַבֵּר
alayhem, shöm'ru aydosöv v'chok	אֲלֵיהֶם, שָׁמְרוּ עֵדֹתָיו וְחֹק
nösan lömo. Adonöy elohaynu	נָתַן לָמוֹ: יְיָ אֱלֹהֵינוּ
atöh anisöm, ayl nosay hö-yisö	אַתָּה עֲנִיתָם, אֵל נֹשֵׂא הָיִיתָ
lö-hem, v'nokaym al ali-losöm.	לָהֶם, וְנֹקֵם עַל עֲלִילוֹתָם:

the Lord. The sea and its fullness will roar in joy, the earth and its inhabitants. The rivers will clap their hands, the mountains will sing together. [They will rejoice] before the Lord, for He has come to judge the earth; He will judge the world with justice, and the nations with righteousness.

INSIGHT

מֶלֶךְ — Speaking of God's Holiness and the laws of justice and morality which He has established, King David recalls Moses, Aaron, and Samuel to indicate that it was thanks to such leaders that the Jewish People were able to maintain their high standards of morality and justice. We are reminded that the leaders and all the Jewish People are beholden to the same set of laws. Each and every Jew is equally obligated to fulfill the commandments of the Torah, regardless of spiritual or political positions.

יְיָ — When the Lord will reveal His kingship, the nations will tremble; the earth will quake before Him who is enthroned upon the kruvim, [before] the Lord who is in Zion, who is great and exalted above all the peoples. They will extol Your Name which is great, awesome and holy. And [they will praise] the might of the King who loves justice. You have established uprightness; You have made [the laws of] justice and righteousness in Jacob. Exalt the Lord our God, and bow down at His footstool; He is holy. Moses and Aaron among His priests, and Samuel among those who invoke His Name, would call upon the Lord and He would answer them. He would speak to them from a pillar of cloud; they observed His testimonies and the decrees which He gave them. Lord our God, You have answered them; You were a forgiving God for their sake, yet bringing retribution for their

Rom'mu adonöy elohaynu
v'hishta-chavu l'har köd-sho,
ki ködosh adonöy elohaynu.

רוֹמְמוּ יְיָ אֱלֹהֵינוּ
וְהִשְׁתַּחֲווּ לְהַר קָדְשׁוֹ,
כִּי קָדוֹשׁ יְיָ אֱלֹהֵינוּ:

Recited standing

Mizmor l'dövid, hövu la-donöy
b'nay aylim, hövu la-donöy kövod
vö-oz. Hövu la-donöy k'vod sh'mo,
hish-tachavu la-donöy b'had'ras
kodesh. Kol adonöy al hamö-yim,
ayl ha-kövod hir-im, adonöy al
ma-yim rabim. Kol adonöy
bako-ach, kol adonöy be-hödör.
Kol adonöy shovayr arözim,
va-y'sha-bayr adonöy es ar'zay
ha-l'vönon. Va-yar-kidaym k'mo
aygel, l'vönon v'siryon k'mo
ven r'aymim. Kol adonöy
cho-tzayv la-havos aysh.
Kol adonöy yöchil midbör,
yöchil adonöy midbar ködaysh.
Kol adonöy y'cholayl a-yölos
va-yechesof y'öros, uv'hay-chölo,
kulo omayr kövod.
Adonöy la-mabul yöshöv,
va-yayshev adonöy melech l'olöm.
Adonöy oz l'amo yitayn, adonöy
y'vöraych es amo va-shölom.

מִזְמוֹר לְדָוִד, הָבוּ לַיְיָ
בְּנֵי אֵלִים, הָבוּ לַיְיָ כָּבוֹד
וָעֹז: הָבוּ לַיְיָ כְּבוֹד שְׁמוֹ,
הִשְׁתַּחֲווּ לַיְיָ בְּהַדְרַת
קֹדֶשׁ: קוֹל יְיָ עַל הַמָּיִם,
אֵל הַכָּבוֹד הִרְעִים, יְיָ עַל
מַיִם רַבִּים: קוֹל יְיָ
בַּכֹּחַ, קוֹל יְיָ בֶּהָדָר:
קוֹל יְיָ שֹׁבֵר אֲרָזִים,
וַיְשַׁבֵּר יְיָ אֶת אַרְזֵי
הַלְּבָנוֹן: וַיַּרְקִידֵם כְּמוֹ
עֵגֶל, לְבָנוֹן וְשִׂרְיוֹן כְּמוֹ
בֶן רְאֵמִים: קוֹל יְיָ
חֹצֵב לַהֲבוֹת אֵשׁ:
קוֹל יְיָ יָחִיל מִדְבָּר,
יָחִיל יְיָ מִדְבַּר קָדֵשׁ:
קוֹל יְיָ יְחוֹלֵל אַיָּלוֹת
וַיֶּחֱשֹׂף יְעָרוֹת, וּבְהֵיכָלוֹ,
כֻּלּוֹ אֹמֵר כָּבוֹד:
יְיָ לַמַּבּוּל יָשָׁב,
וַיֵּשֶׁב יְיָ מֶלֶךְ לְעוֹלָם:
יְיָ עֹז לְעַמּוֹ יִתֵּן, יְיָ
יְבָרֵךְ אֶת עַמּוֹ בַשָּׁלוֹם:

↑
STANDING

own misdeeds. Exalt the Lord our God, and bow down at His holy mountain, for the Lord our God is holy.

INSIGHT

מִזְמוֹר — The following Psalm contains God's name 18 times, which is significant since it is the same as the numerical value of the Hebrew word *chai*, life. The seven repetitions of the words '*Kol Hashem*' (Voice of the Lord) in the Psalm correspond to the seven days of Creation, when everything was created by God's Word. In the Kabbalah (Jewish mysticism) we are told that when this Psalm is recited with concentration and joy, it reverberates with tremendous spiritual force in the upper spiritual worlds.

Recited standing

STANDING
מִזְמוֹר — A Psalm by David. Render to the Lord, children of the mighty, render to the Lord honor and strength. Render to the Lord the honor due to His Name; bow down to the Lord in resplendent holiness. The voice of the Lord is over the waters, the God of glory thunders; the Lord is over mighty waters. The voice of the Lord resounds with might; the voice of the Lord resounds with majesty. The voice of the Lord breaks cedars; the Lord shatters the cedars of Lebanon. He makes them leap like a calf; Lebanon and Sirion like a young wild ox. The voice of the Lord strikes flames of fire. The voice of the Lord makes the desert tremble; the Lord causes the desert of Kadesh to tremble. The voice of the Lord causes the does to calve, and strips the forests bare; and in His Sanctuary all proclaim His glory. The Lord sat [as King] at the Flood; the Lord will sit as King forever. The Lord will give strength to His people; the Lord will bless His people with peace.

Kabbalat Shabbat

Önö, b'cho-ach	אָנָּא, בְּכֹחַ
g'dulas y'min'chö,	גְּדֻלַּת יְמִינְךָ,
tatir tz'ruröh. Kabayl rinas	תַּתִּיר צְרוּרָה: קַבֵּל רִנַּת
am'chö, sag'vaynu, taha-raynu,	עַמְּךָ, שַׂגְּבֵנוּ, טַהֲרֵנוּ,
noröh. Nö gibor, dor'shay	נוֹרָא: נָא גִבּוֹר, דּוֹרְשֵׁי
yichud'chö, k'vövas shöm'raym.	יִחוּדְךָ, כְּבָבַת שָׁמְרֵם:
Bö-r'chaym taha-raym,	בָּרְכֵם טַהֲרֵם,
racha-may tzid'kös'chö tömid	רַחֲמֵי צִדְקָתְךָ תָּמִיד
göm'laym. Chasin ködosh,	גָּמְלֵם: חֲסִין קָדוֹשׁ,
b'rov tuv'chö na-hayl	בְּרוֹב טוּבְךָ נַהֵל
adö-sechö. Yöchid, gay-eh,	עֲדָתֶךָ: יָחִיד, גֵּאֶה,
l'am'chö p'nay, zoch'ray	לְעַמְּךָ פְּנֵה, זוֹכְרֵי
k'dushö-sechö. Shav-ösaynu	קְדֻשָּׁתֶךָ: שַׁוְעָתֵנוּ
kabayl, ush'ma tza-akö-saynu,	קַבֵּל, וּשְׁמַע צַעֲקָתֵנוּ,
yoday-a ta-alumos. Böruch shaym	יוֹדֵעַ תַּעֲלֻמוֹת: בָּרוּךְ שֵׁם
k'vod mal'chuso l'olöm vö-ed.	כְּבוֹד מַלְכוּתוֹ לְעוֹלָם וָעֶד:

L'chöh dodi lik'ras kalöh,	לְכָה דוֹדִי לִקְרַאת כַּלָּה,
p'nay shabös n'kab'löh.	פְּנֵי שַׁבָּת נְקַבְּלָה:
L'chöh dodi lik'ras kalöh,	לְכָה דוֹדִי לִקְרַאת כַּלָּה,
p'nay shabös n'kab'löh.	פְּנֵי שַׁבָּת נְקַבְּלָה:

Shömor v'zöchor b'dibur echöd,	שָׁמוֹר וְזָכוֹר בְּדִבּוּר אֶחָד,
hish-mi-önu ayl ha-m'yuchöd,	הִשְׁמִיעָנוּ אֵל הַמְיֻחָד,
adonöy echöd ush'mo echöd,	יְיָ אֶחָד וּשְׁמוֹ אֶחָד,
l'shaym ul'sif-eres v'lis'hilöh.	לְשֵׁם וּלְתִפְאֶרֶת וְלִתְהִלָּה:
L'chöh dodi lik'ras kalöh,	לְכָה דוֹדִי לִקְרַאת כַּלָּה,
p'nay shabös n'kab'löh.	פְּנֵי שַׁבָּת נְקַבְּלָה:

INSIGHT

אָנָּא — This prayer was composed by Rabbi Nechunya the son of Hakaneh, in the end of the 2nd Temple era, as a prayer of entreaty to God to help the Jews. Some communities recite the following paragraph silently others sing the passage in unison.

אָנָּא — We implore you, by the great power of Your right hand, release the captive. Accept the prayer of Your people; strengthen us, purify us, Awesome One. Mighty One, we beseech You, guard as the apple of the eye those who seek Your Oneness. Bless them, cleanse them; bestow upon them forever Your merciful righteousness. Powerful, Holy One, in Your abounding goodness, guide Your congregation. Only and Exalted One, turn to Your people who are mindful of Your holiness. Accept our supplication and hear our cry, You who know secret thoughts. Blessed be the name of the glory of His kingdom forever and ever.

INSIGHT

לְכָה דוֹדִי — The composer, Rabbi Shlomo Halevi Alkabetz compares the welcoming of Shabbat to the air of intense anticipation, blessing, joy, love and celebration as a groom welcomes his bride.

לְכָה — Come, my Beloved, to meet the Bride; let us welcome the Shabbat. Come, my Beloved, to meet the Bride; let us welcome the Shabbat.

שָׁמוֹר — "Observe" and "Remember," the one and only God caused us to hear in a single utterance; the Lord is One and His name is One, for renown, for glory and for praise. Come, my Beloved, to meet the Bride; let us welcome the Shabbat.

Lik'ras shabös l'chu v'nayl'chöh,	לִקְרַאת שַׁבָּת לְכוּ וְנֵלְכָה,
ki hi m'kor ha-b'röchöh,	כִּי הִיא מְקוֹר הַבְּרָכָה,
may-rosh mi-kedem	מֵרֹאשׁ מִקֶּדֶם
n'suchöh, sof ma-aseh	נְסוּכָה, סוֹף מַעֲשֶׂה
b'ma-chashövöh t'chilöh.	בְּמַחֲשָׁבָה תְּחִלָּה:
L'chöh dodi lik'ras kalöh,	לְכָה דוֹדִי לִקְרַאת כַּלָּה,
p'nay shabös n'kab'löh.	פְּנֵי שַׁבָּת נְקַבְּלָה:

Mikdash melech ir m'luchöh, kumi	מִקְדַּשׁ מֶלֶךְ עִיר מְלוּכָה, קוּמִי
kumi tz'i mitoch ha-hafaychöh,	צְאִי מִתּוֹךְ הַהֲפֵכָה,
rav löch sheves b'aymek ha-böchö,	רַב לָךְ שֶׁבֶת בְּעֵמֶק הַבָּכָא,
v'hu yachmol öla-yich chemlöh.	וְהוּא יַחֲמוֹל עָלַיִךְ חֶמְלָה:
L'chöh dodi lik'ras kalöh,	לְכָה דוֹדִי לִקְרַאת כַּלָּה,
p'nay shabös n'kab'löh.	פְּנֵי שַׁבָּת נְקַבְּלָה:

Hisna-ari may-öför kumi,	הִתְנַעֲרִי מֵעָפָר קוּמִי,
liv'shi big'day sif-artaych ami,	לִבְשִׁי בִּגְדֵי תִפְאַרְתֵּךְ עַמִּי,
al yad ben yishai bays ha-lachmi,	עַל יַד בֶּן יִשַׁי בֵּית הַלַּחְמִי,
kör'vöh el nafshi g'ölöh.	קָרְבָה אֶל נַפְשִׁי גְאָלָהּ:
L'chöh dodi lik'ras kalöh,	לְכָה דוֹדִי לִקְרַאת כַּלָּה,
p'nay shabös n'kab'löh.	פְּנֵי שַׁבָּת נְקַבְּלָה:

His-or'ri his-or'ri,	הִתְעוֹרְרִי הִתְעוֹרְרִי,
ki vö oraych kumi ori,	כִּי בָא אוֹרֵךְ קוּמִי אוֹרִי,
u-ri u-ri shir da-bayri,	עוּרִי עוּרִי שִׁיר דַּבֵּרִי,
k'vod adonöy öla-yich niglöh.	כְּבוֹד יְיָ עָלַיִךְ נִגְלָה:
L'chöh dodi lik'ras kalöh,	לְכָה דוֹדִי לִקְרַאת כַּלָּה,
p'nay shabös n'kab'löh.	פְּנֵי שַׁבָּת נְקַבְּלָה:

לִקְרַאת — Come, let us go to welcome the Shabbat, for it is the source of blessing; from the beginning, from aforetime, it was chosen; last in creation, first in [God's] thought. Come, my Beloved, to meet the Bride; let us welcome the Shabbat.

מִקְדַּש — Sanctuary of the King, royal city, arise, go forth from the ruins; too long have you dwelt in the vale of tears; He will show you abounding mercy. Come, my Beloved, to meet the Bride; let us welcome the Shabbat.

הִתְנַעֲרִי — Shake the dust off yourself, arise, don your glorious garments — my people. Through the son of Yishai of Beis Lechem, draw near to my soul and redeem it. Come, my Beloved, to meet the Bride; let us welcome the Shabbat.

הִתְעוֹרְרִי — Arouse yourself, arouse yourself, for your light has come; arise, shine. Awake, awake, utter a song; the glory of the Lord is revealed upon you. Come, my Beloved, to meet the Bride; let us welcome the Shabbat.

📖

INSIGHT

לִקְרַאת שַׁבָּת — In this stanza, the poet calls us to join him in welcoming the Shabbat. In bygone days, it was actually the custom to welcome the Shabbat under the open sky.

The poet reminds us that the Shabbat is the source of blessing. The Zohar, the classical work of Kabbalah, explains the verse *"and God blessed the seventh day"* to mean that *"all blessings of the upper and lower worlds derive from the seventh day."*

Shabbat is not only blessed, but bestows blessings and holiness on all those who observe it.

Lo say-voshi v'lo siköl'mi,   לֹא תֵבוֹשִׁי וְלֹא תִכָּלְמִי,

mah tish-tochachi umah te-hemi,   מַה תִּשְׁתּוֹחֲחִי וּמַה תֶּהֱמִי,

böch ye-chesu ani-yay ami,   בָּךְ יֶחֱסוּ עֲנִיֵּי עַמִּי,

v'niv-n'söh hö-ir al tilöh: וְנִבְנְתָה הָעִיר עַל תִּלָּהּ:

L'chöh dodi lik'ras kalöh,   לְכָה דוֹדִי לִקְרַאת כַּלָּה,

p'nay shabös n'kab'löh: פְּנֵי שַׁבָּת נְקַבְּלָה:

V'höyu lim'shisöh sho-sö-yich,   וְהָיוּ לִמְשִׁסָּה שֹׁאסָיִךְ,

v'röchaku köl m'val'ö-yich,   וְרָחֲקוּ כָּל מְבַלְּעָיִךְ,

yösis öla-yich elohö-yich,   יָשִׂישׂ עָלַיִךְ אֱלֹהָיִךְ,

kim'sos chösön al kalöh: כִּמְשׂוֹשׂ חָתָן עַל כַּלָּה:

L'chöh dodi lik'ras kalöh,   לְכָה דוֹדִי לִקְרַאת כַּלָּה,

p'nay shabös n'kab'löh: פְּנֵי שַׁבָּת נְקַבְּלָה:

Yömin us'mol tifro-tzi,   יָמִין וּשְׂמֹאל תִּפְרוֹצִי,

v'es adonöy ta-ari-tzi,   וְאֶת יְיָ תַּעֲרִיצִי,

al yad ish ben par-tzi,   עַל יַד אִישׁ בֶּן פַּרְצִי,

v'nis-m'chöh v'nögilöh: וְנִשְׂמְחָה וְנָגִילָה:

L'chöh dodi lik'ras kalöh,   לְכָה דוֹדִי לִקְרַאת כַּלָּה,

p'nay shabös n'kab'löh: פְּנֵי שַׁבָּת נְקַבְּלָה:

Turn around, greeting the "Shabbat Queen"
while reciting the following paragraph:

Bo-i v'shölom ateres ba-löh,   בּוֹאִי בְשָׁלוֹם עֲטֶרֶת בַּעְלָהּ,

gam b'rinöh (On Festivals   גַּם בְּרִנָּה (ביו״ט:

substitute: b'simchöh) uv'tzöhölöh,   בְּשִׂמְחָה) וּבְצָהֳלָה,

toch emunay am s'gulöh,   תּוֹךְ אֱמוּנֵי עַם סְגֻלָּה,

(Bow right) > bo-i chalöh,   > בּוֹאִי כַלָּה,

(Bow left) < bo-i chalöh,   < בּוֹאִי כַלָּה,

לֹא — Do not be ashamed nor confounded; why are you down-cast and why are you agitated? The afflicted of my people will find refuge in you; the city will be rebuilt on its former site. Come, my Beloved, to meet the Bride; let us welcome the Shabbat.

וְהָיוּ — Those who despoil you will be despoiled, and all who would destroy you will be far away. Your God will rejoice over you as a bridegroom rejoices over his bride. Come, my Beloved, to meet the Bride; let us welcome the Shabbat.

יָמִין — To the right and to the left you shall spread out, and the Lord you shall extol. And we shall rejoice and exult, through the man who is a descendant of Peretz. Come, my Beloved, to meet the Bride; let us welcome the Shabbat.

**Turn around, greeting the "Shabbat Queen"
while reciting the following paragraph:**

בּוֹאִי — Come in peace, O crown of her Husband, both with songs (On Festivals substitute: rejoicing) and gladness; among the faithful, the beloved people, (Bow right) > Come, O Bride, (Bow left) < come, O

DID YOU KNOW?

לְכָה דוֹדִי — This beautiful hymn was composed by the saintly kabbalist, Rabbi Shlomo Halevi Alkabetz, who died in Tsfat, in the Holy Land, in the year 1584.

He was one of the leading kabbalist in Tsfat, a contemporary of Rabbi Moshe Cordovero, Rabbi Moshe Alshich and Rabbi Yitzhak Luria also known as the Holy Ari, founder of the Lurianic School of Kabbalah. It was due to the great authority of Rabbi Luria that the hymn Lecha Dodi was adopted and included in the Kabbalat Shabbat. The author "signed" his name in the initial letters of the eight stanzas of the hymn, beginning with the letter *shin*, thus spelling out his name, Shlomo Halevi.

Kabbalat Shabbat

Turn back, bow forward, and say:

(Say silently a third time:) bo-i chalöh shabös mal-k'sö.

(וְיֹאמַר בְּלַחַשׁ פַּעַם שְׁלִישִׁית בּוֹאִי כַלָּה שַׁבָּת מַלְכְּתָא:)

L'chöh dodi lik'ras kalöh, p'nay shabös n'kab'löh.

לְכָה דוֹדִי לִקְרַאת כַּלָּה, פְּנֵי שַׁבָּת נְקַבְּלָה:

Mizmor shir l'yom ha-shabös. — מִזְמוֹר שִׁיר לְיוֹם הַשַּׁבָּת:

Tov l'hodos la-donöy, — טוֹב לְהֹדוֹת לַיְיָ,

ul'zamayr l'shim'chö elyon. — וּלְזַמֵּר לְשִׁמְךָ עֶלְיוֹן:

L'hagid ba-boker chas-dechö, — לְהַגִּיד בַּבֹּקֶר חַסְדֶּךָ,

ve-emunös'chö ba-lay-los. — וֶאֱמוּנָתְךָ בַּלֵּילוֹת:

Alay ösor va-alay növel, — עֲלֵי עָשׂוֹר וַעֲלֵי נָבֶל,

alay higö-yon b'chinor. Ki — עֲלֵי הִגָּיוֹן בְּכִנּוֹר: כִּי

simach-tani adonöy b'fö-ölechö, — שִׂמַּחְתַּנִי יְיָ בְּפָעֳלֶךָ,

b'ma-asay yödechö ara-nayn. — בְּמַעֲשֵׂי יָדֶיךָ אֲרַנֵּן:

Mah göd'lu ma-asechö adonöy, — מַה גָּדְלוּ מַעֲשֶׂיךָ יְיָ,

m'od öm'ku mach-sh'vosechö. — מְאֹד עָמְקוּ מַחְשְׁבֹתֶיךָ:

Ish ba-ar lo yaydö, — אִישׁ בַּעַר לֹא יֵדָע,

uch'sil lo yövin es zos. — וּכְסִיל לֹא יָבִין אֶת זֹאת:

Bifro-ach r'shö-im k'mo aysev, — בִּפְרֹחַ רְשָׁעִים כְּמוֹ עֵשֶׂב,

va-yö-tzi-tzu köl po-alay öven, — וַיָּצִיצוּ כָּל פֹּעֲלֵי אָוֶן,

l'hishöm'döm aday ad. — לְהִשָּׁמְדָם עֲדֵי עַד:

V'atöh mörom l'olöm adonöy. — וְאַתָּה מָרוֹם לְעֹלָם יְיָ:

Ki hinay oy-vechö adonöy, — כִּי הִנֵּה אֹיְבֶיךָ יְיָ,

ki hinay o-y'vechö yo-vaydu, — כִּי הִנֵּה אֹיְבֶיךָ יֹאבֵדוּ,

yispör'du köl po-alay öven. — יִתְפָּרְדוּ כָּל פֹּעֲלֵי אָוֶן:

Va-törem kir'aym karni, — וַתָּרֶם כִּרְאֵים קַרְנִי,

ba-losi b'shemen ra-anön. — בַּלֹּתִי בְּשֶׁמֶן רַעֲנָן:

↓ MAY BE SEATED

94

Bride, (Say silently a third time: come, O Bride; Shabbat Queen). Turn back, bow forward, and say: Come, my Beloved, to meet the Bride; let us welcome the Shabbat.

 מִזְמוֹר — A Psalm, a song for the Shabbat day. It is good to praise the Lord, and to sing to Your Name, O Most High; to proclaim Your kindness in the morning, and Your faithfulness in the nights, with a ten-stringed instrument and lyre, to the melody of a harp. For You, Lord, have gladdened me with Your deeds; I sing for joy at the works of Your hand. How great are Your works, O Lord; how very profound Your thoughts! A brutish man cannot know, a fool cannot comprehend this: When the wicked thrive like grass, and all evildoers flourish — it is in order that they may be destroyed forever. But You, Lord, are exalted forever. Indeed, Your enemies, O Lord, indeed Your enemies shall perish; all evildoers shall be scattered. But You have increased my might like that of a wild ox; I am anointed with fresh oil. My eyes have seen [the downfall of] my watchful enemies; my ears

INSIGHT

מִזְמוֹר שִׁיר — This Psalm celebrates the Shabbat Day; a day on which we cease 'creating,' as God did on the seventh day of creation. This means not doing any of thirty nine kinds of creative physical activities and their derivatives, as explained in the Code of Jewish Law.

According to our Sages, this hymn to the Shabbat was composed by Adam himself. Indeed, who can better appreciate the spirit of Shabbat and the spirit of holiness than the first man, the creation of God's own hands?

Va-tabayt ayni b'shuröy,	וַתַּבֵּט עֵינִי בְּשׁוּרָי,
ba-kömim ölai m'rayim,	בַּקָּמִים עָלַי מְרֵעִים,
tish-ma-nöh öznöy.	תִּשְׁמַעְנָה אָזְנָי:
Tzadik ka-tömör yifröch,	צַדִּיק כַּתָּמָר יִפְרָח,
k'erez ba-l'vönon yisgeh.	כְּאֶרֶז בַּלְּבָנוֹן יִשְׂגֶּה:
Sh'sulim b'vays adonöy,	שְׁתוּלִים בְּבֵית יְיָ,
b'chatz'ros elohaynu yafrichu.	בְּחַצְרוֹת אֱלֹהֵינוּ יַפְרִיחוּ:
Od y'nuvun b'sayvöh d'shaynim	עוֹד יְנוּבוּן בְּשֵׂיבָה, דְּשֵׁנִים
v'ra-ananim yihyu.	וְרַעֲנַנִּים יִהְיוּ:
L'hagid ki yöshör adonöy,	לְהַגִּיד כִּי יָשָׁר יְיָ,
tzuri v'lo avlösöh bo.	צוּרִי וְלֹא עַוְלָתָה בּוֹ:
Adonöy mölöch gay-us lö-vaysh,	יְיָ מָלָךְ גֵּאוּת לָבֵשׁ,
lö-vaysh adonöy, oz his-azör,	לָבֵשׁ יְיָ, עֹז הִתְאַזָּר,
af tikon tay-vayl bal timot.	אַף תִּכּוֹן תֵּבֵל בַּל תִּמּוֹט:
Nöchon kis-achö may-öz,	נָכוֹן כִּסְאֲךָ מֵאָז,
may-olöm ötöh. Nös'u n'höros	מֵעוֹלָם אָתָּה: נָשְׂאוּ נְהָרוֹת
adonöy, nös'u n'höros kolöm,	יְיָ, נָשְׂאוּ נְהָרוֹת קוֹלָם,
yis'u n'höros döch-yöm.	יִשְׂאוּ נְהָרוֹת דָּכְיָם:
Mikolos ma-yim rabim	מִקֹּלוֹת מַיִם רַבִּים
adirim mishb'ray yöm,	אַדִּירִים מִשְׁבְּרֵי יָם,
adir ba-mörom adonöy.	אַדִּיר בַּמָּרוֹם יְיָ:
Aydo-sechö ne-em'nu m'od,	עֵדֹתֶיךָ נֶאֶמְנוּ מְאֹד,
l'vays'chö nö-avöh kodesh,	לְבֵיתְךָ נָאֲוָה קֹדֶשׁ,
adonöy, l'orech yömim.	יְיָ, לְאֹרֶךְ יָמִים:

Mourners stand and recite the "Mourner's Kaddish" (following page).

have heard [the doom of] the wicked who rise against me. The righteous will flourish like a palm tree, grow tall like a cedar in Lebanon. Planted in the House of the Lord, they shall blossom in the courtyards of our God. They shall be fruitful even in old age; they shall be full of sap and freshness. That is to say that the Lord is just; He is my Strength, and there is no injustice in Him.

INSIGHT

יְיָ מָלָךְ — The following Psalm expresses the theme of God's sovereignty and strength. On the sixth day of Creation, God completed the "work of Creation" when He formed the first human beings and "breathed" into them a soul. Adam and Eve were the first intelligent beings, endowed with the gift of speech. Our Sages relate that the first thing Adam did was to proclaim the Creator as King of the Universe, dedicating himself and the world around him to the service of God.

יְיָ — The Lord is King; He has garbed Himself with grandeur; the Lord has robed Himself, He has girded Himself with strength; He has also established the world firmly that it shall not falter. Your throne stands firm from of old; You have existed forever. The rivers have raised, O Lord, the rivers have raised their voice; the rivers raise their raging waves. More than the sound of many waters, than the mighty breakers of the sea, is the Lord mighty on High. Your testimonies are most trustworthy; Your House will be resplendent in holiness, O Lord, forever.

Mourners stand and recite the "Mourner's Kaddish" (following page).

MOURNER'S KADDISH

It is customary for the one saying Kaddish to bow the head while reciting certain words. These words are bracketed by the following symbol: "°". When the symbol appears before a word, bow the head forward, and remain bowed until the word that ends with the same symbol, then raise the head.

Yis-gadal v'yis-kadash °sh'may rabö°. | יִתְגַּדַּל וְיִתְקַדַּשׁ °שְׁמֵהּ רַבָּא°:
    (Cong.: Ömayn.) | אמן

B'öl'mö di v'rö chir'u-say | בְּעָלְמָא דִּי בְרָא כִרְעוּתֵהּ
v'yam-lich mal'chusay, | וְיַמְלִיךְ מַלְכוּתֵהּ,
Nussach Sfard: v'yatz-mach pur-könay | נוסח ספרד: וְיַצְמַח פּוּרְקָנֵהּ
°vikö-rayv m'shi-chay°. | °וִיקָרֵב מְשִׁיחֵהּ°:
    (Cong.: Ömayn.) | אמן

B'cha-yay-chon uv'yomay-chon uv'cha-yay | בְּחַיֵּיכוֹן וּבְיוֹמֵיכוֹן וּבְחַיֵּי
d'chöl bays yisrö-ayl, ba-agölö uviz'man | דְכָל בֵּית יִשְׂרָאֵל, בַּעֲגָלָא וּבִזְמַן
köriv °v'im'ru ömayn°. | קָרִיב °וְאִמְרוּ אָמֵן°:
    (Cong.: Ömayn. Y'hay sh'may rabö | אמן. יְהֵא שְׁמֵהּ רַבָּא
    m'vörach l'ölam ul'öl'may | מְבָרַךְ לְעָלַם וּלְעָלְמֵי עָלְמַיָּא:
    öl'ma-yö. Yisböraych) | יִתְבָּרֵךְ:

°Y'hay sh'may rabö m'vörach | °יְהֵא שְׁמֵהּ רַבָּא מְבָרַךְ
l'ölam ul'öl'may öl'ma-yö. | לְעָלַם וּלְעָלְמֵי עָלְמַיָּא:
Yis-böraych° °v'yish-tabach, v'yispö-ayr, | יִתְבָּרֵךְ° °וְיִשְׁתַּבַּח, וְיִתְפָּאַר,
v'yis-romöm, v'yis-nasay, | וְיִתְרוֹמָם, וְיִתְנַשֵּׂא,
v'yis-hadör, v'yis-aleh, v'yis-halöl°, | וְיִתְהַדָּר, וְיִתְעַלֶּה, וְיִתְהַלָּל°,
°sh'may d'kud-shö b'rich hu°. | °שְׁמֵהּ דְּקֻדְשָׁא בְּרִיךְ הוּא°:
    (Cong.: Ömayn.) | אמן

L'aylö min köl bir'chösö v'shi-rösö, | לְעֵלָּא מִן כָּל בִּרְכָתָא וְשִׁירָתָא,
tush-b'chösö v'neche-mösö, | תֻּשְׁבְּחָתָא וְנֶחֱמָתָא,
da-amirön b'öl'mö, | דַּאֲמִירָן בְּעָלְמָא,
°v'im'ru ömayn°. | °וְאִמְרוּ אָמֵן°:
    (Cong.: Ömayn.) | אמן

INSIGHT

Kaddish means holy. Like most of our prayers it was composed by the Men of the Great Assembly. It is based on the wording of Ezekiel's prophecy in which *Kiddush Hashem*, the sanctification of God's name, is placed at the center of the national duty of Israel, and upon which the deliverance of the Jewish nation was dependent. The word *Amen*, that the congregation responds, is like the word *Emunah*, which means belief. By saying Amen we acknowledge that we agree with what the reader has stated.

At this particular interval, Mourner's Kaddish is recited, usually by a mourner for eleven months after the passing of a parent, and when commemorating the anniversary of the passing (yartzeit).

MOURNER'S KADDISH

It is customary for the one saying Kaddish to bow the head while reciting certain words. These words are bracketed by the following symbol: "°".
When the symbol appears before a word, bow the head forward, and remain bowed until the word that ends with the same symbol, then raise the head.

STANDING יִתְגַּדַּל — Exalted and hallowed be His great Name. (Cong.: Amen)

בְּעָלְמָא — Throughout the world which He has created according to His Will. May He establish His kingship, (Nussach Sfard: bring forth His redemption and hasten the coming of His Moshiach. (Cong.: Amen))

בְּחַיֵּיכוֹן — In your lifetime and in your days and in the lifetime of the entire House of Israel, speedily and soon, and say, Amen. (Cong.: Amen. May His great Name be blessed forever and to all eternity. Blessed)

יְהֵא — May His great Name be blessed forever and to all eternity. Blessed and praised, glorified, exalted and extolled, honored, adored and lauded be the Name of the Holy One, blessed be He. (Cong.: Amen).

לְעֵלָּא — Beyond all the blessings, hymns, praises and consolations that are uttered in the world; and say, Amen. (Cong.: Amen)

Y'hay sh'lömö rabö min sh'ma-yö, יְהֵא שְׁלָמָא רַבָּא מִן שְׁמַיָּא

v'cha-yim tovim ölaynu v'al köl yisrö-ayl וְחַיִּים טוֹבִים עָלֵינוּ וְעַל כָּל יִשְׂרָאֵל

°v'im'ru ömayn.° °וְאִמְרוּ אָמֵן°:

(Cong: Ömayn) אמן

The one reciting Kaddish takes three steps back and says the following, while bowing the head to the right, straight ahead, left, straight ahead, and bow down (as indicated):

> O-seh *shölom (*Between Rosh Hashana and > עֹשֶׂה שָׁלוֹם (בעשי״ת:

Yom Kippur: ha- shölom) bim' romöv, ^ hu הַשָּׁלוֹם) בִּמְרוֹמָיו,^ הוּא > יַעֲשֶׂה שָׁלוֹם

< ya-aseh shölom ölaynu v'al köl yisrö-ayl, עָלֵינוּ וְעַל כָּל יִשְׂרָאֵל,

°v'im'ru ömayn.° °וְאִמְרוּ אָמֵן°:

Take three steps forward.

For Nussach Ari, continue below.
For Nussach Ashkenaz, proceed to Bameh Madlikin (page 102)

K'gavnö d'inun mis-yachadin כְּגַוְנָא דְּאִנּוּן מִתְיַחֲדִין

l'aylö b'echöd uf höchi ihi לְעֵלָּא בְּאֶחָד אוּף הָכִי אִיהִי

isya-chadas l'satö b'rözö אִתְיַחֲדַת לְתַתָּא בְּרָזָא

d'echöd l'mehevay im'hon דְּאֶחָד לְמֶהֱוֵי עִמְּהוֹן

l'aylö chöd lökövayl chöd, לְעֵלָּא חָד לָקֳבֵל חָד,

kud-shö b'rich hu echöd l'aylö קוּדְשָׁא בְּרִיךְ הוּא אֶחָד לְעֵלָּא

lö y'siv al kursa-yö diköray לָא יְתִיב עַל כּוּרְסַיָּא דִּיקָרֵיהּ

ad d'is-avidas ihi b'rözö עַד דְּאִתְעֲבִידַת אִיהִי בְּרָזָא

d'echöd k'gavnö dilay l'mehevay דְּאֶחָד כְּגַוְנָא דִּילֵיהּ לְמֶהֱוֵי

echöd b'echöd. V'hö ukimnö rözö אֶחָד בְּאֶחָד. וְהָא אוּקִימְנָא רָזָא

da-adonöy echöd ush'mö echöd. דַּיְיָ אֶחָד וּשְׁמוֹ אֶחָד.

Rözö d'shabös ihi shabös רָזָא דְּשַׁבָּת אִיהִי שַׁבָּת

d'is-öchödas b'rözö d'echöd דְּאִתְאַחֲדַת בְּרָזָא דְּאֶחָד

l'mishray alöh rözö d'echöd. לְמִשְׁרֵי עֲלַהּ רָזָא דְּאֶחָד.

Tz'losö d'ma-alay shabatö d'hö צְלוֹתָא דְּמַעֲלֵי שַׁבַּתָּא דְּהָא

MAY BE SEATED

יְהֵא — May there be abundant peace from heaven, and a good life for us and for all Israel; and say, Amen. (Cong: Amen.)

עֹשֶׂה — He Who makes peace (Between Rosh Hashana and Yom Kippur say: the peace) in His heavens, may He make peace for us and for all Israel; and say, Amen. (Cong: Amen.)

INSIGHT

Before praying the Maariv service, it is customary to learn portions concerning Shabbat observances. The Sefardic custom (Nussach Ari) is to study a text from the Zohar expounding the kabbalistic meaning of the Shabbat. Ashkenazim study some of the Laws of Shabbat from the Mishna. Both are presented below.

For *Nussach Ari*, continue below.
For *Nussach Ashkenaz*, proceed to *Bemeh Madlikin* (page 102

↓
MAY BE
SEATED

כְּגַוְנָא — Just as they [the six *sefirot* (Divine attributes)] unite above into oneness, so she [*malchut* (kingship)] unites below into the mystery of oneness, so as to be with them above — unity paralleling unity. The Holy One, blessed be He, who is One above, does not take His seat upon His Throne of Glory until she enters into the mystery of oneness, similar to His, to be oneness corresponding to Oneness. This, as we have stated, is the esoteric meaning of the words: "The Lord is One, and His Name is One."

רָזָא — The mystery of Shabbat: She [the *Sefira* of *malchut*] is on Shabbat united within the mystery of Oneness so that the [supernal] mystery of Oneness may rest upon her. [This takes

is-öchödas kursa-yö yakirö	אִתְאָחֲדַת כּוּרְסַיָא יַקִּירָא
kadishö b'rözö d'echöd,	קַדִּישָׁא בְּרָזָא דְאֶחָד,
v'ista-könas l'mishray alöh malkö	וְאִתְתַּקָּנַת לְמִשְׁרֵי עֲלַהּ מַלְכָּא
kadishö ilö-ö. Kad a-yil shabatö	קַדִּישָׁא עִלָּאָה. כַּד עַיִל שַׁבַּתָּא
ihi is-yöchödas v'isp'röshas	אִיהִי אִתְיָחֲדַת וְאִתְפְּרָשַׁת
mi-sitrö öchörö. V'chöl dinin	מִסִּטְרָא אָחֳרָא. וְכָל דִּינִין
mis-ab'rin minöh v'ihi ish-t'öras	מִתְעַבְּרִין מִנַּהּ וְאִיהִי אִשְׁתְּאָרַת
b'yi-chudö din'hiru ka-dishö	בְּיִחוּדָא דִנְהִירוּ קַדִּישָׁא
v'is-at'ras b'chamö itrin l'gabay	וְאִתְעַטְּרַת בְּכַמָּה עִטְּרִין לְגַבֵּי
malkö kadishö. V'chöl shul-tönay	מַלְכָּא קַדִּישָׁא. וְכָל שׁוּלְטָנֵי
rug-zin umöray d'dinö kul'hu	רוּגְזִין וּמָארֵי דְדִינָא כֻּלְּהוּ
arkin v'is-aböru minöh. V'lays	עַרְקִין וְאִתְעַבָּרוּ מִנַּהּ. וְלֵית
shul-tönö öchörö b'chul'hu öl'min,	שׁוּלְטָנָא אָחֳרָא בְּכֻלְּהוּ עָלְמִין,
v'anpöhö n'hirin bin'hiru	וְאַנְפָּהָא נְהִירִין בִּנְהִירוּ
ilö-ö v'is-at'ras l'satö b'amö	עִלָּאָה וְאִתְעַטְּרַת לְתַתָּא בְּעַמָּא
ka-dishö. V'chul'hu mis-at'rin	קַדִּישָׁא. וְכֻלְּהוּ מִתְעַטְּרִין
b'nish-mösin chadatin. K'dayn	בְּנִשְׁמָתִין חֲדַתִּין. כְּדֵין
shay-rusö ditz'losö l'vör'chö löh	שֵׁירוּתָא דִצְלוֹתָא לְבָרְכָא לַהּ
b'chedvöh bin'hiru d'anpin.	בְּחֶדְוָה בִּנְהִירוּ דְאַנְפִּין:

Continue with HALF-KADDISH and *Bor'chu* (page 112)

"BAMEH MADLIKIN"
Those following *Nussach Ashkenaz* recite the following.

Bameh madlikin uva-meh ayn ma-dlikin,	א) בַּמֶּה מַדְלִיקִין וּבַמֶּה אֵין מַדְלִיקִין,
ayn ma-dlikin lo v'lechesh v'lo v'chosen	אֵין מַדְלִיקִין לֹא בְלֶכֶשׁ וְלֹא בְחֹסֶן
v'lo v'chalöch, v'lo bif-silas hö-i-dön,	וְלֹא בְכַלָּךְ, וְלֹא בִּפְתִילַת הָאִידָן,
v'lo bif-silas ha-midbör, v'lo vi-rokö	וְלֹא בִּפְתִילַת הַמִּדְבָּר, וְלֹא בִירוֹקָה
she-al p'nai ha-mö-yim, lo v'zefes	שֶׁעַל פְּנֵי הַמָּיִם, לֹא בְזֶפֶת
v'lo v'sha-avöh, v'lo v'shemen kik,	וְלֹא בְשַׁעֲוָה, וְלֹא בְשֶׁמֶן קִיק,

place during] the Maariv Prayer of Shabbat eve, for then the holy Throne of Glory merges into the mystery of Oneness, and is ready for the holy transcendent King to rest upon it. As Shabbat arrives, she merges into Oneness, and is separated from the "other side," and all strict judgments are severed from her. And she remains in unity with the holy light, and crowns herself with many crowns for the holy King. Then all powers of wrath and all adversaries flee from her and vanish, and no other power reigns in any of the worlds. Her countenance is irradiated with a supernal light, and she crowns herself here below with the holy people, all of whom are crowned with new souls. Then the commencement of the prayer is to bless her with joy and radiant countenance.

Continue with HALF-KADDISH and *Bor'chu* (page 112)

INSIGHT

כְּגַוְנָא — The Shabbat hymns are followed by an excerpt in Aramaic from the Zohar (the classical work of Jewish mysticism), beginning with the word K'gavna.

It is a poetic passage, describing the holiness of Shabbat in the complex and poetic language of Kabbalah.

"BAMEH MADLIKIN"
Those following nussach Ahkanaz recite the following.

בַּמֶּה — With what may one light a lamp on the Shabbat and with what may one not light? One may not light

v'lo v'shemen s'rayföh, v'lo v'alyöh,
v'lo v'chay-lev nöchum ha-mödi omayr
ma-dlikin b'chay-lev m'vushöl
va-chachömim om'rim echöd m'vushöl
v'echöd she-ayno m'vushöl ayn ma-dlikin
bo. Ayn ma-dlikin b'shemen s'rayföh
b'yom tov, rabi yishmö-ayl omayr ain
ma-dlikin b'it-rön mi-p'nay k'vod
ha-shabös, va-chachömim ma-tirim
b'chöl hash-mönim, b'shemen
sum-s'min b'shemen egozim
b'shemen tz'nonos, b'shemen dögim,
b'shemen paku-os, b'itrön u-v'nayft,
rabi tarfon omayr ayn ma-dlikin
elö v'shemen zayis bil'vöd.
Köl ha-yotzay min hö-aytz ayn
ma-dlikin bo elö fish-tön, v'chöl
hayotzy min hö-aytz ayno mi-tamay
tum'as ohölim elö fishtön, p'silas
ha-beged she-kiplöh v'lo hiv-havövöh,
rabi eli-ezer omayr t'may-öh hi v'ayn
ma-dlikin böh, rabi akivö omayr t'horöh
hi umad'likin vöh. Lo yikov ödöm
sh'fo-feres shel baytzöh vimal-enöh
shemen v'yit-nenöh al pi ha-nayr
bish-vil shet'hay m'natefes va-afilu hi
shel cheres v'rabi yehodöh matir, avöl
im chibro ha-yotzayr mit'cholöh mutör
mip-nay she-hu k'li echöd. Lo yima-lay
ödöm k'öröh shemen v'yit-nenöh b'tzad
ha-nayr v'yitayn rosh ha-p'silöh b'sochöh
bish-vil shet'hay sho-eves v'rabi yehudöh
matir. Ha-m'chabeh es hanayr mip'nay
she-hu misyöray mip-nay goyim,
mip-nay listim, mip-nay ruach rö-öh,

וְלֹא בְשֶׁמֶן שְׂרֵפָה, וְלֹא בְאַלְיָה,
וְלֹא בְחֵלֶב, נַחוּם הַמָּדִי אוֹמֵר
מַדְלִיקִין בְּחֵלֶב מְבֻשָּׁל,
וַחֲכָמִים אוֹמְרִים אֶחָד מְבֻשָּׁל
וְאֶחָד שֶׁאֵינוֹ מְבֻשָּׁל אֵין מַדְלִיקִין
בּוֹ: ב) אֵין מַדְלִיקִין בְּשֶׁמֶן שְׂרֵפָה
בְּיוֹם טוֹב, רַבִּי יִשְׁמָעֵאל אוֹמֵר אֵין
מַדְלִיקִין בְּעִטְרָן מִפְּנֵי כְּבוֹד
הַשַּׁבָּת, וַחֲכָמִים מַתִּירִים
בְּכָל הַשְּׁמָנִים, בְּשֶׁמֶן
שֻׁמְשְׁמִין, בְּשֶׁמֶן אֱגוֹזִים,
בְּשֶׁמֶן צְנוֹנוֹת, בְּשֶׁמֶן דָּגִים,
בְּשֶׁמֶן פַּקּוּעוֹת, בְּעִטְרָן וּבְנֶפְט,
רַבִּי טַרְפוֹן אוֹמֵר אֵין מַדְלִיקִין
אֶלָּא בְשֶׁמֶן זַיִת בִּלְבָד:
ג) כָּל הַיּוֹצֵא מִן הָעֵץ אֵין
מַדְלִיקִין בּוֹ אֶלָּא פִּשְׁתָּן, וְכָל
הַיּוֹצֵא מִן הָעֵץ אֵינוֹ מְטַמֵּא
טֻמְאַת אֹהָלִים אֶלָּא פִשְׁתָּן, פְּתִילַת
הַבֶּגֶד שֶׁקִּפְּלָהּ וְלֹא הִבְהֲבָהּ,
רַבִּי אֱלִיעֶזֶר אוֹמֵר טְמֵאָה הִיא וְאֵין
מַדְלִיקִין בָּהּ, רַבִּי עֲקִיבָא אוֹמֵר טְהוֹרָה
הִיא וּמַדְלִיקִין בָּהּ: ד) לֹא יִקֹּב אָדָם
שְׁפוֹפֶרֶת שֶׁל בֵּיצָה וִימַלְאֶנָּה
שֶׁמֶן וְיִתְּנֶנָּה עַל פִּי הַנֵּר
בִּשְׁבִיל שֶׁתְּהֵא מְנַטֶּפֶת וַאֲפִלּוּ הִיא
שֶׁל חֶרֶס וְרַבִּי יְהוּדָה מַתִּיר, אֲבָל
אִם חִבְּרָהּ הַיּוֹצֵר מִתְּחִלָּה מֻתָּר
מִפְּנֵי שֶׁהוּא כְּלִי אֶחָד: לֹא יְמַלֵּא
אָדָם קְעָרָה שֶׁמֶן וְיִתְּנֶנָּה בְּצַד
הַנֵּר וְיִתֵּן רֹאשׁ הַפְּתִילָה בְּתוֹכָהּ
בִּשְׁבִיל שֶׁתְּהֵא שׁוֹאֶבֶת וְרַבִּי יְהוּדָה
מַתִּיר: ה) הַמְכַבֶּה אֶת הַנֵּר מִפְּנֵי
שֶׁהוּא מִתְיָרֵא מִפְּנֵי גוֹיִם,
מִפְּנֵי לִסְטִים, מִפְּנֵי רוּחַ רָעָה,

with bast of ceder, uncombed flax, silk, bast of willow, desert silk, nor seaweed. Nor may one light with pitch, wax, cottonseed oil, oil that must be destroyed by fire, fat from sheeps' tails, nor with tallow. Nachman from Mede says: One may light with boiled tallow. But the sages say: Whether it is boiled or not, we may not light with it.

אֵין — One may not light on festivals with oil that must be destroyed by fire. Rabbi Yishmael says: One may not light with tar, out of respect for the honor of the Shabbat. But the Sages permit lighting with the following oils: sesame oil, nut oil, radish oil, fish oil, gourd oil, tar, or naphta. Rabbi Tarfon says: One may light only with olive oil.

כָּל — One may not light with any product of a tree, except linen. And tree by-products do not become impure from tumas oholim (contamination from sheltering with an impure object) , with the exception of linen. If a wick was made from a cloth that was twisted but not singed, Rabbi Eliezer says: It can become impure and thus we may not light with it. Rabbi Akiva says: It does not become impure and thus we may light with it.

לֹא — One may not pierce an eggshell, fill it with oil, and place it over the mouth or a lamp so that the oil may drip down, even if the lamp is made from earthenware. Rabbi Yehuda permits this. But if the candle-maker created it so from the outset, it is permitted because it is now a single vessel. One may not fill a bowl with oil and lay it next to the lamp, placing the end of the wick from the candle into it so that it will draw fuel. Rabbi Yehudah permits this.

הַמְכַבֶּה — If one extinguishes a lamp due to fear of idolaters, bandits, malevolent spirits, or to help an ill person fall asleep, he is not libel. But if he does so to spare the lamp, to spare the oil, to spare the wick he is libel. Rabbi Yose absolves in all those cases, except that of the wick, because he produces charcoal.

mip-nay hacholeh she-yishön pötur, מִפְּנֵי הַחוֹלֶה שֶׁיִּשָׁן פָּטוּר,

k'chös al ha-nayr k'chös al ha-shemen, כְּחָס עַל הַנֵּר כְּחָס עַל הַשֶּׁמֶן,

k'cöhos al hap-silöh cha-yöv v'rabi yosay כְּחָס עַל הַפְּתִילָה חַיָּב וְרַבִּי יוֹסֵי

potayr b'chulön chutz min ha-psilöh, פּוֹטֵר בְּכֻלָּן חוּץ מִן הַפְּתִילָה

mip-nay she-hu osöh pechöm: מִפְּנֵי שֶׁהוּא עוֹשֶׂה פֶּחָם:

Al shölosh avayros nöshim may-sos ו) עַל שָׁלֹשׁ עֲבֵירוֹת נָשִׁים מֵתוֹת

bish-as laydöson, al she-aynon z'hiros בִּשְׁעַת לֵידָתָן, עַל שֶׁאֵינָן זְהִירוֹת

b'nidöh b'chalöh uv'had'lökas ha-nayr. בְּנִדָּה בְּחַלָּה וּבְהַדְלָקַת הַנֵּר:

Shloshöh d'vörim tzörich ödöm lomar ז) שְׁלֹשָׁה דְבָרִים צָרִיךְ אָדָם לוֹמַר

b'soch bayso erev shabös im chashaychöh, בְּתוֹךְ בֵּיתוֹ עֶרֶב שַׁבָּת עִם חֲשֵׁכָה,

isartem, ayravtem, hadliku es hanayr, עִשַּׂרְתֶּם, עֵרַבְתֶּם, הַדְלִיקוּ אֶת הַנֵּר,

söfayk cha-shaychö söfayk aynö cha- סָפֵק חֲשֵׁכָה, סָפֵק אֵינָהּ חֲשֵׁכָה,

shaychöh, ayn m'asrin as hava-döy, v'ayn אֵין מְעַשְּׂרִין אֶת הַוַּדַּאי, וְאֵין

matbilin es hakaylim, v'ayn madlikin מַטְבִּילִין אֶת הַכֵּלִים, וְאֵין מַדְלִיקִין

es hanayros, avöl m'asrin es had-möy, אֶת הַנֵּרוֹת, אֲבָל מְעַשְּׂרִין אֶת הַדְּמַאי,

um'örvin v'tom'nin es ha-chamin. וּמְעָרְבִין וְטוֹמְנִין אֶת הַחַמִּין:

Tanyö chananyö omayr, chayöv ödöm תַּנְיָא חֲנַנְיָא אוֹמֵר, חַיָּב אָדָם

l'mash-maysh biv'gödöv b'erev shabös im לְמַשְׁמֵשׁ בְּבְגָדָיו בְּעֶרֶב שַׁבָּת עִם

cha-shaychö shemö yish-kach v'yaytzay, חֲשֵׁכָה שֶׁמָּא יִשְׁכַּח וְיֵצֵא,

ömar rav yosayf hilch'sö rab'sö l'shab'sö. אָמַר רַב יוֹסֵף הִלְכְתָא רַבְּתָא לְשַׁבְּתָא:

Ömar rabi el-özör ömar rabi cha-ninö, אָמַר רַבִּי אֶלְעָזָר אָמַר רַבִּי חֲנִינָא,

talmiday cha-chömim marbim תַּלְמִידֵי חֲכָמִים מַרְבִּים

shölom bö-olöm, she-ne-emar v'chöl שָׁלוֹם בָּעוֹלָם, שֶׁנֶּאֱמַר וְכָל

bö-na-yich limuday adonöy v'rav בָּנַיִךְ לִמּוּדֵי יְיָ, וְרַב

sh'lom bönö-yich. Al tikray bönö-yich, שְׁלוֹם בָּנָיִךְ: אַל תִּקְרֵי בָּנָיִךְ,

elö bonö-yich. Shölom röv l'ohavai אֶלָּא בּוֹנָיִךְ: שָׁלוֹם רָב לְאֹהֲבֵי

sorösechö, v'ayn lömo mich-shol. תוֹרָתֶךָ, וְאֵין לָמוֹ מִכְשׁוֹל:

Y'hi shölom b'chay-laych, shalvöh יְהִי שָׁלוֹם בְּחֵילֵךְ, שַׁלְוָה

b'arm'nosöyich. L'ma-an achai v'rai-öi בְּאַרְמְנוֹתָיִךְ: לְמַעַן אַחַי וְרֵעָי

adab'röh nö shölom böch. L'ma-an bays אֲדַבְּרָה נָּא שָׁלוֹם בָּךְ: לְמַעַן בֵּית

adonöy elohaynu, avak-shöh tov löch. יְיָ אֱלֹהֵינוּ, אֲבַקְשָׁה טוֹב לָךְ:

Adonöy oz l'amo yitayn, adonöy יְיָ עֹז לְעַמּוֹ יִתֵּן, יְיָ

y'vöraych es amo vashölom. יְבָרֵךְ אֶת עַמּוֹ בַשָּׁלוֹם:

Mourners stand and recite *Kaddish D'Rabanan* (page 60).

עַל — For three transgressions women die during child-bearing labor: for being careless regarding the laws of Niddah (family purity), the tithe from the dough, and kindling the [Shabbat] light.

שְׁלֹשָׁה — A person must say three things in his home on the eve of Shabbat before dark: "Have you tithed? Have you prepared the Eruv? Kindle the [Shabbat] lights." If there is doubt whether it is dark or not dark, one may not tithe definitely untithed produce, one may not immerse vessels, and one may not kindle the lights; but one may tithe questionable produce, make an Eruv, and insulate hot food.

תַּנְיָא — It has been taught, Rabbi Chanania said: A person must check his clothing (i.e. pockets) on the eve of Shabbat just before dark, for he may forget and go out (thus carrying objects on the Shabbat). Rav Yosef said: This is a significant law regarding the Shabbat.

אָמַר — Rabbi Elazar said in the name of Rabbi Chanina: Torah scholars increase peace in the world, for it is said: And all your children shall be learners of the [Torah of the] Lord, and great will be the peace of banayich (your children). Do not read banayich, but bonayich (your builders). Those who love Your Torah have abundant peace, and there is no stumbling for them. May there be peace within your walls, serenity within your mansions. For the sake of my brethren and friends, I ask that there be peace within you. For the sake of the House of the Lord our God, I seek your well-being. The Lord will give strength to His people; the Lord will bless His people with peace.

Mourners stand and recite *Kaddish D'Rabanan* (page 60).

Maariv
L'Shabbat V'Yom Tov

Evening Service for Shabbat and Festivals

INSIGHT

The three daily prayers — *Shacharit*, *Mincha*, and *Maariv* — were originally instituted by our three Patriarchs, Abraham, Isaac, and Jacob respectively.

As a result of the destruction of the first Holy Temple and the subsequent dispersion and assimilation, the sages, beginning with Ezra the Scribe, saw the need to establish a formal prayer service, the core being the Amidah prayer, which was simple, lucid, yet eloquent.

The *Maariv* service consists of:

1. *Shema* — with two blessings before and two after it.

2 *Amidah* — Silent central prayer.

3. *Vay'chulu* — Special Shabbat portions.

4. *Olaynu* — Concluding prayer

FOR SHABBAT

When praying with 10 Jewish males over the age of 13 (a Minyan), the leader begins with HALF KADDISH (following page) followed with *BOR'CHU*.

FOR PESACH, SHAVOUT, OR SUKKOT

The service begins on the bottom of this page.

"VELOMAR BOR'CHU"

Recited when praying alone or without a Minyan.
It is meant to substitute for the *Bor'chu* call to prayer,
which can only be recited with a Minyan.

V'lomar bö-r'chu es adonöy	וְלוֹמַר בָּרְכוּ אֶת יְיָ
ha-m'voröch, es daikö dö shabös	הַמְבוֹרָךְ, אֶת דַּיְקָא דָא שַׁבָּת
d'ma-alay sha-batö. Böruch adonöy	דְּמֵעֲלֵי שַׁבַּתָּא: בָּרוּךְ יְיָ
ha-m'voröch dö apiku d'vir-chö-ön	הַמְבֹרָךְ דָּא אַפִּיקוּ דְּבִרְכָאן
mim'korö d'cha-yay va-asar d'nöfik	מִמְּקוֹרָא דְּחַיֵּי וַאֲתַר דְּנָפִיק
minay köl shak-yu l'ashkö-ö l'cholö.	מִנֵּיהּ כָּל שַׁקְיוּ לְאַשְׁקָאָה לְכֹלָּא.
Uv'gin d'ihu m'korö b'rözö d'ös	וּבְגִין דְּאִיהוּ מְקוֹרָא בְּרָזָא דְאָת
ka-yömö körinön lay ha-m'voröch	קַיָּמָא קָרִינָן לֵיהּ הַמְבֹרָךְ
ihu mabu-ö d'vayrö v'chayvön	אִיהוּ מַבּוּעָא דְּבֵירָא וְכֵיוָן
dim'tö-ön hösöm hö chul'hu l'olöm	דְּמִטְאָן הָתָם הָא כֻלְּהוּ לְעוֹלָם
vö-ed. V'dö ihu Böruch adonöy	וָעֶד. וְדָא אִיהוּ בָּרוּךְ יְיָ
ha-m'voröch l'olöm vö-ed.	הַמְבֹרָךְ לְעוֹלָם וָעֶד:

Continue with *"Böruch Atöh"* (page 114)

On Pesach, Shavout, or Sukkot

Weekday festival services begin here. When a Festival occurs on Shabbat, the services begin earlier with *"Mizmor L'dovid"* (A Psalm by David) on page 86.

Shir ha-ma-alos, hinay bö-r'chu es adonöy	שִׁיר הַמַּעֲלוֹת, הִנֵּה בָּרְכוּ אֶת יְיָ
köl av'day adonöy hö-öm'dim b'vays	כָּל עַבְדֵי יְיָ הָעֹמְדִים בְּבֵית
adonöy ba-laylos. S'u y'daychem kodesh,	יְיָ בַּלֵּילוֹת: שְׂאוּ יְדֵכֶם קֹדֶשׁ,
uvö-r'chu es adonöy. Y'vö-rech'chö adonöy	וּבָרְכוּ אֶת יְיָ: יְבָרֶכְךָ יְיָ
mitziyon, osay shöma-yim vö-öretz.	מִצִּיּוֹן, עֹשֵׂה שָׁמַיִם וָאָרֶץ:
Yomöm y'tza-veh adonöy chasdo	יוֹמָם יְצַוֶּה יְיָ חַסְדּוֹ
uvalai-löh shiroh imi t'filöh l'ayl cha-yöy.	וּבַלַּיְלָה שִׁירֹה עִמִּי תְּפִלָּה לְאֵל חַיָּי:

FOR SHABBAT
When praying with 10 Jewish males over the age of 13 (a Minyan), the leader
begins with HALF KADDISH (following page) followed with *BOR'CHU*.

FOR PESACH, SHAVOUT, OR SUKKOT
The service begins on the bottom of this page.

"VELOMAR BOR'CHU"
**Recited when praying alone or without a Minyan.
It is meant to substitute for the** *Bor'chu* **call to prayer,
which can only be recited with a Minyan.**

וְלוֹמַר — And say: "Bless the Lord who is blessed". The word "the" refers
to Shabbat eve. "Blessed be the Lord who is blessed" is that which elicits
the blessings from the source of life and the place from whence issue all
streams to irrigate all things. And because it is the source, the mystery of
the "sign," it is called "the blessed." It is the stream of the wellspring. And
since they [the blessings] reach there, they all [flow] "for all eternity." And
this is [the meaning of]: "Blessed be the Lord who is blessed for all eternity."

Continue with *"Blessed are You"* **(page 114)**

On Pesach, Shavout, or Sukkot
Weekday festival services begin here. When a Festival occurs
on Shabbat, the services begin earlier with *"Mizmor L'dovid"*
(A Psalm by David) on page 86.

שִׁיר — A Song of Ascents. Bless the Lord, all servants of the Lord who
stand in the house of the Lord at night. Raise your hands in holiness and
bless the Lord. May the Lord, Maker of heaven and earth, bless you from
Zion. By day the Lord ordains His kindness, and at night His song is with

Us'shu-as tzadikim may-adonöy וּתְשׁוּעַת צַדִּיקִים מֵיְיָ

mö-uzöm b'ays tzöröh. Va-ya-z'raym מָעוּזָם בְּעֵת צָרָה: וַיַּעְזְרֵם

adonöy va-y'fal'taym, y'fal'taym יְיָ וַיְפַלְּטֵם, יְפַלְּטֵם

may-r'shö-im v'yoshi-aym, ki chösu vo. מֵרְשָׁעִים וְיוֹשִׁיעֵם, כִּי חָסוּ בוֹ:

Say three times: Adonöy tz'vö-os imönu, יְיָ צְבָאוֹת עִמָּנוּ

misgöv lönu elohay ya-akov selöh. מִשְׂגָּב לָנוּ אֱלֹהֵי יַעֲקֹב סֶלָה ג׳׳פ:

Say three times: Adonöy tzvö-os יְיָ צְבָאוֹת

ash-ray ödöm botay-ach böch. אַשְׁרֵי אָדָם בֹּטֵחַ בָּךְ ג׳׳פ:

Say three times: Adonöy ho-shi-öh, יְיָ הוֹשִׁיעָה,

ha-melech ya-ananyu v'yom kör'aynu. הַמֶּלֶךְ יַעֲנֵנוּ בְיוֹם קָרְאֵנוּ ג׳׳פ:

All rise. The leader recites Half-Kaddish, followed by "*Bö-r'chu.*"

HALF-KADDISH

↑ STANDING

Yis-gadal v'yis-kadash °sh'may rabö°. יִתְגַּדַּל וְיִתְקַדַּשׁ °שְׁמֵהּ רַבָּא°:

(Cong.: Ömayn.) אמן

B'öl'mö di v'rö chir'u-say בְּעָלְמָא דִּי בְרָא כִרְעוּתֵהּ

v'yam-lich mal'chusay, וְיַמְלִיךְ מַלְכוּתֵהּ,

Nussach Sfard: v'yatz-mach pur-könay נוסח ספרד: וְיַצְמַח פּוּרְקָנֵהּ

°vikö-rayv m'shi-chay°. °וִיקָרֵב מְשִׁיחֵהּ°:

(Cong.: Ömayn.) אמן

B'cha-yay-chon uv'yomay-chon uv'cha-yay בְּחַיֵּיכוֹן וּבְיוֹמֵיכוֹן וּבְחַיֵּי

d'chöl bays yisrö-ayl, ba-agölö uviz'man דְכָל בֵּית יִשְׂרָאֵל, בַּעֲגָלָא וּבִזְמַן

köriv °v'im'ru ömayn°. קָרִיב °וְאִמְרוּ אָמֵן°:

(Cong.: Ömayn. Y'hay sh'may rabö m'vörach אמן. יְהֵא שְׁמֵהּ רַבָּא מְבָרַךְ

l'ölam ul'öl'may öl'ma-yö. לְעָלַם וּלְעָלְמֵי עָלְמַיָּא:

Yisböraych) יִתְבָּרַךְ:

°Y'hay sh'may rabö m'vörach °יְהֵא שְׁמֵהּ רַבָּא מְבָרַךְ

l'ölam ul'öl'may öl'ma-yö. לְעָלַם וּלְעָלְמֵי עָלְמַיָּא:

Yis-böraych° °v'yish-tabach, v'yispö-ayr, יִתְבָּרַךְ° °וְיִשְׁתַּבַּח, וְיִתְפָּאַר,

v'yis-romöm, v'yis-nasay, וְיִתְרוֹמַם, וְיִתְנַשֵּׂא,

v'yis-hadör, v'yis-aleh, v'yis-halöl°, °sh'may וְיִתְהַדָּר, וְיִתְעַלֶּה, וְיִתְהַלָּל°, °שְׁמֵהּ

d'kud-shö b'rich hu°. דְּקֻדְשָׁא בְּרִיךְ הוּא°:

(Cong.: Ömayn.) אמן

me, a prayer to the God of my life. The deliverance of the righteous is from the Lord; He is their strength in time of distress. The Lord helps them and delivers them; He delivers them from the wicked and saves them, because they have put their trust in Him. Say three times: The Lord of hosts is with us; the God of Jacob is our stronghold forever. Say three times: Lord of hosts, happy is the man who trusts in You. Say three times: Lord, deliver us; may the King answer us on the day we call.

All rise. The leader recites Half-Kaddish, followed by "Bö-r'chu."

INSIGHT

בָּרְכוּ — The Kabbalah explains "*All sacred acts require summoning,*" meaning that all mitzvot require proper preparation — including prayer. As we have to be in the right frame of mind, we take time to pause and consider the significance of the mitzvah we're about to perform. Historically, the public prayers began with the blessings of the Shema. Therefore when the congregation would gather for the prayers, the leader would 'summon' the congregation with *Bor'chu*, a call to praise God, which is also a call to prepare for prayer. We respond by acknowledging the sanctity of God for all eternity.

STANDING

HALF-KADDISH

יִתְגַּדַּל — Exalted and hallowed be His great Name. (Cong.: Amen)

בְּעָלְמָא — Throughout the world which He has created according to His Will. May He establish His kingship, (Nussach Sfard: bring forth His redemption and hasten the coming of His Moshiach. (Cong.: Amen))

בְּחַיֵּיכוֹן — In your lifetime and in your days and in the lifetime of the entire House of Israel, speedily and soon, and say, Amen. (Cong.: Amen. May His great Name be blessed forever and to all eternity. Blessed)

יְהֵא — May His great Name be blessed forever and to all eternity. Blessed and praised, glorified, exalted and extolled, honored, adored and lauded be the Name of the Holy One, blessed be He. (Cong.: Amen).

L'aylö min köl bir'chösö v'shi-rösö,   לְעֵלָּא מִן כָּל בִּרְכָתָא וְשִׁירָתָא,

tush-b'chösö v'neche-mösö,   תֻּשְׁבְּחָתָא וְנֶחֱמָתָא,

da-amirön b'öl'mö,   דַּאֲמִירָן בְּעָלְמָא,

°v'im'ru ömayn°.   °וְאִמְרוּ אָמֵן°:

(Cong.: Ömayn.)   אמן

The leader bows his head and recites:

Bö-r'chu es adonöy ha-m'voröch.   בָּרְכוּ אֶת יְיָ הַמְבֹרָךְ:

↑ STANDING

Congregation bows their head and recites the following, follwed by the leader:

Böruch adonöy ha-m'voröch   בָּרוּךְ יְיָ הַמְבֹרָךְ

l'olöm vö-ed.   לְעוֹלָם וָעֶד:

Böruch atöh adonöy   בָּרוּךְ אַתָּה יְיָ

↓ MAY BE SEATED

elo-haynu melech hö-olöm,   אֱלֹהֵינוּ מֶלֶךְ הָעוֹלָם,

asher bid'vöro ma-ariv arövim,   אֲשֶׁר בִּדְבָרוֹ מַעֲרִיב עֲרָבִים,

b'chöch-möh posay-ach sh'örim,   בְּחָכְמָה פּוֹתֵחַ שְׁעָרִים,

uvis-vunöh m'sha-neh itim,   וּבִתְבוּנָה מְשַׁנֶּה עִתִּים,

umacha-lif es ha-z'manim,   וּמַחֲלִיף אֶת הַזְּמַנִּים,

um'sader es ha-kochövim,   וּמְסַדֵּר אֶת הַכּוֹכָבִים,

b'mish-m'rosay-hem böröki-a,   בְּמִשְׁמְרוֹתֵיהֶם בָּרָקִיעַ,

kir'tzono. Boray yom völöy-löh,   כִּרְצוֹנוֹ. בּוֹרֵא יוֹם וָלָיְלָה,

golayl or mip'nay cho-shech,   גּוֹלֵל אוֹר מִפְּנֵי חֹשֶׁךְ,

v'cho-shech mip'nay or,   וְחֹשֶׁךְ מִפְּנֵי אוֹר,

uma-avir yom umay-vi löy-löh,   וּמַעֲבִיר יוֹם וּמֵבִיא לָיְלָה,

umavdil bayn yom uvayn löy-löh,   וּמַבְדִּיל בֵּין יוֹם וּבֵין לָיְלָה,

adonöy tzvö-os sh'mo. Böruch   יְיָ צְבָאוֹת שְׁמוֹ. בָּרוּךְ

atöh adonöy, ha-ma-ariv arövim.   אַתָּה יְיָ, הַמַּעֲרִיב עֲרָבִים:

לְעֵלָּא — Beyond all the blessings, hymns, praises and consolations that are uttered in the world; and say, Amen. (Cong.: Amen)

STANDING

The leader bows his head and recites:

בָּרְכוּ — Bless the Lord who is blessed.

Congregation bows their head and recites the following, follwed by the leader:

בָּרוּךְ — Blessed be the Lord who is blessed for all eternity.

MAY BE SEATED

בָּרוּךְ — Blessed are You, Lord our God, King of the universe, who by His word causes the evenings to become dark. With wisdom He opens the [heavenly] gates; with understanding He changes the periods [of the day], varies the times, and arranges the stars in their positions in the sky according to His will. He creates day and night; He rolls away light before darkness and darkness before light; He causes the day to pass and brings on the night, and separates between day and night; the Lord of hosts is His Name. Blessed are You Lord, who causes the evenings to become dark.

INSIGHT

בָּרוּךְ — This is the first blessing before the Shema. With this blessing we acknowledge the awesome change from day to night. The opening verse refers to the first evening which God created, as it is written in Genesis, *"And it was evening, and it was morning, one day."* What may seem as a 'natural' and ordinary change from day to night and from night to day, from summer to winter, and so on, is really a wonderful act of Creation by God, not something to be taken for granted.

Ahavas olöm bays yisrö-ayl	אַהֲבַת עוֹלָם בֵּית יִשְׂרָאֵל
am'chö öhövtö, toröh umitzvos,	עַמְּךָ אָהָבְתָּ, תּוֹרָה וּמִצְוֹת,
chukim umish-pötim osönu	חֻקִּים וּמִשְׁפָּטִים אוֹתָנוּ
limad-tö. Al kayn adonöy	לִמַּדְתָּ. עַל כֵּן יְיָ
elohaynu, b'shöch'vaynu	אֱלֹהֵינוּ, בְּשָׁכְבֵנוּ
uv'kumaynu nösi-ach b'chukechö,	וּבְקוּמֵנוּ נָשִׂיחַ בְּחֻקֶּיךָ,
v'nismach b'div'ray sorös'chö	וְנִשְׂמַח בְּדִבְרֵי תוֹרָתֶךָ
uv'mitzvo-sechö l'olöm vö-ed.	וּבְמִצְוֹתֶיךָ לְעוֹלָם וָעֶד.
Ki haym cha-yaynu v'orech	כִּי הֵם חַיֵּינוּ וְאֹרֶךְ
yömaynu, uvöhem neh-geh	יָמֵינוּ, וּבָהֶם נֶהְגֶּה
yomöm völöy-lö, v'ahavös'chö	יוֹמָם וָלָיְלָה, וְאַהֲבָתְךָ
lo sösur (*Nussach Ashkenaz:* al tösir)	לֹא תָסוּר (נוסח אשכנז: אַל תָּסִיר)
mi-menu l'olömim. Böruch atöh	מִמֶּנּוּ לְעוֹלָמִים. בָּרוּךְ אַתָּה
adonöy, ohayv amo yisrö-ayl.	יְיָ, אוֹהֵב עַמּוֹ יִשְׂרָאֵל:

It is customary to cover the eyes with the right hand while reciting the first verse of the Shema, in order to avoid distractions and promote deep concentration.

Sh'ma yisrö-ayl,	שְׁמַע יִשְׂרָאֵל,
adonöy elohaynu,	יְיָ אֱלֹהֵינוּ,
adonöy echöd.	יְיָ אֶחָד:

Uncover the eyes and say the following in an undertone:

Böruch shaym k'vod	בָּרוּךְ שֵׁם כְּבוֹד
mal'chuso l'olöm vö-ed.	מַלְכוּתוֹ לְעוֹלָם וָעֶד:

Continue in a regular tone below:

V'öhavtö ays adonöy elohechö,	וְאָהַבְתָּ אֵת יְיָ אֱלֹהֶיךָ,
b'chöl l'vöv'chö, uv'chöl naf-sh'chö,	בְּכָל לְבָבְךָ, וּבְכָל נַפְשְׁךָ,
uv'chöl m'odechö. V'hö-yu	וּבְכָל מְאֹדֶךָ: וְהָיוּ

INSIGHT

אַהֲבַת עוֹלָם — This blessing is a fitting introduction to the Shema. It speaks of God's love of His people, and reminds us that the Torah and mitzvot are not merely additions to our life, but our very life and cause for existence.

אַהֲבַת — With everlasting love have You loved the House of Israel Your people. You have taught us Torah and mitzvot, decrees and laws. Therefore, Lord our God, when we lie down and when we rise, we will speak of Your statutes and rejoice in the words of Your Torah and in Your mitzvot forever. For they are our life and the length of our days, and we will meditate on them day and night. May Your love never depart from us. Blessed are You Lord, who loves His people Israel.

INSIGHT

שְׁמַע — The Shema expresses the essence of the Jewish faith, and consists of three paragraphs from the Torah (Bible). The first begins with the proclamation "The Lord is One." It goes on to tell us that we must love God and dedicate our lives to carrying out His will, and bring up our children in this belief. It also contains the mitzvot of *Tefillin* (phylacteries, worn weekdays on head and arm) and *Mezuzah* (placed on all doorposts), which remind us that we are Jews and of our responsibilities as Jews.

It is customary to cover the eyes with the right hand while reciting the first verse of the Shema, in order to avoid distractions and promote deep concentration.

שְׁמַע — Hear, O Israel, the Lord is our God, the Lord is One.

Uncover the eyes and say the following in an undertone:

בָּרוּךְ — Blessed be the name of the glory of His kingdom forever and ever.

Continue in a regular tone below:

וְאָהַבְתָּ — You shall love the Lord your God with all your heart, with all your soul, and with all your might. And these words

ha-d'vörim hö-ay-leh asher	הַדְּבָרִים הָאֵלֶּה אֲשֶׁר
önochi m'tzav'chö ha-yom,	אָנֹכִי מְצַוְּךָ הַיּוֹם,
al l'vö-vechö. V'shinan-töm	עַל לְבָבֶךָ: וְשִׁנַּנְתָּם
l'vö-nechö v'dibartö böm,	לְבָנֶיךָ וְדִבַּרְתָּ בָּם,
b'shiv-t'chö b'vaysechö,	בְּשִׁבְתְּךָ בְּבֵיתֶךָ,
uv'lech-t'chö va-derech,	וּבְלֶכְתְּךָ בַדֶּרֶךְ,
uv'shöch-b'chö, uv'kumechö.	וּבְשָׁכְבְּךָ, וּבְקוּמֶךָ:
Uk'shartöm l'os al yö-dechö,	וּקְשַׁרְתָּם לְאוֹת עַל יָדֶךָ,
v'hö-yu l'totöfos bayn ay-nechö.	וְהָיוּ לְטֹטָפֹת בֵּין עֵינֶיךָ:
Uch'savtöm al m'zuzos	וּכְתַבְתָּם עַל מְזֻזוֹת
bay-sechö, uvish'örechö.	בֵּיתֶךָ, וּבִשְׁעָרֶיךָ:

V'hö-yöh im shömo-a tish-m'u	וְהָיָה אִם שָׁמֹעַ תִּשְׁמְעוּ
el mitzvo-sai asher önochi	אֶל מִצְוֹתַי אֲשֶׁר אָנֹכִי
m'tza-veh es'chem ha-yom,	מְצַוֶּה אֶתְכֶם הַיּוֹם,
l'ahavöh es adonöy elo-haychem	לְאַהֲבָה אֶת יְיָ אֱלֹהֵיכֶם
ul'öv'do, b'chöl l'vav'chem uv'chöl	וּלְעָבְדוֹ, בְּכָל לְבַבְכֶם וּבְכָל
naf-sh'chem. V'nösati m'tar	נַפְשְׁכֶם: וְנָתַתִּי מְטַר
artz'chem b'ito yo-reh umal-kosh,	אַרְצְכֶם בְּעִתּוֹ יוֹרֶה וּמַלְקוֹשׁ,
v'ösaftö d'gönechö v'sirosh'chö	וְאָסַפְתָּ דְגָנֶךָ וְתִירֹשְׁךָ
v'yitz-hörechö. V'nösati aysev	וְיִצְהָרֶךָ: וְנָתַתִּי עֵשֶׂב
b'söd'chö liv'hemtechö, v'öchaltö	בְּשָׂדְךָ לִבְהֶמְתֶּךָ, וְאָכַלְתָּ
v'sövö-tö. Hishöm'ru löchem pen	וְשָׂבָעְתָּ: הִשָּׁמְרוּ לָכֶם פֶּן
yifteh l'vav'chem, v'sartem	יִפְתֶּה לְבַבְכֶם, וְסַרְתֶּם
va-avad-tem elohim a-chayrim	וַעֲבַדְתֶּם אֱלֹהִים אֲחֵרִים
v'hish-tacha-visem löhem.	וְהִשְׁתַּחֲוִיתֶם לָהֶם:
V'chöröh af adonöy böchem	וְחָרָה אַף יְיָ בָּכֶם
v'ötzar es ha-shöma-yim v'lo	וְעָצַר אֶת הַשָּׁמַיִם וְלֹא

118

which I command you today shall be upon your heart. You shall teach them thoroughly to your children, and you shall speak of them when you sit in your house and when you walk on the road, when you lie down and when you rise. You shall bind them as a sign upon your hand, and they shall be for a reminder between your eyes. And you shall write them upon the doorposts of your house and upon your gates.

INSIGHT

וְהָיָה — The first chapter of the Shema emphasizes faith and the belief in God, whilst the second chapter calls for implementing this faith through the practical observance of the mitzvot.

This paragraph highlights the Jewish belief of reward and punishment, where God promises to send His blessings when we fulfill His will and withhold them, and the heavenly consequences when ignored.

The mitzvot of *Tefillin* and *Mezuzah* are once again mentioned because they are tangible symbols of God's commandments.

וְהָיָה — And it will be, if you will diligently obey My commandments which I enjoin upon you this day, to love the Lord your God and to serve Him with all your heart and with all your soul, I will give rain for your land at the proper time, the early rain and the late rain, and you will gather in your grain, your wine and your oil. And I will give grass in your fields for your cattle, and you will eat and be sated. Take care lest your heart be lured away, and you turn astray and worship alien gods and bow down to them. For then the Lord's wrath will flare up against you, and

yih-yeh mötör v'hö-adömöh lo	יִהְיֶה מָטָר וְהָאֲדָמָה לֹא
sitayn es y'vulöh, va-avad-tem	תִתֵּן אֶת יְבוּלָהּ וַאֲבַדְתֶּם
m'hayröh may-al hö-öretz	מְהֵרָה מֵעַל הָאָרֶץ
ha-tovöh asher adonöy no-sayn	הַטֹּבָה אֲשֶׁר יְיָ נֹתֵן
löchem. V'samtem es d'vörai	לָכֶם: וְשַׂמְתֶּם אֶת דְּבָרַי
ayleh al l'vav'chem v'al	אֵלֶּה עַל לְבַבְכֶם וְעַל
naf-sh'chem uk'shartem osöm	נַפְשְׁכֶם וּקְשַׁרְתֶּם אֹתָם
l'os al yed'chem v'hö-yu l'totöfos	לְאוֹת עַל יֶדְכֶם וְהָיוּ לְטוֹטָפֹת
bayn aynaychem. V'limad-tem	בֵּין עֵינֵיכֶם: וְלִמַּדְתֶּם
osöm es b'naychem l'dabayr böm,	אֹתָם אֶת בְּנֵיכֶם לְדַבֵּר בָּם,
b'shiv-t'chö b'vaysechö	בְּשִׁבְתְּךָ בְּבֵיתֶךָ
uv'lech-t'chö va-derech	וּבְלֶכְתְּךָ בַדֶּרֶךְ
uv'shöch-b'chö uv'kumechö.	וּבְשָׁכְבְּךָ וּבְקוּמֶךָ:
Uch'savtöm al m'zuzos bay-sechö	וּכְתַבְתָּם עַל מְזוּזוֹת בֵּיתֶךָ
uvish'örechö. L'ma-an yirbu	וּבִשְׁעָרֶיךָ: לְמַעַן יִרְבּוּ
y'maychem vimay v'naychem	יְמֵיכֶם וִימֵי בְנֵיכֶם
al hö-adömöh asher nishba	עַל הָאֲדָמָה אֲשֶׁר נִשְׁבַּע
adonöy la-avosaychem lösays	יְיָ לַאֲבֹתֵיכֶם לָתֵת
löhem, kimay ha-shöma-yim	לָהֶם, כִּימֵי הַשָּׁמַיִם
al hö-öretz.	עַל הָאָרֶץ:

Va-yomer adonöy el mosheh	וַיֹּאמֶר יְיָ אֶל מֹשֶׁה
laymor. Dabayr el b'nay yisrö-ayl	לֵּאמֹר: דַּבֵּר אֶל בְּנֵי יִשְׂרָאֵל
v'ömartö alay-hem v'ösu lö-hem	וְאָמַרְתָּ אֲלֵהֶם וְעָשׂוּ לָהֶם
tzitzis al kan'fay vig'dayhem	צִיצִת עַל כַּנְפֵי בִגְדֵיהֶם
l'dorosöm, v'nös'nu al tzitzis	לְדֹרֹתָם, וְנָתְנוּ עַל צִיצִת הַכָּנָף,
ha-könöf, p'sil t'chayles.	פְּתִיל תְּכֵלֶת:
V'hö-yöh löchem l'tzitzis,	וְהָיָה לָכֶם לְצִיצִת,

He will close the heavens so that there will be no rain and the earth will not yield its produce, and you will swiftly perish from the good land which the Lord gives you. Therefore, place these words of Mine upon your heart and upon your soul, and bind them for a sign on your hand, and they shall be for a reminder between your eyes. You shall teach them to your children, to speak of them when you sit in your house and when you walk on the road, when you lie down and when you rise. And you shall inscribe them on the doorposts of your house and on your gates — so that your days and the days of your children may be prolonged on the land which the Lord swore to your fathers to give to them for as long as the heavens are above the earth.

INSIGHT

וַיֹּאמֶר — The third chapter contains the commandment of *Tzitzit*, the distinctive four-cornered garment Jewish males wear with fringes on the four corners, as constant reminder of all the precepts of the Torah.

In addition, the passage contains the Biblical precept to *'remember the Exodus from Egypt'* which requires every Jew to remember the historic event each and every day.

וַיֹּאמֶר — The Lord spoke to Moses, saying: Speak to the children of Israel and tell them to make for themselves fringes on the corners of their garments throughout their generations, and to attach a thread of blue on the fringe of each corner. They shall be to you as tzitzit, and you shall look upon them and remember

ur'isem oso uz'chartem es	וּרְאִיתֶם אֹתוֹ וּזְכַרְתֶּם אֶת
köl mitzvos adonöy va-asisem	כָּל מִצְוֹת יְיָ וַעֲשִׂיתֶם
osöm, v'lo sösuru acha-ray	אֹתָם, וְלֹא תָתוּרוּ אַחֲרֵי
l'vav'chem v'acharay aynay-chem	לְבַבְכֶם וְאַחֲרֵי עֵינֵיכֶם
asher atem zonim acha-rayhem.	אֲשֶׁר אַתֶּם זֹנִים אַחֲרֵיהֶם:
L'ma-an tiz-k'ru va-asisem es	לְמַעַן תִּזְכְּרוּ וַעֲשִׂיתֶם אֶת
köl mitzvo-söy, vih-yisem	כָּל מִצְוֹתָי, וִהְיִיתֶם
k'doshim laylo-hay-chem.	קְדֹשִׁים לֵאלֹהֵיכֶם:
Ani adonöy elo-haychem asher	אֲנִי יְיָ אֱלֹהֵיכֶם אֲשֶׁר
ho-tzaysi es'chem may-eretz	הוֹצֵאתִי אֶתְכֶם מֵאֶרֶץ
mitzra-yim lih-yos löchem	מִצְרַיִם לִהְיוֹת לָכֶם
lay-lohim, ani adonöy	לֵאלֹהִים, אֲנִי יְיָ
elo-haychem. Emes.	אֱלֹהֵיכֶם: אֱמֶת.

Ve-emunöh köl zos, v'ka-yöm	וֶאֱמוּנָה כָּל זֹאת, וְקַיָּם
ölaynu, ki hu adonöy elohaynu	עָלֵינוּ, כִּי הוּא יְיָ אֱלֹהֵינוּ
v'ayn zulöso, va-anach-nu	וְאֵין זוּלָתוֹ, וַאֲנַחְנוּ
yisrö-ayl amo, ha-podaynu	יִשְׂרָאֵל עַמּוֹ, הַפּוֹדֵנוּ
mi-yad m'löchim, mal-kaynu	מִיַּד מְלָכִים, מַלְכֵּנוּ
ha-go-alay-nu mi-kaf köl	הַגּוֹאֲלֵנוּ מִכַּף כָּל
he-öri-tzim. Hö-ayl ha-nifrö	הֶעָרִיצִים. הָאֵל הַנִּפְרָע
lönu mitzö-raynu, v'ham'shalaym	לָנוּ מִצָּרֵינוּ, וְהַמְשַׁלֵּם
g'mul l'chöl o-y'vay naf-shaynu,	גְּמוּל לְכָל אֹיְבֵי נַפְשֵׁנוּ,
hö-oseh g'dolos ad ayn chay-ker,	הָעֹשֶׂה גְדֹלוֹת עַד אֵין חֵקֶר,
v'niflö-os ad ayn mispör. Ha-söm	וְנִפְלָאוֹת עַד אֵין מִסְפָּר. הַשָּׂם
naf-shaynu bacha-yim, v'lo nösan	נַפְשֵׁנוּ בַּחַיִּים, וְלֹא נָתַן
lamot rag-laynu, ha-madri-chaynu	לַמּוֹט רַגְלֵנוּ, הַמַּדְרִיכֵנוּ
al bömos oy'vaynu, va-yörem	עַל בָּמוֹת אֹיְבֵנוּ, וַיָּרֶם

all the commandments of the Lord and fulfill them, and you will not follow after your heart and after your eyes by which you go astray — so that you may remember and fulfill all My commandments and be holy to your God. I am the Lord your God who brought you out of the land of Egypt to be your God; I, the Lord, am your God. Truth.

INSIGHT

וֶאֱמוּנָה — This section refers to the Shema we just read. It reinforces our connection and belief in God and recounts the numerous miracles He has wrought for the Jewish People, which enable us to be here today.

וֶאֱמוּנָה — And belief is all this; it is established with us that He is the Lord our God, there is no other, and that we Israel are His people. It is He who redeems us from the hand of kings; our King, who delivers us from the grip of all the tyrants; the benevolent God, who avenges us against our persecutors, and brings retribution on all our mortal enemies. He does great things beyond limit, and wonders beyond number. He has kept us alive, and did not allow our feet to falter. He led us upon the high places of our

kar-naynu, al köl son'aynu.
Hö-ayl hö-oseh lönu n'kömö
b'far-oh, v'osos umof'sim
b'ad'mas b'nay chöm. Ha-ma-keh
v'evröso köl b'choray mitzrö-yim,
va-yotzay es amo yisrö-ayl
mi-tochöm l'chayrus olöm.
Ha-ma-avir bönöv bayn giz'ray
yam suf, v'es rod'fayhem v'es
son'ayhem bis'homos tiba,
v'rö-u vönöv g'vuröso,
shib'chu v'hodu lish'mo.
Umal'chuso v'rötzon kib'lu
alayhem, mosheh uv'nay yisro-ayl
l'chö önu shirö b'simchöh raböh,
v'öm'ru chulöm.

קָרְנֵנוּ, עַל כָּל שׂנְאֵינוּ.
הָאֵל הָעֹשֶׂה לָּנוּ נְקָמָה
בְּפַרְעֹה, וְאֹותֹות וּמֹופְתִים
בְּאַדְמַת בְּנֵי חָם. הַמַּכֶּה
בְּעֶבְרָתֹו כָּל בְּכֹורֵי מִצְרָיִם,
וַיֹּוצֵא אֶת עַמֹו יִשְׂרָאֵל
מִתֹּוכָם לְחֵרוּת עֹולָם.
הַמַּעֲבִיר בָּנָיו בֵּין גִּזְרֵי
יַם סוּף, וְאֶת רֹודְפֵיהֶם וְאֶת
שֹׂונְאֵיהֶם בִּתְהֹומֹות טִבַּע,
וְרָאוּ בָנָיו גְּבוּרָתֹו,
שִׁבְּחוּ וְהֹודוּ לִשְׁמֹו.
וּמַלְכוּתֹו בְּרָצֹון קִבְּלוּ
עֲלֵיהֶם, מֹשֶׁה וּבְנֵי יִשְׂרָאֵל
לְךָ עָנוּ שִׁירָה בְּשִׂמְחָה רַבָּה,
וְאָמְרוּ כֻלָּם:

Mi chö-mochöh bö-aylim
adonöy, mi kö-mochö ne-dör
ba-kodesh, norö s'hilos, osay
fe-le. Mal'chus'chö rö-u vö-nechö,
bokay-a yöm lif'nay mosheh,
zeh ayli önu v'öm'ru, adonöy
yim-loch l'olöm vö-ed. V'ne-emar,
ki födöh adonöy es ya-akov,
ug'ölo mi-yad chözök mi-menu.
Böruch atöh adonöy,
gö-al yisrö-ayl.

מִי כָמֹכָה בָּאֵלִם
יְיָ, מִי כָּמֹכָה נֶאְדָּר
בַּקֹּדֶשׁ, נֹורָא תְהִלֹּת, עֹשֵׂה
פֶלֶא: מַלְכוּתְךָ רָאוּ בָנֶיךָ,
בֹּוקֵעַ יָם לִפְנֵי מֹשֶׁה,
זֶה אֵלִי עָנוּ וְאָמְרוּ: יְיָ
יִמְלֹךְ לְעֹלָם וָעֶד. וְנֶאֱמַר:
כִּי פָדָה יְיָ אֶת יַעֲקֹב,
וּגְאָלֹו מִיַּד חָזָק מִמֶּנוּ:
בָּרוּךְ אַתָּה יְיָ,
גָּאַל יִשְׂרָאֵל:

foes, and increased our strength over all our adversaries. He is the benevolent God who, in our behalf, brought retribution upon Pharaoh, and signs and miracles in the land of the Hamites; who, in His wrath, struck all the first-born of Egypt and brought out His people Israel from their midst to everlasting freedom; who led His children through the divided parts of the Sea of Reeds, and drowned their pursuers and their enemies in the depths. As His children beheld His might, they extolled and offered praise to His Name, and willingly accepted His sovereignty; Moses and the children of Israel with great joy raised their voices in song to You, and they all proclaimed:

INSIGHT

מִי כָמֹכָה — This prayer continues the themes of the preceding prayers. In it we proclaim the uniqueness of God and make reference to the redemption that God has brought — and continues to bring — to the Jewish People. The prayer highlights the great miracle of the Godly Revelation and splitting of the Reed Sea upon the Exodus from Egypt.

מִי — Who is like You among the supernal beings, O Lord! Who is like You, resplendent in holiness, awesome in praise, performing wonders! Your children beheld Your sovereignty as You split the sea before Moses. "This is my God!" they exclaimed, and declared, "The Lord shall reign forever and ever." And it is said: For the Lord has redeemed Jacob, and delivered him from a power mightier than he. Blessed are You Lord, who has delivered Israel.

Hash-kivaynu övinu l'shölom,	הַשְׁכִּיבֵנוּ אָבִינוּ לְשָׁלוֹם,
v'ha-amidaynu mal-kaynu	וְהַעֲמִידֵנוּ מַלְכֵּנוּ
l'cha-yim tovim ul'shölom,	לְחַיִּים טוֹבִים וּלְשָׁלוֹם,
v'sak'naynu b'ay-tzöh tovöh	וְתַקְּנֵנוּ בְּעֵצָה טוֹבָה
mil'fönechö, v'hoshi-aynu	מִלְּפָנֶיךָ, וְהוֹשִׁיעֵנוּ
m'hayröh l'ma-an sh'mechö,	מְהֵרָה לְמַעַן שְׁמֶךָ,
uf'ros ölaynu sukas sh'lomechö.	וּפְרוֹשׂ עָלֵינוּ סֻכַּת שְׁלוֹמֶךָ:
Böruch atöh adonöy,	בָּרוּךְ אַתָּה יְיָ,
ha-porays sukas shölom	הַפּוֹרֵשׂ סֻכַּת שָׁלוֹם
ölaynu v'al köl amo yisrö-ayl	עָלֵינוּ וְעַל כָּל עַמּוֹ יִשְׂרָאֵל
v'al y'rushölö-yim.	וְעַל יְרוּשָׁלָיִם:

"V'SHAM'RU"
Those following *Nussach Ashkenaz* recite the following:

V'shöm'ru v'nay yisrö-ayl	וְשָׁמְרוּ בְנֵי יִשְׂרָאֵל
es ha-shabös, la-asos es	אֶת הַשַּׁבָּת, לַעֲשׂוֹת אֶת
ha-shabös l'dorosöm b'ris olöm.	הַשַּׁבָּת לְדֹרֹתָם בְּרִית עוֹלָם.
Bayni uvayn b'nay yisrö-ayl	בֵּינִי וּבֵין בְּנֵי יִשְׂרָאֵל
os hi l'olöm, ki shay-shes yömim	אוֹת הִיא לְעֹלָם, כִּי שֵׁשֶׁת יָמִים
ösöh adonöy es ha-shöma-yim	עָשָׂה יְיָ אֶת הַשָּׁמַיִם
v'es hö-öretz uva-yom ha-sh'vi-i	וְאֶת הָאָרֶץ, וּבַיּוֹם הַשְּׁבִיעִי
shövas va-yinöfash.	שָׁבַת וַיִּנָּפַשׁ:

On festivals, those following *Nussach Ashkenaz* recite the following:

Va-y'dabayr mosheh es mo-adai	וַיְדַבֵּר מֹשֶׁה אֶת מוֹעֲדֵי
adonöy el b'nay yisrö-ayl.	יְיָ, אֶל בְּנֵי יִשְׂרָאֵל:

INSIGHT

הַשְׁכִּיבֵנוּ — It is interesting to note how in the following prayer we refer to God as 'Our Father,' but upon waking in the morning we address Him as "Our King." The reason for this is that in the course of the day we have learnt, from all that has happened to us, that God has been more than a King to us; He has shown us many kindnesses and has taken care of us like a loving parent, because, when we are about to retire for the night, we feel confident and secure in God, as a child feels secure in the arms of his father.

הַשְׁכִּיבֵנוּ — Our Father, let us lie down in peace; our King, raise us up to a good life and peace. Improve us with Your good counsel, help us speedily for the sake of Your Name, and spread over us the shelter of Your peace. Blessed are You Lord, who spreads the shelter of peace over us, over His entire people Israel, and over Jerusalem.

"V'SHAM'RU"
Those following *Nussach Ashkenaz* recite the following

ON SHABBAT

וְשָׁמְרוּ And the children of Israel shall observe the Shabbat, establishing the Shabbat throughout their generations as an everlasting covenant. It is a sign between Me and the children of Israel for all time, for in six days the Lord made the heavens and the earth, and on the seventh day He ceased from work and rested.

ON FESTIVALS

וַיְדַבֵּר And Moses declared the festivals of the Lord to the children of Israel.

The leader recites Half-Kaddish.

HALF-KADDISH

↑ STANDING

Yis-gadal v'yis-kadash °sh'may rabö°.   יִתְגַּדַּל וְיִתְקַדַּשׁ °שְׁמֵהּ רַבָּא°:

(Cong.: Ömayn.)   אָמֵן

B'öl'mö di v'rö chir'u-say   בְּעָלְמָא דִּי בְרָא כִרְעוּתֵהּ

v'yam-lich mal'chusay,   וְיַמְלִיךְ מַלְכוּתֵהּ,

Nussach Sfard: v'yatz-mach pur-könay   נוסח ספרד: וְיַצְמַח פּוּרְקָנֵהּ

°vikö-rayv m'shi-chay°.   °וִיקָרֵב מְשִׁיחֵהּ°:

(Cong.: Ömayn.)   אָמֵן

B'cha-yay-chon uv'yomay-chon uv'cha-yay   בְּחַיֵּיכוֹן וּבְיוֹמֵיכוֹן וּבְחַיֵּי

d'chöl bays yisrö-ayl, ba-agölö uviz'man   דְכָל בֵּית יִשְׂרָאֵל, בַּעֲגָלָא וּבִזְמַן

köriv °v'im'ru ömayn°.   קָרִיב °וְאִמְרוּ אָמֵן°:

(Cong.: Ömayn. Y'hay sh'may rabö m'vörach   אָמֵן. יְהֵא שְׁמֵהּ רַבָּא מְבָרַךְ

l'ölam ul'öl'may öl'ma-yö.   לְעָלַם וּלְעָלְמֵי עָלְמַיָּא:

Yisböraych)   יִתְבָּרֵךְ:

°Y'hay sh'may rabö m'vörach   °יְהֵא שְׁמֵהּ רַבָּא מְבָרַךְ

l'ölam ul'öl'may öl'ma-yö.   לְעָלַם וּלְעָלְמֵי עָלְמַיָּא:

Yis-böraych° °v'yish-tabach, v'yispö-ayr,   יִתְבָּרֵךְ° °וְיִשְׁתַּבַּח, וְיִתְפָּאַר,

v'yis-romöm, v'yis-nasay,   וְיִתְרוֹמַם, וְיִתְנַשֵּׂא,

v'yis-hadör, v'yis-aleh, v'yis-halöl°, °sh'may   וְיִתְהַדָּר, וְיִתְעַלֶּה, וְיִתְהַלָּל°,

d'kud-shö b'rich hu°.   °שְׁמֵהּ דְקֻדְשָׁא בְּרִיךְ הוּא°:

(Cong.: Ömayn.)   אָמֵן

L'aylö min köl bir'chösö v'shi-rösö,   לְעֵלָּא מִן כָּל בִּרְכָתָא וְשִׁירָתָא,

tush-b'chösö v'neche-mösö,   תֻּשְׁבְּחָתָא וְנֶחֱמָתָא,

da-amirön b'öl'mö,   דַּאֲמִירָן בְּעָלְמָא,

°v'im'ru ömayn°.   °וְאִמְרוּ אָמֵן°:

(Cong.: Ömayn.)   אָמֵן

FOR SHABBAT: Continue on following page.
FOR PESACH, SHAVOUT, AND SUKKOT: Recite the Amidah on page 182.

The leader recites Half-Kaddish.

STANDING

HALF-KADDISH

יִתְגַּדַּל Exalted and hallowed be His great Name. (Cong.: Amen)

בְּעָלְמָא Throughout the world which He has created according to His Will. May He establish His kingship, (Nussach Sfard: bring forth His redemption and hasten the coming of His Moshiach. (Cong.: Amen))

בְּחַיֵּיכוֹן In your lifetime and in your days and in the lifetime of the entire House of Israel, speedily and soon, and say, Amen. (Cong.: Amen. May His great Name be blessed forever and to all eternity. Blessed)

יְהֵא May His great Name be blessed forever and to all eternity. Blessed and praised, glorified, exalted and extolled, honored, adored and lauded be the Name of the Holy One, blessed be He. (Cong.: Amen).

לְעֵלָּא Beyond all the blessings, hymns, praises and consolations that are uttered in the world; and say, Amen. (Cong.: Amen)

INSIGHT

The sanctification of God's name is one of the most essential requirements of the Jewish faith. It is the purpose of each and every Jew to testify to God's existence.

A simple way of achieving this is by making a public declaration that God is exalted and holy. This public declaration is expressed by the congregation in the first response of the Kaddish: "*May His great Name be blessed for ever and ever.*" In fact, one reason for reciting Kaddish is to elicit this response from all who listen to it.

FOR SHABBAT: Continue on following page.
FOR PESACH, SHAVOUT, AND SUKKOT: Recite the Amidah on page 182.

THE AMIDAH FOR SHABBAT
The Amidah is recited while standing, with both feet together.
Before beginning, take three steps back, then three steps forward,
and say:

STANDING

Adonöy, s'fösai tif-töch ufi   אֲדֹנָי, שְׂפָתַי תִּפְתָּח וּפִי

yagid t'hilö-sechö.   יַגִּיד תְּהִלָּתֶךְ:

At the word "Böruch" bend the knee; at "Atöh" bow forward;
and at "Adonöy" straighten up.

RECALLING OUR PATRIARCHS

Böruch atöh adonöy elo-haynu   בָּרוּךְ אַתָּה יְיָ אֱלֹהֵינוּ

vay-lohay avosaynu,   וֵאלֹהֵי אֲבוֹתֵינוּ,

elo-hay avröhöm, elo-hay   אֱלֹהֵי אַבְרָהָם, אֱלֹהֵי

yitzchök, vay-lohay ya-akov,   יִצְחָק, וֵאלֹהֵי יַעֲקֹב,

hö-ayl ha-gödol ha-gibor   הָאֵל הַגָּדוֹל הַגִּבּוֹר

v'hanorö, ayl el-yon, gomayl   וְהַנּוֹרָא, אֵל עֶלְיוֹן, גּוֹמֵל

cha-södim tovim, ko-nay ha-kol,   חֲסָדִים טוֹבִים, קוֹנֵה הַכֹּל,

v'zochayr chas'day övos,   וְזוֹכֵר חַסְדֵי אָבוֹת,

umay-vi go-ayl liv'nay v'nayhem   וּמֵבִיא גוֹאֵל לִבְנֵי בְנֵיהֶם

l'ma-an sh'mo b'ahavöh.   לְמַעַן שְׁמוֹ בְּאַהֲבָה:

Between Rosh Hashana and Yom Kippur add:

Zöch'raynu l'cha-yim, melech chöfaytz   זָכְרֵנוּ לְחַיִּים, מֶלֶךְ חָפֵץ

ba-cha-yim, v'chös'vaynu b'sayfer   בַּחַיִּים, וְכָתְבֵנוּ בְּסֵפֶר

ha-cha-yim, l'ma-an'chö elohim cha-yim.   הַחַיִּים, לְמַעַנְךָ אֱלֹהִים חַיִּים.

At the word "*Böruch*" bend the knee; at "*Atöh*" bow forward;
and at "*Adonöy*" straighten up.

Melech ozayr   מֶלֶךְ עוֹזֵר

umo-shi-a umö-gayn.   וּמוֹשִׁיעַ וּמָגֵן:

Böruch atöh adonöy,   בָּרוּךְ אַתָּה יְיָ,

mö-gayn avröhöm.   מָגֵן אַבְרָהָם:

INTRODUCTION

The Shabbat Amidah differs significantly from the daily Amidah in that we do not submit our regular mundane requests. The weekday Amidah blessings express our daily needs and requests, connected with worldly worries and desires. Because Shabbat and Festivals are days of sanctity and joy, our prayers take on a more spiritual tone. The Shabbat Amidah contains only seven blessings, since Shabbat is the seventh day of the week.

THE AMIDAH FOR SHABBAT
The Amidah is recited while standing, with both feet together.
Before beginning, take three steps back, then three steps forward,
and say:

↑
STANDING

אֲדֹנָי — My Lord, open my lips, and my mouth shall declare Your praise.

At the word "Blessed" bend the knee; at "You" bow forward;
and at "Lord" straighten up.

RECALLING OUR PATRIARCHS

בָּרוּךְ — **Blessed** are **You**, **Lord** our God and God of our fathers, God of Abraham, God of Isaac and God of Jacob, the great, mighty and awesome God, exalted God, Who bestows bountiful kindness, Who creates all things, Who remembers the piety of the Patriarchs, and Who, in love, brings a redeemer to their children's children, for the sake of His Name.

> **Between Rosh Hashana and Yom Kippur add:**
>
> זָכְרֵנוּ — Remember us for life, King Who desires life; inscribe us in the Book of Life, for Your sake, O living God.

At the word "Blessed" bend the knee; at "You" bow forward;
and at "Lord" straighten up.

מֶלֶךְ — King, [You are] a helper, a savior and a shield. **Blessed** are **You Lord**, Shield of Abraham.

GOD'S MIGHT

Atöh gibor l'olöm adonöy,　　אַתָּה גִבּוֹר לְעוֹלָם אֲדֹנָי,

m'cha-yeh maysim atöh,　　מְחַיֶּה מֵתִים אַתָּה,

rav l'hoshi-a.　　רַב לְהוֹשִׁיעַ:

In summer say: Morid ha-töl.　　בקיץ: מוֹרִיד הַטָּל:

In winter say: Mashiv höru-ach　　בחורף: מַשִּׁיב הָרוּחַ

umo-rid ha-geshem.　　וּמוֹרִיד הַגֶּשֶׁם:

M'chal-kayl cha-yim b'chesed,　　מְכַלְכֵּל חַיִּים בְּחֶסֶד,

m'cha-yeh may-sim b'racha-mim　　מְחַיֶּה מֵתִים בְּרַחֲמִים

rabim, so-maych nof'lim,　　רַבִּים, סוֹמֵךְ נוֹפְלִים,

v'rofay cholim, uma-tir　　וְרוֹפֵא חוֹלִים, וּמַתִּיר

asu-rim, um'ka-yaym emu-nöso　　אֲסוּרִים, וּמְקַיֵּם אֱמוּנָתוֹ לִישֵׁנֵי

li-shaynay öför, mi chö-mochö　　עָפָר, מִי כָמוֹךָ

ba-al g'vuros umi do-meh löch,　　בַּעַל גְּבוּרוֹת וּמִי דוֹמֶה לָךְ,

melech may-mis um'cha-yeh　　מֶלֶךְ מֵמִית וּמְחַיֶּה

umatz-mi-ach y'shu-öh.　　וּמַצְמִיחַ יְשׁוּעָה:

Between Rosh Hashana and Yom Kippur add:

Mi chömochö öv hörachamön zochayr　　מִי כָמוֹךָ אַב הָרַחֲמָן זוֹכֵר

y'tzuröv l'cha-yim b'racha-mim.　　יְצוּרָיו לְחַיִּים בְּרַחֲמִים:

V'ne-emön atöh l'ha-cha-yos　　וְנֶאֱמָן אַתָּה לְהַחֲיוֹת

may-sim. Böruch atöh adonöy,　　מֵתִים: בָּרוּךְ אַתָּה יְיָ,

m'cha-yeh ha-amaysim.　　מְחַיֶּה הַמֵּתִים:

HOLINESS OF GOD'S NAME

Atöh ködosh v'shim'chö　　אַתָּה קָדוֹשׁ וְשִׁמְךָ

ködosh uk'doshim b'chöl yom　　קָדוֹשׁ וּקְדוֹשִׁים בְּכָל יוֹם

GOD'S MIGHT

אַתָּה — You are mighty forever, my Lord; You resurrect the dead; You are powerful to save.

In summer say: He causes the dew to descend.

In winter say: He causes the wind to blow and the rain to fall.

He sustains the living with lovingkindness, resurrects the dead with great mercy, supports the falling, heals the sick, releases the bound, and fulfills His trust to those who sleep in the dust. Who is like You, mighty One! And who can be compared to You, King, Who brings death and restores life, and causes deliverance to spring forth!

Between Rosh Hashana and Yom Kippur add:

מִי — Who is like You, merciful Father, Who in compassion remembers His creatures for life.

וְנֶאֱמָן — You are trustworthy to revive the dead. Blessed are You Lord, Who revives the dead.

INSIGHT

אַתָּה גִבּוֹר — The belief in 'the revival of the dead' is one of the thirteen principles of the Jewish faith enumerated by Maimonides.

On a deeper level, it not only refers to the physically dead but also to those who feel spiritually deadened. We beseech God to help those in need to "restore life", to rejuvenate them spiritually.

HOLINESS OF GOD'S NAME

אַתָּה — You are holy and Your Name is holy, and holy beings

y'ha-l'luchö selöh. Böruch atöh
adonöy, *hö-ayl ha-ködosh.
(*Between Rosh Hashana and Yom Kippur
substitute: Ha-melech ha-ködosh.)

יְהַלְלוּךְ סֶּלָה. בָּרוּךְ אַתָּה
יְיָ, הָאֵל הַקָּדוֹשׁ:
(בעשי״ת:
הַמֶּלֶךְ הַקָּדוֹשׁ)

HOLINESS OF THE SEVENTH DAY

Atöh kidashtö es yom ha-sh'vi-i
lish'mechö, tachlis ma-asay
shöma-yim vö-öretz,
bay-rachto miköl ha-yömim,
v'kidashto miköl ha-z'manim,
v'chayn kösuv b'sörösechö.

אַתָּה קִדַּשְׁתָּ אֶת יוֹם הַשְּׁבִיעִי
לִשְׁמֶךָ, תַּכְלִית מַעֲשֶׂה
שָׁמַיִם וָאָרֶץ,
בֵּרַכְתּוֹ מִכָּל הַיָּמִים,
וְקִדַּשְׁתּוֹ מִכָּל הַזְּמַנִּים,
וְכֵן כָּתוּב בְּתוֹרָתֶךָ:

Va-y'chulu ha-shöma-yim
v'hö-öretz v'chöl tz'vö-öm.
Va-y'chal elohim ba-yom ha-sh'vi-i,
m'lachto asher ösöh, va-yishbos
ba-yom ha-sh'vi-i mi-köl
m'lachto asher ösöh.
Va-y'vörech elohim es yom
ha-sh'vi-i, va-y'kadaysh oso,
ki vo shövas miköl m'lachto,
asher börö elohim la-asos.

וַיְכֻלּוּ הַשָּׁמַיִם
וְהָאָרֶץ וְכָל צְבָאָם:
וַיְכַל אֱלֹהִים בַּיּוֹם הַשְּׁבִיעִי,
מְלַאכְתּוֹ אֲשֶׁר עָשָׂה, וַיִּשְׁבֹּת
בַּיּוֹם הַשְּׁבִיעִי מִכָּל
מְלַאכְתּוֹ אֲשֶׁר עָשָׂה:
וַיְבָרֶךְ אֱלֹהִים אֶת יוֹם
הַשְּׁבִיעִי וַיְקַדֵּשׁ אֹתוֹ,
כִּי בוֹ שָׁבַת מִכָּל מְלַאכְתּוֹ
אֲשֶׁר בָּרָא אֱלֹהִים לַעֲשׂוֹת:

Those following *Nussach Ashkenaz* omit the following paragraph.

Yis-m'chu v'mal'chus'chö
shom'ray shabös v'kor'ay oneg,
am m'kad'shay sh'vi-i, kulöm

יִשְׂמְחוּ בְמַלְכוּתְךָ
שׁוֹמְרֵי שַׁבָּת וְקוֹרְאֵי עֹנֶג,
עַם מְקַדְּשֵׁי שְׁבִיעִי, כֻּלָּם

praise You daily for all eternity. Blessed are You Lord, *the holy God. (*Between Rosh Hashana and Yom Kippur substitute: the holy King.)

INSIGHT

אַתָּה קִדַּשְׁתָּ — This blessing is a form of introduction to the quotation from the Torah where the Shabbat was first instituted. The word used to describe God consecrating His name to the Shabbat is the same word used for betrothal (*Kiddushin*).

This implies that God 'betrothed', so to speak, the Shabbat to the Jewish people. Its holiness and sanctity are enjoyed by them through the proper observance of its laws and traditions.

HOLINESS OF THE SEVENTH DAY

אַתָּה — You have consecrated to Your Name the Seventh Day, the purpose of the creation of heaven and earth. You have blessed it above all days and sanctified it above all festivals. And thus it is written in Your Torah:

וַיְכֻלּוּ — The heavens and the earth and all their hosts were completed. And God finished by the Seventh Day His work which He had done, and He rested on the Seventh Day from all His work which He had done. And God blessed the Seventh Day and made it holy, for on it He rested from all His work which God created to function.

Those following *Nussach Ashkenaz* omit the following paragraph.

יִשְׂמְחוּ — Those who observe the Shabbat and call it a delight shall rejoice in Your kingship; the nation which hallows the

yis-b'u v'yis-an'gu mi-tuvechö,	יִשְׂבְּעוּ וְיִתְעַנְּגוּ מִטּוּבֶךָ,
uvash'vi-i rö-tzisö bo v'kidashto,	וּבַשְּׁבִיעִי רָצִיתָ בּוֹ וְקִדַּשְׁתּוֹ,
chem-das yömim oso kö-rösö,	חֶמְדַּת יָמִים אוֹתוֹ קָרָאתָ,
zaycher l'ma-asay v'rayshis.	זֵכֶר לְמַעֲשֵׂה בְרֵאשִׁית:

Elohaynu vay-lohay	אֱלֹהֵינוּ וֵאלֹהֵי
avosay-nu, r'tzay nö	אֲבוֹתֵינוּ, רְצֵה נָא
vim'nuchö-saynu,	בִמְנוּחָתֵנוּ,
kad'shaynu b'mitzvo-sechö	קַדְּשֵׁנוּ בְּמִצְוֹתֶיךָ
v'sayn chel-kaynu b'sorö-sechö,	וְתֵן חֶלְקֵנוּ בְּתוֹרָתֶךָ,
sab'aynu mitu-vechö v'samay-ach	שַׂבְּעֵנוּ מִטּוּבֶךָ וְשַׂמֵּחַ
naf-shaynu bishu-ösechö,	נַפְשֵׁנוּ בִּישׁוּעָתֶךָ,
v'tahayr li-baynu l'öv-d'chö	וְטַהֵר לִבֵּנוּ לְעָבְדְּךָ
be-emes, v'han-chi-laynu	בֶּאֱמֶת, וְהַנְחִילֵנוּ
adonöy elohaynu b'ahavöh	יְיָ אֱלֹהֵינוּ בְּאַהֲבָה
uv'rö-tzon shabas köd-shechö,	וּבְרָצוֹן שַׁבַּת קָדְשֶׁךָ,
v'yönuchu vöh köl yisrö-ayl	וְיָנוּחוּ בָהּ כָּל יִשְׂרָאֵל
m'kad'shay sh'mechö.	מְקַדְּשֵׁי שְׁמֶךָ:
Böruch atöh adonöy,	בָּרוּךְ אַתָּה יְיָ,
m'kadaysh ha-shabös.	מְקַדֵּשׁ הַשַּׁבָּת:

TEMPLE SERVICE

R'tzay adonöy elo-haynu b'am'chö	רְצֵה יְיָ אֱלֹהֵינוּ בְּעַמְּךָ
yisrö-ayl v'lis'filösöm sh'ay,	יִשְׂרָאֵל וְלִתְפִלָּתָם שְׁעֵה,
v'hö-shayv hö-avodöh lid'vir	וְהָשֵׁב הָעֲבוֹדָה לִדְבִיר
bay-sechö, v'ishay yisrö-ayl	בֵּיתֶךָ, וְאִשֵּׁי יִשְׂרָאֵל
us'fi-lösöm b'aha-vöh s'kabayl	וּתְפִלָּתָם בְּאַהֲבָה תְקַבֵּל
b'rö-tzon, us'hi l'rö-tzon tömid	בְּרָצוֹן, וּתְהִי לְרָצוֹן תָּמִיד
avodas yisrö-ayl a-mechö.	עֲבוֹדַת יִשְׂרָאֵל עַמֶּךָ:

Seventh Day — all shall be satiated and delighted with Your goodness. You were pleased with the Seventh Day and made it holy; You called it the most desirable of days, in remembrance of the work of Creation.

אֱלֹהֵינוּ — Our God and God of our fathers, please find favor in our rest, make us holy with Your commandments and grant us our portion in Your Torah; satiate us with Your goodness, gladden our soul with Your salvation, and make our heart pure to serve You in truth; and, Lord our God, grant as our heritage, in love and goodwill, Your holy Shabbat, and may all Israel who sanctify Your Name rest thereon. Blessed are You Lord, who sanctifies the Shabbat.

TEMPLE SERVICE

רְצֵה — Look with favor, Lord our God, on Your people Israel and pay heed to their prayer; restore the service to Your Sanctuary and accept with love and favor Israel's fire-offerings and prayer; and may the service of Your people Israel always find favor.

INSIGHT

יַעֲלֶה וְיָבֹא — On Rosh Chodesh (the first day of each month) and on all the Festivals, this prayer is included in the Amidah and Grace After Meals. We ask God to remember us and Jerusalem and to bring deliverance and peace in our times, because on these special days it is natural to miss the Holy Temple even more.

The prayer opens with eight expressions of ascent, (*Ya-aleh* means Ascend). These expressions refer to the eight stages that our prayers ascend to come before God.

On Rosh Chodesh, intermediate days of Passover or Sukkot, add the following:

Elo-haynu vay-lohay avo-saynu	אֱלֹהֵינוּ וֵאלֹהֵי אֲבוֹתֵינוּ
ya-aleh v'yövo, v'yagi-a v'yayrö-eh	יַעֲלֶה וְיָבֹא, וְיַגִּיעַ וְיֵרָאֶה
v'yay-rö-tzeh, v'yishöma v'yipökayd	וְיֵרָצֶה, וְיִשָּׁמַע וְיִפָּקֵד
v'yizöchayr, zichro-naynu ufik'do-naynu,	וְיִזָּכֵר, זִכְרוֹנֵנוּ וּפִקְדוֹנֵנוּ,
v' zichron avo-saynu, v'zichron	וְזִכְרוֹן אֲבוֹתֵינוּ, וְזִכְרוֹן
möshi-ach ben dövid av-dechö,	מָשִׁיחַ בֶּן דָּוִד עַבְדֶּךָ,
v'zichron y'rushöla-yim ir köd-shechö,	וְזִכְרוֹן יְרוּשָׁלַיִם עִיר קָדְשֶׁךָ,
v' zichron köl am'chö bays yisrö-ayl	וְזִכְרוֹן כָּל עַמְּךָ בֵּית יִשְׂרָאֵל
l'fönechö lif'laytöh l'tovöh, l'chayn	לְפָנֶיךָ לִפְלֵיטָה לְטוֹבָה, לְחֵן
ul'chesed ul'racha-mim ul' cha-yim	וּלְחֶסֶד וּלְרַחֲמִים וּלְחַיִּים
tovim ul'shölom b'yom	טוֹבִים וּלְשָׁלוֹם, בְּיוֹם
On Rosh Chodesh: Rosh ha-chodesh ha-zeh.	בר״ח: רֹאשׁ הַחֹדֶשׁ הַזֶּה.
On Passover: Chag ha-matzos ha-zeh.	בחה״מ פסח: חַג הַמַּצּוֹת הַזֶּה.
On Sukkot: Chag ha-sukos ha-zeh.	בחה״מ סוכות: חַג הַסֻּכּוֹת הַזֶּה.
Zöch'raynu adonöy elo-haynu bo l'tovöh,	זָכְרֵנוּ יְיָ אֱלֹהֵינוּ בּוֹ לְטוֹבָה,
ufök'daynu vo liv'röchöh, v'hoshi-aynu	וּפָקְדֵנוּ בוֹ לִבְרָכָה, וְהוֹשִׁיעֵנוּ
vo l'cha-yim tovim. Uvid'var y'shu-öh	בוֹ לְחַיִּים טוֹבִים: וּבִדְבַר יְשׁוּעָה
v'rachamim chus v'chö-naynu v'ra-chaym	וְרַחֲמִים חוּס וְחָנֵּנוּ וְרַחֵם
ölaynu v'hoshi-aynu ki ay-lechö ay-naynu,	עָלֵינוּ וְהוֹשִׁיעֵנוּ כִּי אֵלֶיךָ עֵינֵינוּ,
ki ayl melech cha-nun v'rachum ötöh.	כִּי אֵל מֶלֶךְ חַנּוּן וְרַחוּם אָתָּה:

V'se-chezenöh ay-naynu	וְתֶחֱזֶינָה עֵינֵינוּ
b'shuv'chö l'tziyon b'racha-mim.	בְּשׁוּבְךָ לְצִיּוֹן בְּרַחֲמִים:
Böruch atöh adonöy, ha-machazir	בָּרוּךְ אַתָּה יְיָ, הַמַּחֲזִיר
sh'chinöso l'tziyon.	שְׁכִינָתוֹ לְצִיּוֹן:

Bow forward while reciting the first five words:

THANKSGIVING

Modim anachnu löch,	מוֹדִים אֲנַחְנוּ לָךְ,
shö-atöh hu adonöy elo-haynu	שָׁאַתָּה הוּא יְיָ אֱלֹהֵינוּ
vay-lohay avo-saynu l'olöm	וֵאלֹהֵי אֲבוֹתֵינוּ לְעוֹלָם

On Rosh Chodesh, intermediate days of Passover or Sukkot, add the following:

Our God and God of our fathers, may there ascend, come and reach, be seen, accepted, and heard, recalled and remembered before You, the remembrance and recollection of us, the remembrance of our fathers, the remembrance of Moshiach the son of David Your servant, the remembrance of Jerusalem Your holy city, and the remembrance of all Your people the House of Israel, for deliverance, well-being, grace, kindness, mercy, good life and peace, on this day On Rosh Chodesh: Rosh Chodesh. On Passover: the Festival of Matzot. On Sukkot: the Festival of Sukkot. Remember us on this [day], Lord our God, for good; be mindful of us on this [day] for blessing; help us on this [day] for good life. With the promise of deliverance and compassion, spare us and be gracious to us; have mercy upon us and deliver us; for our eyes are directed to You, for You, God, are a gracious and merciful King.

וְתֶחֱזֶינָה May our eyes behold Your return to Zion in mercy. Blessed are You Lord, Who restores His Divine Presence to Zion.

INSIGHT

מוֹדִים — We conclude the Amidah with blessings of thanksgiving. We thank God for giving us the means to communicate with Him through prayer, and for all the miracles He does daily, irrespective, of whether we are conscious of them or not.

One of the basic values that Judaism encourages is appreciation to both God and to man, acknowledging the blessings that we have received with humility. We also bow at this prayer perhaps as a tangible expression of this sense of humility before God.

Bow forward while reciting the words in bold below:

THANKSGIVING

מוֹדִים **We thankfully acknowledge that You are** the Lord our God and God of our fathers forever. You are the strength of our

vö-ed, tzur cha-yaynu mö-gayn	וָעֶד, צוּר חַיֵּינוּ מָגֵן
yish-aynu, atöh hu l'dor vödor,	יִשְׁעֵנוּ, אַתָּה הוּא לְדוֹר וָדוֹר,
no-deh l'chö un'sapayr	נוֹדֶה לְּךָ וּנְסַפֵּר
t'hilö-sechö, al cha-yaynu	תְּהִלָּתֶךָ, עַל חַיֵּינוּ
ha-m'surim b'yödechö,	הַמְּסוּרִים בְּיָדֶךָ,
v'al nish'mosaynu ha-p'kudos	וְעַל נִשְׁמוֹתֵינוּ הַפְּקוּדוֹת
löch, v'al ni-sechö sheb'chöl	לָךְ, וְעַל נִסֶּיךָ שֶׁבְּכָל
yom imönu, v'al nif-l'ösechö	יוֹם עִמָּנוּ, וְעַל נִפְלְאוֹתֶיךָ
v'tovosechö sheb'chöl ays,	וְטוֹבוֹתֶיךָ שֶׁבְּכָל עֵת,
erev vö-voker v'tzöhö-rö-yim,	עֶרֶב וָבֹקֶר וְצָהֳרָיִם,
ha-tov, ki lo chölu racha-mechö,	הַטּוֹב, כִּי לֹא כָלוּ רַחֲמֶיךָ,
ham'rachaym, ki lo samu	הַמְרַחֵם, כִּי לֹא תַמּוּ
chasö-dechö, ki may-olöm	חֲסָדֶיךָ, כִּי מֵעוֹלָם
kivinu löch.	קִוִּינוּ לָךְ:

On Chanukah, add the following:

V'al ha-nisim v'al ha-purkön	וְעַל הַנִּסִּים וְעַל הַפֻּרְקָן
v'al ha-g'vuros v'al ha-t'shu-os	וְעַל הַגְּבוּרוֹת וְעַל הַתְּשׁוּעוֹת
v'al ha-niflö-os she-ösisö la-avosaynu	וְעַל הַנִּפְלָאוֹת שֶׁעָשִׂיתָ לַאֲבוֹתֵינוּ
ba-yömim hö-haym biz'man ha-zeh.	בַּיָּמִים הָהֵם בִּזְמַן הַזֶּה:

Bi-may matis-yöhu ben yochö-nön	בִּימֵי מַתִּתְיָהוּ בֶּן יוֹחָנָן
ko-hayn gödol chash- monö-i uvönöv,	כֹּהֵן גָּדוֹל, חַשְׁמוֹנַאי וּבָנָיו,
k'she- öm'döh mal'chus yövön	כְּשֶׁעָמְדָה מַלְכוּת יָוָן
hö-r'shö-öh al am'chö yisrö-ayl,	הָרְשָׁעָה, עַל עַמְּךָ יִשְׂרָאֵל,
l'hash-kichöm torö-sechö ul'ha-aviröm	לְהַשְׁכִּיחָם תּוֹרָתֶךָ וּלְהַעֲבִירָם
may-chukay r'tzo-nechö,	מֵחֻקֵּי רְצוֹנֶךָ,
v'atöh b'racha-mechö hö-rabim ömad-tö	וְאַתָּה בְּרַחֲמֶיךָ הָרַבִּים עָמַדְתָּ
löhem b'ays tzörösöm. Ravtö es rivöm,	לָהֶם בְּעֵת צָרָתָם. רַבְתָּ אֶת רִיבָם,
dantö es dinöm, nökam-tö es nik'mösöm.	דַּנְתָּ אֶת דִּינָם, נָקַמְתָּ אֶת נִקְמָתָם.
Mösartö gi-borim b'yad chalöshim,	מָסַרְתָּ גִבּוֹרִים בְּיַד חַלָּשִׁים,
v'rabim b' yad m'atim, ut'may-im b'yad	וְרַבִּים בְּיַד מְעַטִּים, וּטְמֵאִים בְּיַד

life, the shield of our salvation in every generation. We will give thanks to You and recount Your praise, evening, morning and noon, for our lives which are committed into Your hand, for our souls which are entrusted to You, for Your miracles which are with us daily, and for Your continual wonders and beneficence. You are the Beneficent One, for Your mercies never cease; and the Merciful One, for Your kindnesses never end; for we always place our hope in You.

On Chanukah, add the following:

And [we thank You] for the miracles, for the redemption, for the mighty deeds, for the saving acts, and for the wonders which You have wrought for our ancestors in those days, at this time.

In the days of Matityohu, the son of Yochonon the High Priest, the Hasmonean and his sons, when the wicked Hellenic government rose up against Your people Israel to make them forget Your Torah and violate the decrees of Your Will. But You, in Your abounding mercies, stood by them in the time of their distress. You waged their battles, defended their rights and avenged the wrong done to them. You delivered the mighty into the hands of the weak, the many into the hands of the few, the impure into the hands

INSIGHT

וְעַל הַנִּסִּים — During Chanukah we remember the miraculous events that occurred on those days. This is when the small band of Maccabees overcame the powerful Greeks and the Temple was restored to its sanctity.

t'horim, ur'shö-im b'yad tzadikim,	טְהוֹרִים, וּרְשָׁעִים בְּיַד צַדִּיקִים,
v'zaydim b'yad os'kay sorö-sechö.	וְזֵדִים בְּיַד עוֹסְקֵי תוֹרָתֶךָ.
Ul'chö ösisö shaym gödol v'ködosh	וּלְךָ עָשִׂיתָ שֵׁם גָּדוֹל וְקָדוֹשׁ
bö-olömechö, ul'am'chö yisrö-ayl ösisö	בְּעוֹלָמֶךָ, וּלְעַמְּךָ יִשְׂרָאֵל עָשִׂיתָ
t'shu-öh g'dolöh ufurkön k'ha-yom	תְּשׁוּעָה גְדוֹלָה וּפֻרְקָן כְּהַיּוֹם
ha-zeh. V'achar kach bö-u vö-nechö	הַזֶּה. וְאַחַר כַּךְ בָּאוּ בָנֶיךָ
lid'vir bay-sechö, ufinu es hay-chölechö,	לִדְבִיר בֵּיתֶךָ, וּפִנּוּ אֶת הֵיכָלֶךָ,
v'tiharu es mik-döshechö, v'hid-liku	וְטִהֲרוּ אֶת מִקְדָּשֶׁךָ, וְהִדְלִיקוּ
nayros b'chatz'ros köd-shechö,	נֵרוֹת בְּחַצְרוֹת קָדְשֶׁךָ,
v'köv'u sh'monas y'may chanuköh aylu	וְקָבְעוּ שְׁמוֹנַת יְמֵי חֲנֻכָּה אֵלּוּ
l'hodos ul'halayl l'shim'chö hagödol.	לְהוֹדוֹת וּלְהַלֵּל לְשִׁמְךָ הַגָּדוֹל:

V'al kulöm yis-böraych	וְעַל כֻּלָּם יִתְבָּרַךְ
v'yisromöm v'yisnasay shim'chö	וְיִתְרוֹמַם וְיִתְנַשֵּׂא שִׁמְךָ
malkaynu tömid l'olöm vö-ed.	מַלְכֵּנוּ תָּמִיד לְעוֹלָם וָעֶד:

Between Rosh Hashana and Yom Kippur add:

Uch'sov l'cha-yim tovim	וּכְתוֹב לְחַיִּים טוֹבִים
köl b'nay v'risechö.	כָּל בְּנֵי בְרִיתֶךָ:

**At the word "Böruch" bend the knee; at "Atöh" bow forward;
and at "Adonöy" straighten up.**

V'chöl ha-cha-yim yo-duchö selöh	וְכָל הַחַיִּים יוֹדוּךָ סֶּלָה
viha-l'lu shim'chö ha-gödol l'olöm	וִיהַלְלוּ שִׁמְךָ הַגָּדוֹל לְעוֹלָם
ki tov, hö-ayl y'shu-ösaynu	כִּי טוֹב, הָאֵל יְשׁוּעָתֵנוּ
v'ezrö-saynu selöh, hö-ayl ha-tov.	וְעֶזְרָתֵנוּ סֶלָה, הָאֵל הַטּוֹב:
ha-tov. Böruch atöh adonöy,	בָּרוּךְ אַתָּה יְיָ,
ha-tov shim'chö ul'chö	הַטּוֹב שִׁמְךָ וּלְךָ
nö-eh l'hodos.	נָאֶה לְהוֹדוֹת:

of the pure, the wicked into the hands of the righteous, and the wanton sinners into the hands of those who occupy themselves with Your Torah. You made a great and holy name for Yourself in Your world, and effected a great deliverance and redemption for Your people to this very day. Then Your children entered the shrine of Your House, cleansed Your Temple, purified Your Sanctuary, kindled lights in Your holy courtyards, and instituted these eight days of Chanukah to give thanks and praise to Your great Name.

וְעַל — And for all these, may Your Name, our King, be continually blessed, exalted and extolled forever and all time.

Between Rosh Hashana and Yom Kippur add:

וּכְתוֹב — Inscribe all the children of Your Covenant for a good life.

At the word "Blessed" bend the knee; at "You" bow forward; and at "Lord" straighten up.

וְכָל — And all living things shall forever thank You, and praise Your great Name eternally, for You are good. God, You are our everlasting salvation and help, O benevolent God. Blessed are You Lord, Beneficent is Your Name, and to You it is fitting to offer thanks.

INSIGHT

שִׂים שָׁלוֹם — This prayer contains the essence of the Priestly Blessing, *"Peace, goodness, life, graciousness, kindness and mercy."* We all want these blessings in our personal lives and we ask God to bestow them upon us and all of Israel.

The blessing also reminds us of our communal responsibility to each other. Despite the fact that we are scattered around the world, we are one nation, and one body.

PEACE

Sim shölom tovöh uv'röchöh,	שִׂים שָׁלוֹם, טוֹבָה וּבְרָכָה,
cha-yim chayn vöchesed	חַיִּים חֵן וָחֶסֶד
v'rachamim, ölaynu v'al köl	וְרַחֲמִים, עָלֵינוּ וְעַל כָּל
yisrö-ayl amechö. Bö-r'chaynu	יִשְׂרָאֵל עַמֶּךְ: בָּרְכֵנוּ
övinu kulönu k'echöd b'or	אָבִינוּ כֻּלָּנוּ כְּאֶחָד, בְּאוֹר
pönechö, ki v'or pönechö,	פָּנֶיךָ, כִּי בְאוֹר פָּנֶיךָ,
nösatö lönu, adonöy el-ohaynu,	נָתַתָּ לָּנוּ יְיָ אֱלֹהֵינוּ,
toras cha-yim v'ahavas	תּוֹרַת חַיִּים, וְאַהֲבַת
chesed utz'dököh uv'röchöh	חֶסֶד, וּצְדָקָה וּבְרָכָה
v'rachamim v'cha-yim v'shölom.	וְרַחֲמִים וְחַיִּים וְשָׁלוֹם:
V'tov b'aynechö l'vöraych	וְטוֹב בְּעֵינֶיךָ לְבָרֵךְ
es am'chö yisrö-ayl b'chöl ays	אֶת עַמְּךָ יִשְׂרָאֵל בְּכָל עֵת
uv'chöl shö-öh bish'lomechö.	וּבְכָל שָׁעָה בִּשְׁלוֹמֶךָ:

Between Rosh Hashana and Yom Kippur add:

Uv'sayfer cha-yim b'röchöh v'shölom	וּבְסֵפֶר חַיִּים בְּרָכָה וְשָׁלוֹם
ufar- nösöh tovöh, y'shu-öh v'nechömöh,	וּפַרְנָסָה טוֹבָה יְשׁוּעָה וְנֶחָמָה
ug'zayros tovos, ni-zöchayr v'nikösayv	וּגְזֵרוֹת טוֹבוֹת נִזָּכֵר וְנִכָּתֵב
l'fönechö, anachnu v'chöl am'chö	לְפָנֶיךָ, אֲנַחְנוּ וְכָל עַמְּךָ
bays yisrö-ayl, l'cha-yim tovim ul'shölom.	בֵּית יִשְׂרָאֵל, לְחַיִּים טוֹבִים וּלְשָׁלוֹם:

Böruch atöh adonöy,	בָּרוּךְ אַתָּה יְיָ,
ha-m'vöraych es amo	הַמְבָרֵךְ אֶת עַמּוֹ
yisrö-ayl ba-shölom.	יִשְׂרָאֵל בַּשָּׁלוֹם:

Yih-yu l'rö-tzon im'ray fi,	יִהְיוּ לְרָצוֹן אִמְרֵי פִי,
v'heg-yon libi l'fönechö,	וְהֶגְיוֹן לִבִּי לְפָנֶיךָ,
adonöy tzuri v'go-ali.	יְיָ צוּרִי וְגוֹאֲלִי:

PEACE

שִׂים — Bestow peace, goodness and blessing, life, graciousness, kindness and mercy, upon us and upon all Your people Israel. Bless us, our Father, all of us as one, with the light of Your countenance. For by the light of Your countenance You gave us, Lord our God, the Torah of life and lovingkindness, righteousness, blessing, mercy, life and peace. May it be favorable in Your eyes to bless Your people Israel, at all times and at every moment, with Your peace.

Between Rosh Hashana and Yom Kippur add:

וּבְסֵפֶר — And in the Book of Life, blessing, peace and prosperity, deliverance, consolation and favorable decrees, may we and all Your people the House of Israel be remembered and inscribed before You for a happy life and for peace.

בָּרוּךְ — Blessed are You Lord, Who blesses His people Israel with peace.

יִהְיוּ — May the words of my mouth and the meditation of my heart be acceptable before You, Lord, my Strength and my Redeemer.

INSIGHT

אֱלֹהַי — This prayer was composed by the Sage Mar the son of Ravina, who used to conclude his prayer with this petition.

The Torah places a great emphasis on creating harmony between people. Therefore it is critical that we constantly train ourselves and pray to God to "guard my tongue from evil and my lips from speaking with deceit." However, it is insufficient to only abstain from evil, we must also strive to do good and add light through the lessons of the Torah and therefore we beseech God to "open my heart to Your Torah."

Elohai, n'tzor l'shoni may-rö,   אֱלֹהַי, נְצוֹר לְשׁוֹנִי מֵרָע,

us'fösai midabayr mirmöh.   וּשְׂפָתַי מִדַּבֵּר מִרְמָה:

V'lim'kal'lai, nafshi sidom,   וְלִמְקַלְלַי, נַפְשִׁי תִדּוֹם,

v'nafshi ke-öför la-kol tih-yeh.   וְנַפְשִׁי כֶּעָפָר לַכֹּל תִּהְיֶה:

P'sach libi b'sorö-sechö,   פְּתַח לִבִּי בְּתוֹרָתֶךָ,

uv'mitzvosechö tirdof nafshi,   וּבְמִצְוֹתֶיךָ תִּרְדּוֹף נַפְשִׁי,

v'chöl ha-chosh'vim ölai   וְכָל הַחוֹשְׁבִים עָלַי

rö-öh, m'hayröh hö-fayr atz-ösöm   רָעָה, מְהֵרָה הָפֵר עֲצָתָם

v'kalkayl ma-chashavtöm.   וְקַלְקֵל מַחֲשַׁבְתָּם:

Yih-yu k'motz lif'nay ru-ach   יִהְיוּ כְּמוֹץ לִפְנֵי רוּחַ

umal-ach adonöy do-cheh.   וּמַלְאַךְ יְיָ דּוֹחֶה:

L'ma-an yay-chöl'tzun y'didechö,   לְמַעַן יֵחָלְצוּן יְדִידֶיךָ,

hoshi-öh y'min'chö va-anayni.   הוֹשִׁיעָה יְמִינְךָ וַעֲנֵנִי:

Asay l'ma-an sh'mechö,   עֲשֵׂה לְמַעַן שְׁמֶךָ,

asay l'ma-an y'minechö,   עֲשֵׂה לְמַעַן יְמִינֶךָ,

asay l'ma-an torösechö,   עֲשֵׂה לְמַעַן תּוֹרָתֶךָ,

asay l'ma-an k'dusho-sechö.   עֲשֵׂה לְמַעַן קְדֻשָּׁתֶךָ:

Yih-yu l'rö-tzon im'ray fi,   יִהְיוּ לְרָצוֹן אִמְרֵי פִי,

v'heg-yon libi l'fönechö,   וְהֶגְיוֹן לִבִּי לְפָנֶיךָ,

adonöy tzuri v'go-ali.   יְיָ צוּרִי וְגוֹאֲלִי:

Take three steps back and say the following, while bowing the head to the left, straight ahead, right, straight ahead, and bow down (as indicated):

< O-seh *shölom (*Between Rosh Hashana   <עֹשֶׂה שָׁלוֹם (בעשי״ת)

and Yom Kippur: ha- shölom) bim' romöv,   הַשָּׁלוֹם) בִּמְרוֹמָיו,

hu > ya-aseh shölom ölaynu v'al   הוּא > יַעֲשֶׂה שָׁלוֹם עָלֵינוּ וְעַל

köl yisrö-ayl, °v'im'ru ömayn.°   כָּל יִשְׂרָאֵל, °וְאִמְרוּ אָמֵן:°

אֱלֹהַי — My God, guard my tongue from evil and my lips from speaking deceitfully. Let my soul be silent to those who curse me; let my soul be as dust to all. Open my heart to Your Torah, and let my soul eagerly pursue Your commandments. As for all those who plot evil against me, hasten to annul their counsel and frustrate their design. Let them be as chaff before the wind; let the angel of the Lord thrust them away. That Your beloved ones may be delivered, help with Your right hand and answer me. Do it for the sake of Your Name; do it for the sake of Your right hand; do it for the sake of Your Torah; do it for the sake of Your holiness. May the words of my mouth and the meditation of my heart be acceptable before You, Lord, my Strength and my Redeemer.

INSIGHT

עֹשֶׂה שָׁלוֹם — Our Sages say that in the heavens there are hosts of angels, whose nature are as contrary as fire and water, yet they live and worship side by side in complete peace and harmony. Thus we pray *"He Who makes peace in His heavens, may He make peace for us and for all Israel."* First we are asking for our own peace — inner peace and harmony in the struggle between our body and soul, our heart and mind. This peace is a prelude to the collective peace among our people Israel.

Take three steps back and say the following, while bowing the head to the left, straight ahead, right, straight ahead, and bow down (as indicated):

עֹשֶׂה — <He Who makes peace (Between Rosh Hashana and Yom Kippur substitute: the peace) in His heavens, may He > make peace for us and for all Israel; °and say: Amen°.

Y'hi rö-tzon mil'fö-nechö, adonöy	יְהִי רָצוֹן מִלְּפָנֶיךָ, יְיָ
elo-haynu vay-lohay avo-saynu,	אֱלֹהֵינוּ וֵאלֹהֵי אֲבוֹתֵינוּ,
she-yibö- neh bays ha-mikdösh	שֶׁיִּבָּנֶה בֵּית הַמִּקְדָּשׁ
bim' hayröh v'yö-maynu,	בִּמְהֵרָה בְיָמֵינוּ,
v'sayn chel-kaynu b'sorö-sechö.	וְתֵן חֶלְקֵנוּ בְּתוֹרָתֶךָ:

Take three steps forward. This concludes the Amidah.

↑
STANDING

Va-y'chulu ha-shöma-yim	וַיְכֻלּוּ הַשָּׁמַיִם
v'hö-öretz v'chöl tz'vö-öm.	וְהָאָרֶץ וְכָל צְבָאָם:
Va-y'chal elohim ba-yom ha-sh'vi-i,	וַיְכַל אֱלֹהִים בַּיוֹם הַשְּׁבִיעִי,
m'lachto asher ösöh, va-yishbos	מְלַאכְתּוֹ אֲשֶׁר עָשָׂה, וַיִּשְׁבֹּת
ba-yom ha-sh'vi-i mi-köl	בַּיוֹם הַשְּׁבִיעִי מִכָּל
m'lachto asher ösöh.	מְלַאכְתּוֹ אֲשֶׁר עָשָׂה:
Va-y'vörech elohim es yom	וַיְבָרֶךְ אֱלֹהִים אֶת יוֹם
ha-sh'vi-i, va-y'kadaysh oso,	הַשְּׁבִיעִי וַיְקַדֵּשׁ אֹתוֹ,
ki vo shövas miköl m'lachto,	כִּי בוֹ שָׁבַת מִכָּל מְלַאכְתּוֹ,
asher börö elohim la-asos.	אֲשֶׁר בָּרָא אֱלֹהִים לַעֲשׂוֹת:

When praying with a Minyan, the leader recites the following:

Böruch atöh adonöy elohaynu	בָּרוּךְ אַתָּה יְיָ, אֱלֹהֵינוּ
vay-lohay avosaynu, elohay	וֵאלֹהֵי אֲבוֹתֵינוּ, אֱלֹהֵי
avröhöm, elohay yitzchök,	אַבְרָהָם, אֱלֹהֵי יִצְחָק,
vay-lohay ya-akov, hö-ayl ha-gödol	וֵאלֹהֵי יַעֲקֹב, הָאֵל הַגָּדוֹל
ha-gibör v'ha-noröh ayl el-yon,	הַגִּבּוֹר וְהַנּוֹרָא אֵל עֶלְיוֹן,
konay shöma-yim vö-retz.	קוֹנֵה שָׁמַיִם וָאָרֶץ:

יְהִי — May it be Your will, Lord our God and God of our fathers, that the *Beit Hamikdash* (Holy Temple) be speedily rebuilt in our days, and grant us our portion in Your Torah.

Take three steps forward. This concludes the Amidah.

↑
STANDING וַיְכֻלּוּ — The heavens and the earth and all their hosts were completed. And God finished by the Seventh Day His work which He had done, and He rested on the Seventh Day from all His work which He had done. And God blessed the Seventh Day and made it holy, for on it He rested from all His work which God created to function.

When praying with a Minyan, the leader recites the following:

בָּרוּךְ — Blessed are You, Lord our God and God of our fathers, God of Abraham, God of Isaac and God of Jacob, the great, mighty and awesome God, exalted God, Creator of heaven and earth.

INSIGHT

וַיְכֻלּוּ — After the conclusion of the Amidah we stand, like witnesses who are giving testimony, and recite "Vay'chulu" as a congregation. These biblical verses express the very essence of the Shabbat, describing God creating the world in six days and resting on the seventh.

Resting does not necessarily mean refraining from all physical activity, but rather from specific activities which are considered 'creative work' as listed in the Torah and the Code of Jewish Law, including writing, cooking and gardening. Shabbat is a day where we focus our energy towards our family and spiritual growth.

Maariv for Shabbat and Festivals

The congregation recites the following, followed by the leader:

Mögayn övos bid'vöro	מָגֵן אָבוֹת בִּדְבָרוֹ
m'cha-yeh maysim b'ma-amöro	מְחַיֶּה מֵתִים בְּמַאֲמָרוֹ
hö-ayl (bet. Rosh Hashana and Yom Kippur	הָאֵל (בש״ת הַמֶּלֶךְ)
substitute: ha-melech) ha-ködosh	הַקָּדוֹשׁ
she-ayn kömohu ha-mayni-ach	שֶׁאֵין כָּמוֹהוּ הַמֵּנִיחַ
l'amo b'yom shabas köd-sho,	לְעַמּוֹ בְּיוֹם שַׁבַּת קָדְשׁוֹ,
ki vöm rötzöh l'höni-ach löhem,	כִּי בָם רָצָה לְהָנִיחַ לָהֶם,
l'fönöv na-avod b'yir-öh	לְפָנָיו נַעֲבוֹד בְּיִרְאָה
vö-fachad v'no-deh lish'mo	וָפַחַד וְנוֹדֶה לִשְׁמוֹ
b'chöl yom tömid, may-ayn	בְּכָל יוֹם תָּמִיד, מֵעֵין
ha-b'röchos, ayl ha-hodö-os	הַבְּרָכוֹת, אֵל הַהוֹדָאוֹת
adon ha-shölom, m'kadaysh	אֲדוֹן הַשָּׁלוֹם, מְקַדֵּשׁ
ha-shabös um'vöraych sh'vi-i,	הַשַּׁבָּת וּמְבָרֵךְ שְׁבִיעִי,
umayni-ach bik'dushöh,	וּמֵנִיחַ בִּקְדֻשָּׁה,
l'am m'dush'nay oneg,	לְעַם מְדֻשְּׁנֵי עֹנֶג,
zaycher l'ma-asay v'rayshis.	זֵכֶר לְמַעֲשֵׂה בְרֵאשִׁית:

When praying with a Minyan, the leader recites the following:

Elohaynu vay-lohay	אֱלֹהֵינוּ וֵאלֹהֵי
avosay-nu, r'tzay nö	אֲבוֹתֵינוּ, רְצֵה נָא
vim'nuchö-saynu,	בִמְנוּחָתֵנוּ,
kad'shaynu b'mitzvo-sechö	קַדְּשֵׁנוּ בְּמִצְוֹתֶיךָ
v'sayn chel-kaynu b'sorö-sechö,	וְתֵן חֶלְקֵנוּ בְּתוֹרָתֶךָ,
sab'aynu mitu-vechö v'samay-ach	שַׂבְּעֵנוּ מִטּוּבֶךָ וְשַׂמֵּחַ
naf-shaynu bishu-ösechö,	נַפְשֵׁנוּ בִּישׁוּעָתֶךָ,
v'tahayr li-baynu l'öv-d'chö	וְטַהֵר לִבֵּנוּ לְעָבְדְּךָ
be-emes, v'han-chi-laynu	בֶּאֱמֶת, וְהַנְחִילֵנוּ

The congregation recites the following, followed by the leader:

מָגֵן — He was a shield to our fathers with His word; He resurrects the dead by His utterance; He is the holy God (Between Rosh Hashana and Yom Kippur substitute: the holy King) like whom there is none. He gives rest to His people on His holy Shabbat day, for to them He desired to give rest. We will serve Him with awe and fear, and offer thanks to His Name every day, continually, in accordance with the blessings [of that day]. He is the God worthy of thanks, the Master of peace, who sanctifies the Shabbat and blesses the Seventh Day and brings rest with holiness to a people satiated with delight — in remembrance of the work of Creation.

INSIGHT

מָגֵן אָבוֹת — This seven-faceted blessing is a synthesis of the seven blessings of the Shabbat Amidah. The words *Magen Avot* refer to the Shield of Abraham, Isaac and Jacob. The other six blessings are a reference to the resurrection of the dead, the sanctity of the day, the Shabbat blessing, a blessing for acceptance of our Shabbat prayers, thanksgiving, and the last blessing which is for peace.

When praying with a Minyan, the leader recites the following:

אֱלֹהֵינוּ — Our God and God of our fathers, please find favor in our rest, make us holy with Your commandments and grant us our portion in Your Torah; satiate us with Your goodness, gladden our soul with Your salvation, and make our heart pure to serve You in truth; and, Lord our God, grant as our heritage, in

adonöy elohaynu b'ahavöh	יְיָ אֱלֹהֵינוּ בְּאַהֲבָה
uv'rö-tzon shabas köd-shechö,	וּבְרָצוֹן שַׁבַּת קָדְשֶׁךָ,
v'yönuchu vöh köl yisrö-ayl	וְיָנוּחוּ בָהּ כָּל יִשְׂרָאֵל
m'kad'shay sh'mechö.	מְקַדְּשֵׁי שְׁמֶךָ:
Böruch atöh adonöy,	בָּרוּךְ אַתָּה יְיָ,
m'kadaysh ha-shabös.	מְקַדֵּשׁ הַשַּׁבָּת:

WHOLE KADDISH
The leader recites the Kaddish below.

↑ STANDING

Yis-gadal v'yis-kadash °sh'may rabö°.	יִתְגַּדַּל וְיִתְקַדַּשׁ °שְׁמֵהּ רַבָּא°:
(Cong.: Ömayn.)	אמן
B'öl'mö di v'rö chir'u-say	בְּעָלְמָא דִּי בְרָא כִרְעוּתֵהּ
v'yam-lich mal'chusay,	וְיַמְלִיךְ מַלְכוּתֵהּ,
Nussach Sfard: v'yatz-mach pur-könay	נוסח ספרד: וְיַצְמַח פּוּרְקָנֵהּ
°vikö-rayv m'shi-chay°.	°וִיקָרֵב מְשִׁיחֵהּ°:
(Cong.: Ömayn.)	אמן
B'cha-yay-chon uv'yomay-chon uv'cha-yay	בְּחַיֵּיכוֹן וּבְיוֹמֵיכוֹן וּבְחַיֵּי
d'chöl bays yisrö-ayl, ba-agölö uviz'man	דְכָל בֵּית יִשְׂרָאֵל, בַּעֲגָלָא וּבִזְמַן
köriv °v'im'ru ömayn°.	קָרִיב °וְאִמְרוּ אָמֵן°:
(Cong.: Ömayn. Y'hay sh'may rabö m'vörach	אמן. יְהֵא שְׁמֵהּ רַבָּא מְבָרַךְ
l'ölam ul'öl'may öl'ma-yö.	לְעָלַם וּלְעָלְמֵי עָלְמַיָּא:
Yisböraych)	יִתְבָּרַךְ:
°Y'hay sh'may rabö m'vörach	°יְהֵא שְׁמֵהּ רַבָּא מְבָרַךְ
l'ölam ul'öl'may öl'ma-yö.	לְעָלַם וּלְעָלְמֵי עָלְמַיָּא:
Yis-böraych° °v'yish-tabach, v'yispö-ayr,	יִתְבָּרַךְ° °וְיִשְׁתַּבַּח, וְיִתְפָּאַר,
v'yis-romöm, v'yis-nasay,	וְיִתְרוֹמַם, וְיִתְנַשֵּׂא,
v'yis-hadör, v'yis-aleh, v'yis-halöl°,	וְיִתְהַדָּר, וְיִתְעַלֶּה, וְיִתְהַלָּל°,
°sh'may d'kud-shö b'rich hu°.	°שְׁמֵהּ דְּקֻדְשָׁא בְּרִיךְ הוּא°:
(Cong.: Ömayn.)	אמן

love and goodwill, Your holy Shabbat, and may all Israel who sanctify Your Name rest thereon. Blessed are You Lord, who sanctifies the Shabbat.

INSIGHT

אֱלֹהֵינוּ — This prayer is a request to God to find favor in the way we observe the Shabbat. On one hand, we rest by refraining from the thirty-nine categories of work. On the other hand, we create the Shabbat atmosphere by observing the Mitzvot of Shabbat, including lighting the candles before the onset of Shabbat, making Kiddush on wine, the blessing over the the double-loaves of bread, eating the festive meals, prayer, the study of Torah, and celebrating Shabbat with our family.

We are taught that Shabbat provides us with a taste of the World to Come. We pray to God that just as he gave us the Shabbat with love and favor, so may He cause us to inherit eternal life and restfulness with the Messianic era.

STANDING

WHOLE KADDISH
The leader recites the Kaddish below.

יִתְגַּדַּל — Exalted and hallowed be His great Name. (Cong.: Amen)

בְּעָלְמָא — Throughout the world which He has created according to His Will. May He establish His kingship, (Nussach Sfard: bring forth His redemption and hasten the coming of His Moshiach. (Cong.: Amen))

בְּחַיֵּיכוֹן — In your lifetime and in your days and in the lifetime of the entire House of Israel, speedily and soon, and say, Amen. (Cong.: Amen. May His great Name be blessed forever and to all eternity. Blessed)

יְהֵא — May His great Name be blessed forever and to all eternity. Blessed and praised, glorified, exalted and extolled, honored, adored and lauded be the Name of the Holy One, blessed be He. (Cong.: Amen).

L'aylö min köl bir'chösö v'shi-rösö,   לְעֵלָּא מִן כָּל בִּרְכָתָא וְשִׁירָתָא,

tush-b'chösö v'neche-mösö,   תֻּשְׁבְּחָתָא וְנֶחֱמָתָא,

da-amirön b'öl'mö,   דַּאֲמִירָן בְּעָלְמָא,

°v'im'ru ömayn°.   °וְאִמְרוּ אָמֵן°:

(Cong.: Ömayn.)   אמן

Tiskabayl tz'los-hon uvö-us-hon d'chöl   תִּתְקַבֵּל צְלוֹתְהוֹן וּבָעוּתְהוֹן דְּכָל

bays yisrö-ayl, ködöm avu-hon   בֵּית יִשְׂרָאֵל, קֳדָם אֲבוּהוֹן

di vish'ma-yö, °v'im'ru ömayn.°   דִּי בִשְׁמַיָּא, °וְאִמְרוּ אָמֵן°:

(Cong: Ömayn)   אמן

Y'hay sh'lömö rabö min sh'ma-yö,   יְהֵא שְׁלָמָא רַבָּא מִן שְׁמַיָּא,

v'cha-yim tovim ölaynu v'al köl yisrö-ayl   וְחַיִּים טוֹבִים עָלֵינוּ וְעַל כָּל יִשְׂרָאֵל

°v'im'ru ömayn.°   °וְאִמְרוּ אָמֵן°:

(Cong: Ömayn)   אמן

**The leader takes three steps back and says the following,
while bowing the head to the right, straight ahead, left, straight ahead,
and bow down (as indicated):**

> O-seh *shölom (*Between Rosh Hashana and   > עֹשֶׂה שָׁלוֹם (בעשי״ת

Yom Kippur: ha- shölom) bim' romöv, ^ hu   הַשָּׁלוֹם) בִּמְרוֹמָיו,^ הוּא > יַעֲשֶׂה שָׁלוֹם

< ya-aseh shölom ölaynu v'al köl yisrö-ayl,   עָלֵינוּ וְעַל כָּל יִשְׂרָאֵל,

°v'im'ru ömayn.°   °וְאִמְרוּ אָמֵן°:

Take three steps forward.

Those following *Nussach Ashkenaz* omit the following paragraph.

Mizmor l'dövid, adonöy ro-i lo   מִזְמוֹר לְדָוִד, יְיָ רֹעִי לֹא

echsör. Bin'os deshe yarbi-tzayni,   אֶחְסָר: בִּנְאוֹת דֶּשֶׁא יַרְבִּיצֵנִי,

al may m'nuchos y'nahalayni.   עַל מֵי מְנֻחוֹת יְנַהֲלֵנִי:

Nafshi y'shovayv, yan-chayni   נַפְשִׁי יְשׁוֹבֵב, יַנְחֵנִי

לְעֵלָּא — Beyond all the blessings, hymns, praises and consolations that are uttered in the world; and say, Amen. (Cong.: Amen)

תִּתְקַבֵּל — May the prayers and supplications of the entire House of Israel be accepted before their Father in heaven; and say, Amen. (Cong: Amen.)

יְהֵא — May there be abundant peace from heaven, and a good life for us and for all Israel; and say, Amen. (Cong: Amen.)

עֹשֶׂה — He Who makes peace (Between Rosh Hashana and Yom Kippur say: the peace) in His heavens, may He make peace for us and for all Israel; and say, Amen. (Cong: Amen.)

INSIGHT

מִזְמוֹר לְדָוִד — Psalm 23 is one of the most familiar of the book of Psalms. It paints a serene picture of peace and comfort, free from anxiety and fear, reflecting the Shabbat atmosphere.

Another connection is that the holy day of Shabbat is also the 'shepherd' of the entire week, as our Sages taught that Shabbat is the source of blessings for the other six days of the week.

This Psalm is sometimes called the *Parnassah* Psalm (parnassah means sustenance or livelihood), for it reminds us that God is our true Provider, our Shepherd.

Those following *Nussach Ashkenaz* omit the following paragraph.

מִזְמוֹר — A Psalm by David. The Lord is my shepherd; I shall lack nothing. He makes me lie down in green pastures; He leads me beside still waters. He revives my soul; He directs me in the

v'ma-g'lay tzedek l'ma-an sh'mo.   בְּמַעְגְּלֵי צֶדֶק לְמַעַן שְׁמוֹ:

Gam ki ay-laych b'gay tzal-möves   גַּם כִּי אֵלֵךְ בְּגֵיא צַלְמָוֶת

lo irö rö, ki atöh imödi,   לֹא אִירָא רָע, כִּי אַתָּה עִמָּדִי,

shiv-t'chö umish-an-techö   שִׁבְטְךָ וּמִשְׁעַנְתֶּךָ

hay-möh y'nacha-muni.   הֵמָּה יְנַחֲמֻנִי:

Ta-aroch l'fönai shul-chön neged   תַּעֲרֹךְ לְפָנַי שֻׁלְחָן נֶגֶד

tzo-r'röy, dish-antö va-shemen   צֹרְרָי, דִּשַּׁנְתָּ בַשֶּׁמֶן

roshi, kosi r'vö-yöh. Ach tov   רֹאשִׁי, כּוֹסִי רְוָיָה: אַךְ טוֹב

vö-chesed yir-d'funi köl y'may   וָחֶסֶד יִרְדְּפוּנִי כָּל יְמֵי

cha-yöy, v'shavti b'vays   חַיָּי, וְשַׁבְתִּי בְּבֵית

adonöy l'orech yömim.   יְיָ לְאֹרֶךְ יָמִים:

HALF KADDISH
The leader recites the Kaddish below.

Yis-gadal v'yis-kadash °sh'may rabö°.   יִתְגַּדַּל וְיִתְקַדַּשׁ °שְׁמֵהּ רַבָּא°:

(Cong.: Ömayn.)   אמן

B'öl'mö di v'rö chir'u-say   בְּעָלְמָא דִּי בְרָא כִרְעוּתֵהּ

v'yam-lich mal'chusay,   וְיַמְלִיךְ מַלְכוּתֵהּ,

Nussach Sfard: v'yatz-mach pur-könay   נוסח ספרד: וְיַצְמַח פּוּרְקָנֵהּ

°vikö-rayv m'shi-chay°.   °וִיקָרֵב מְשִׁיחֵהּ°:

(Cong.: Ömayn.)   אמן

B'cha-yay-chon uv'yomay-chon uv'cha-yay   בְּחַיֵּיכוֹן וּבְיוֹמֵיכוֹן וּבְחַיֵּי

d'chöl bays yisrö-ayl, ba-agölö uviz'man   דְכָל בֵּית יִשְׂרָאֵל, בַּעֲגָלָא וּבִזְמַן

köriv °v'im'ru ömayn°.   קָרִיב °וְאִמְרוּ אָמֵן°:

(Cong.: Ömayn. Y'hay sh'may rabö   אמן. יְהֵא שְׁמֵהּ רַבָּא מְבָרַךְ

m'vörach l'ölam ul'öl'may   לְעָלַם וּלְעָלְמֵי עָלְמַיָּא

öl'ma-yö. Yisböraych)   יִתְבָּרַךְ:

paths of righteousness for the sake of His Name. Even if I will walk in the valley of the shadow of death, I will fear no evil, for You are with me; Your rod and Your staff — they will comfort me. You will prepare a table for me before my enemies; You have anointed my head with oil; my cup is full. Only goodness and kindness shall follow me all the days of my life, and I shall dwell in the House of the Lord for many long years.

INSIGHT

יִתְגַּדֵּל — The Kaddish is a prayer of praise, expressing our complete faith in God, even though His name is not mentioned. The Kaddish was written in Aramaic which was the common language in Talmudic times The word '*Kaddish*' means holy, reciting it reinforces the holiness of God's name and brings holiness to all those who respond "*Amen.*"

In addition, the prayer highlights the concept of *Kiddush Hashem*, to sanctify and bring reverence to God's name. Throughout history, this was often understood to mean that one died as a martyr, being killed rather than renouncing one's faith. However, in essence to sanctify God's Name publicly' is expressed not only by the way we die, but mainly by the way we live. When we act in such a way as to bring honor to our faith, to the Torah, and to our people, we are sanctifying God's Name.

HALF KADDISH
The leader recites the Kaddish below

יִתְגַּדֵּל — Exalted and hallowed be His great Name. (Cong.: Amen)

בְּעָלְמָא — Throughout the world which He has created according to His Will. May He establish His kingship, (Nussach Sfard: bring forth His redemption and hasten the coming of His Moshiach. (Cong.: Amen))

בְּחַיֵּיכוֹן — In your lifetime and in your days and in the lifetime of the entire House of Israel, speedily and soon, and say, Amen. (Cong.: Amen. May His great Name be blessed forever and to all eternity. Blessed)

°Y'hay sh'may rabö m'vörach °יְהֵא שְׁמֵהּ רַבָּא מְבָרַךְ
l'ölam ul'öl'may öl'ma-yö. לְעָלַם וּלְעָלְמֵי עָלְמַיָּא:
Yis-böraych° °v'yish-tabach, v'yispö-ayr, יִתְבָּרַךְ° °וְיִשְׁתַּבַּח, וְיִתְפָּאַר,
v'yis-romöm, v'yis-nasay, וְיִתְרוֹמָם, וְיִתְנַשֵּׂא,
v'yis-hadör, v'yis-aleh, v'yis-halöl°, וְיִתְהַדָּר, וְיִתְעַלֶּה, וְיִתְהַלָּל°,
°sh'may d'kud-shö b'rich hu°. °שְׁמֵהּ דְּקֻדְשָׁא בְּרִיךְ הוּא°:
(Cong.: Ömayn.) אמן

L'aylö min köl bir'chösö v'shi-rösö, לְעֵלָּא מִן כָּל בִּרְכָתָא וְשִׁירָתָא,
tush-b'chösö v'neche-mösö, תֻּשְׁבְּחָתָא וְנֶחֱמָתָא,
da-amirön b'öl'mö, דַּאֲמִירָן בְּעָלְמָא,
°v'im'ru ömayn°. °וְאִמְרוּ אָמֵן°:
(Cong.: Ömayn.) אמן

The leader bows his head and recites:

Bö-r'chu es adonöy ha-m'voröch. בָּרְכוּ אֶת יְיָ הַמְבֹרָךְ:

Congregation bows their head and recites the following, follwed by the leader:

Böruch adonöy ha-m'voröch בָּרוּךְ יְיָ הַמְבֹרָךְ
l'olöm vö-ed. לְעוֹלָם וָעֶד:

"SEFIRAT HAOMER" - THE COUNTING OF THE OMER
Between Passover and Shavout the Sefirah is counted here (page 171).

Ölaynu l'shabay-ach la-adon עָלֵינוּ לְשַׁבֵּחַ לַאֲדוֹן
ha-kol, lösays g'dulöh l'yo-tzayr הַכֹּל, לָתֵת גְּדֻלָּה לְיוֹצֵר
b'rayshis, shelo ösönu k'go-yay בְּרֵאשִׁית, שֶׁלֹא עָשָׂנוּ כְּגוֹיֵי
hö-arö-tzos, v'lo sömönu הָאֲרָצוֹת, וְלֹא שָׂמָנוּ
k'mish-p'chos hö-adömöh, כְּמִשְׁפְּחוֹת הָאֲדָמָה,
shelo söm chel-kaynu köhem, שֶׁלֹא שָׂם חֶלְקֵנוּ כָּהֶם,
v'gorö-laynu k'chöl ha-monöm וְגֹרָלֵנוּ כְּכָל הֲמוֹנָם

158

יְהֵא — May His great Name be blessed forever and to all eternity. Blessed and praised, glorified, exalted and extolled, honored, adored and lauded be the Name of the Holy One, blessed be He. (Cong.: Amen).

לְעֵלָּא — Beyond all the blessings, hymns, praises and consolations that are uttered in the world; and say, Amen. (Cong.: Amen)

INSIGHT

בָּרְכוּ — Even though *Bör'chu* was recited earlier in the service, it is recited again to afford those who may have missed it earlier the opportunity to offer this special statement of praise to God in the presence of the congregation.

The leader bows his head and recites:

בָּרְכוּ — Bless the Lord who is blessed.

Congregation bows their head and recites the following, follwed by the leader:

בָּרוּךְ — Blessed be the Lord who is blessed for all eternity.

"SEFIRAT HAOMER" - THE COUNTING OF THE OMER
Between Passover and Shavout the Sefirah is counted here (page 171).

עָלֵינוּ — It is incumbent upon us to praise the Master of all things, to exalt the Creator of all existence, that He has not made us like the nations of the world, nor caused us to be like the families of the earth; that He has not assigned us a portion like theirs, nor

she-haym mish-tachavim l'hevel	שֶׁהֵם מִשְׁתַּחֲוִים לְהֶבֶל
v'lörik. Va-anachnu kor'im	וָלָרִיק. וַאֲנַחְנוּ כּוֹרְעִים
umish-tachavim umodim,	וּמִשְׁתַּחֲוִים וּמוֹדִים,
lif'nay melech, mal'chay	לִפְנֵי מֶלֶךְ, מַלְכֵי
ha-m'löchim, ha-ködosh	הַמְּלָכִים, הַקָּדוֹשׁ
böruch hu. She-hu noteh	בָּרוּךְ הוּא. שֶׁהוּא נוֹטֶה
shöma-yim v'yosayd ö-retz,	שָׁמַיִם וְיוֹסֵד אָרֶץ,
umo-shav y'köro ba-shöma-yim	וּמוֹשַׁב יְקָרוֹ בַּשָּׁמַיִם
mima-al, ush'chinas uzo b'göv'hay	מִמַּעַל, וּשְׁכִינַת עֻזּוֹ בְּגָבְהֵי
m'romim, hu elo-haynu ayn	מְרוֹמִים, הוּא אֱלֹהֵינוּ אֵין
od. Emes mal-kaynu, efes zulöso,	עוֹד: אֱמֶת מַלְכֵּנוּ, אֶפֶס זוּלָתוֹ,
kakösuv b'soröso: V'yöda-tö	כַּכָּתוּב בְּתוֹרָתוֹ: וְיָדַעְתָּ
ha-yom va-hashay-vosö el	הַיּוֹם וַהֲשֵׁבֹתָ אֶל
l'vövechö, ki adonöy hu	לְבָבֶךָ, כִּי יְיָ הוּא
hö-elohim ba-shöma-yim	הָאֱלֹהִים בַּשָּׁמַיִם
mima-al, v'al hö-öretz	מִמַּעַל, וְעַל הָאָרֶץ
mi-töchas, ayn od.	מִתָּחַת, אֵין עוֹד:
V'al kayn n'ka-veh l'chö	וְעַל כֵּן נְקַוֶּה לְךָ
adonöy elo-haynu, lir-os	יְיָ אֱלֹהֵינוּ, לִרְאוֹת
m'hayröh b'sif-eres uzechö,	מְהֵרָה בְּתִפְאֶרֶת עֻזֶּךָ,
l'ha-avir gilu-lim min hö-öretz	לְהַעֲבִיר גִּלּוּלִים מִן הָאָרֶץ
v'hö-elilim köros yiköray-sun,	וְהָאֱלִילִים כָּרוֹת יִכָּרֵתוּן,
l'sakayn olöm b'mal'chus	לְתַקֵּן עוֹלָם בְּמַלְכוּת
shadai, v'chöl b'nay vösör	שַׁדַּי, וְכָל בְּנֵי בָשָׂר
yik-r'u vish'mechö, l'hafnos	יִקְרְאוּ בִשְׁמֶךָ, לְהַפְנוֹת
ay-lechö köl rish'ay öretz.	אֵלֶיךָ כָּל רִשְׁעֵי אָרֶץ:
Yakiru v'yay-d'u köl yosh'vay	יַכִּירוּ וְיֵדְעוּ כָּל יוֹשְׁבֵי

a lot like that of all their multitudes, for they bow to vanity and nothingness. But we bend the knee, bow down, and offer praise before the supreme King of kings, the Holy One, blessed be He, Who stretches forth the heavens and establishes the earth, the seat of Whose glory is in the heavens above and the abode of Whose majesty is in the loftiest heights. He is our God; there is none else. Truly, He is our King; there is nothing besides Him, as it is written in His Torah: Know this day and take unto your heart that the Lord is God; in the heavens above and upon the earth below there is nothing else.

INSIGHT

עָלֵינוּ — Authored by Joshua the son of Nun, *Olaynu* is considered to be one of the loftiest prayers in our liturgy. It articulates the Jewish people's unique acceptance of God as the One and Only — the Creator and Master of the Universe.

Because it refers to God as the King of Kings, *Olaynu* was initially only recited on Rosh Hashanah as part of the 'Kingship section' of the Mussaf Amidah. During the thirteenth century it became the closing prayer of every daily service (with the exception of Mussaf and Mincha of Yom Kippur). This is possibly because *Olaynu*, like *Shema Yisrael*, was the final sanctification of God chanted by martyrs during the Crusades.

וְעַל — And therefore we hope to You, Lord our God, that we may speedily behold the splendor of Your might, to banish idolatry from the earth — and false gods will be utterly destroyed; to perfect the world under the sovereignty of the Almighty. All mankind shall invoke Your Name, to turn to You all the wicked of the earth. Then all the inhabitants of the world will recognize

sayvayl ki l'chö tichra köl	תֵבֵל, כִּי לְךָ תִּכְרַע כָּל
berech, ti-shöva köl löshon.	בֶּרֶךְ, תִּשָׁבַע כָּל לָשׁוֹן.
L'fönechö adonöy elo-haynu	לְפָנֶיךָ יְיָ אֱלֹהֵינוּ
yich-r'u v'yipolu, v'lich'vod	יִכְרְעוּ וְיִפּוֹלוּ, וְלִכְבוֹד
shim'chö y'kör yi-taynu,	שִׁמְךָ יְקָר יִתֵּנוּ,
vi-kab'lu chulöm alay-hem	וִיקַבְּלוּ כֻלָּם עֲלֵיהֶם
es ol mal'chu-sechö, v'simloch	אֶת עוֹל מַלְכוּתֶךָ, וְתִמְלוֹךְ
alay-hem m'hayröh l'olöm	עֲלֵיהֶם מְהֵרָה לְעוֹלָם
vö-ed, ki ha-mal'chus shel'chö hi,	וָעֶד, כִּי הַמַּלְכוּת שֶׁלְּךָ הִיא,
ul'ol'may ad tim-loch b'chövod,	וּלְעוֹלְמֵי עַד תִּמְלוֹךְ בְּכָבוֹד,
ka-kösuv b'sorö-sechö,	כַּכָּתוּב בְּתוֹרָתֶךָ:
adonöy yim-loch l'olöm vö-ed.	יְיָ יִמְלֹךְ לְעֹלָם וָעֶד.
V'ne-emar: v'hö-yöh adonöy	וְנֶאֱמַר: וְהָיָה יְיָ
l'melech al köl hö-öretz,	לְמֶלֶךְ עַל כָּל הָאָרֶץ,
ba-yom hahu yih-yeh adonöy	בַּיּוֹם הַהוּא יִהְיֶה יְיָ
echöd ush'mo echöd.	אֶחָד וּשְׁמוֹ אֶחָד:

MOURNER'S KADDISH
Mourners recite the Kaddish below

Yis-gadal v'yis-kadash °sh'may rabö°.	יִתְגַּדַּל וְיִתְקַדַּשׁ °שְׁמֵהּ רַבָּא°:
(Cong.: Ömayn.)	אמן
B'öl'mö di v'rö chir'u-say	בְּעָלְמָא דִּי בְרָא כִרְעוּתֵהּ
v'yam-lich mal'chusay,	וְיַמְלִיךְ מַלְכוּתֵהּ,
Nussach Sfard: v'yatz-mach pur-könay	נוסח ספרד: וְיַצְמַח פּוּרְקָנֵהּ
°vikö-rayv m'shi-chay°.	°וִיקָרֵב מְשִׁיחֵהּ°:
(Cong.: Ömayn.)	אמן
B'cha-yay-chon uv'yomay-chon uv'cha-yay	בְּחַיֵּיכוֹן וּבְיוֹמֵיכוֹן וּבְחַיֵּי
d'chöl bays yisrö-ayl, ba-agölö uviz'man	דְכָל בֵּית יִשְׂרָאֵל, בַּעֲגָלָא וּבִזְמַן

and know that every knee should bend to You, every tongue should swear [by Your Name]. Before You, Lord our God, they will bow and prostrate themselves, and give honor to the glory of Your Name; and they will all take upon themselves the yoke of Your kingdom. May You soon reign over them forever and ever, for kingship is Yours, and to all eternity You will reign in glory, as it is written in Your Torah: The Lord will reign forever and ever. And it is said: The Lord shall be King over the entire earth; on that day the Lord shall be One and His Name One.

INSIGHT

וְעַל כֵּן — In this prayer we express our fervent hope for that Great Day, when all idolatry and wickedness will be abolished and all humanity acknowledges the sovereignty of God.

Then, even the wicked will submit to God's rule, and God in return, will reign upon all the earth. Then, *"the Lord shall be One and His Name One"* will be made truly manifest.

At present many people accept God's rule in theory only. They do not realize or feel deeply that God directly rules the world and the affairs of humanity. So we pray for the day when this recognition will be complete.

MOURNER'S KADDISH
Mourners recite the Kaddish below

יִתְגַּדַּל — Exalted and hallowed be His great Name. (Cong.: Amen)

בְּעָלְמָא — Throughout the world which He has created according to His Will. May He establish His kingship, (Nussach Sfard: bring forth His redemption and hasten the coming of His Moshiach. (Cong.: Amen))

בְּחַיֵּיכוֹן — In your lifetime and in your days and in the lifetime of the entire

köriv °v'im'ru ömayn°. :קָרִיב °וְאִמְרוּ אָמֵן°

(Cong.: Ömayn. Y'hay sh'may rabö אָמֵן. יְהֵא שְׁמֵהּ רַבָּא מְבָרַךְ

m'vörach l'ölam ul'öl'may לְעָלַם וּלְעָלְמֵי עָלְמַיָּא:

öl'ma-yö. Yisböraych) :יִתְבָּרֵךְ

°Y'hay sh'may rabö m'vörach °יְהֵא שְׁמֵהּ רַבָּא מְבָרַךְ

l'ölam ul'öl'may öl'ma-yö. :לְעָלַם וּלְעָלְמֵי עָלְמַיָּא

Yis-böraych° °v'yish-tabach, v'yispö-ayr, יִתְבָּרֵךְ° °וְיִשְׁתַּבַּח, וְיִתְפָּאַר,

v'yis-romöm, v'yis-nasay, וְיִתְרוֹמָם, וְיִתְנַשֵּׂא,

v'yis-hadör, v'yis-aleh, v'yis-halöl°, ,°וְיִתְהַדָּר, וְיִתְעַלֶּה, וְיִתְהַלָּל

°sh'may d'kud-shö b'rich hu°. :°שְׁמֵהּ דְּקֻדְשָׁא בְּרִיךְ הוּא

(Cong.: Ömayn.) אָמֵן

L'aylö min köl bir'chösö v'shi-rösö, לְעֵלָּא מִן כָּל בִּרְכָתָא וְשִׁירָתָא,

tush-b'chösö v'neche-mösö, תֻּשְׁבְּחָתָא וְנֶחֱמָתָא,

da-amirön b'öl'mö, דַּאֲמִירָן בְּעָלְמָא,

°v'im'ru ömayn°. :°וְאִמְרוּ אָמֵן

(Cong.: Ömayn.) אָמֵן

Y'hay sh'lömö rabö min sh'ma-yö, יְהֵא שְׁלָמָא רַבָּא מִן שְׁמַיָּא

v'cha-yim tovim ölaynu v'al köl yisrö-ayl וְחַיִּים טוֹבִים עָלֵינוּ וְעַל כָּל יִשְׂרָאֵל

°v'im'ru ömayn.° :°וְאִמְרוּ אָמֵן

(Cong: Ömayn) אָמֵן

The one reciting Kaddish takes three steps back and says the following, while bowing the head to the right, straight ahead, left, straight ahead, and bow down (as indicated):

> O-seh *shölom (*Between Rosh Hashana and > עֹשֶׂה שָׁלוֹם (בעש״ת:

Yom Kippur: ha- shölom) bim' romöv, ^ hu הַשָּׁלוֹם) בִּמְרוֹמָיו,^ הוּא > יַעֲשֶׂה שָׁלוֹם

< ya-aseh shölom ölaynu v'al köl yisrö-ayl, עָלֵינוּ וְעַל כָּל יִשְׂרָאֵל,

°v'im'ru ömayn.° :°וְאִמְרוּ אָמֵן

Take three steps forward.

House of Israel, speedily and soon, and say, Amen. (Cong.: Amen. May His great Name be blessed forever and to all eternity. Blessed)

יְהֵא — May His great Name be blessed forever and to all eternity. Blessed and praised, glorified, exalted and extolled, honored, adored and lauded be the Name of the Holy One, blessed be He. (Cong.: Amen).

לְעֵלָּא — Beyond all the blessings, hymns, praises and consolations that are uttered in the world; and say, Amen. (Cong.: Amen)

יְהֵא — May there be abundant peace from heaven, and a good life for us and for all Israel; and say, Amen. (Cong: Amen.)

עֹשֶׂה — He Who makes peace (Between Rosh Hashana and Yom Kippur say: the peace) in His heavens, may He make peace for us and for all Israel; and say, Amen. (Cong: Amen.)

DID YOU KNOW?

The Mourner's Kaddish can only be recited in the presence of a Minyan (quorum of ten Jewish males over age thirteen) during a prayer service, or after reciting Psalms or *Mishnayot*. It is normally recited at specific points during each of the three daily services.

Our Tradition teaches that a son who recites Kaddish for his father or mother saves them from certain judgment. One should therefore, do the utmost to recite Kaddish at every opportunity during the first 11 months from the passing, and on each Yahrtzeit (the anniversary of the day of the passing) thereafter.

Women may undertake to do a specific Mitzvah in honor and memory of the loved one. Our sages state that for women, this brings the same merit to the soul as does the recitation of Kaddish by men.

Many mourners make a point of leading the weekday prayer services in their synagogue for the entire 11 months, for then one can recite all the different forms of Kaddish throughout the services. This adds more and more holiness to the soul of the departed. By leading the services, one also joins the merit of all those praying and praising God to the soul of their dear departed.

Al tirö mi-pachad pis-om, אַל תִּירָא מִפַּחַד פִּתְאֹם,

umi-sho-as r'shö-im ki sövo. וּמִשֹּׁאַת רְשָׁעִים כִּי תָבֹא:

Utzu ay-tzöh v'suför, עֻצוּ עֵצָה וְתֻפָר,

dab'ru dövör v'lo yökum, דַּבְּרוּ דָבָר וְלֹא יָקוּם,

ki imönu ayl. V'ad zik-nöh ani כִּי עִמָּנוּ אֵל: וְעַד זִקְנָה אֲנִי

hu, v'ad sayvöh ani esbol, הוּא, וְעַד שֵׂיבָה אֲנִי אֶסְבֹּל,

ani ösisi va-ani esö, אֲנִי עָשִׂיתִי וַאֲנִי אֶשָּׂא,

va-ani esbol va-ama-layt. וַאֲנִי אֶסְבֹּל וַאֲמַלֵּט:

Ach tzadikim yodu lish'mechö אַךְ צַדִּיקִים יוֹדוּ לִשְׁמֶךָ

yay-sh'vu y'shörim es pö-nechö. יֵשְׁבוּ יְשָׁרִים אֶת פָּנֶיךָ:

MOURNER'S KADDISH D'RABBANAN
Mourners recite the Kaddish below

Yis-gadal v'yis-kadash °sh'may rabö°. יִתְגַּדַּל וְיִתְקַדַּשׁ °שְׁמֵהּ רַבָּא°:

(Cong.: Ömayn.) אמן

B'öl'mö di v'rö chir'u-say בְּעָלְמָא דִּי בְרָא כִרְעוּתֵהּ

v'yam-lich mal'chusay, וְיַמְלִיךְ מַלְכוּתֵהּ,

Nussach Sfard: v'yatz-mach pur-könay נוסח ספרד: וְיַצְמַח פּוּרְקָנֵהּ

°vikö-rayv m'shi-chay°. °וִיקָרֵב מְשִׁיחֵהּ°:

(Cong.: Ömayn.) אמן

B'cha-yay-chon uv'yomay-chon uv'cha-yay בְּחַיֵּיכוֹן וּבְיוֹמֵיכוֹן וּבְחַיֵּי

d'chöl bays yisrö-ayl, ba-agölö uviz'man דְּכָל בֵּית יִשְׂרָאֵל, בַּעֲגָלָא וּבִזְמַן

köriv °v'im'ru ömayn°. קָרִיב °וְאִמְרוּ אָמֵן°:

(Cong.: Ömayn. Y'hay sh'may rabö אמן. יְהֵא שְׁמֵהּ רַבָּא מְבָרַךְ

m'vörach l'ölam ul'öl'may לְעָלַם וּלְעָלְמֵי עָלְמַיָּא:

öl'ma-yö. Yisböraych) יִתְבָּרַךְ:

°Y'hay sh'may rabö m'vörach °יְהֵא שְׁמֵהּ רַבָּא מְבָרַךְ

l'ölam ul'öl'may öl'ma-yö. לְעָלַם וּלְעָלְמֵי עָלְמַיָּא:

אַל Do not fear sudden terror, nor the destruction of the wicked when it comes. Contrive a scheme, but it will be foiled; conspire a plot, but it will not materialize, for God is with us. To your old age I am [with you]; to your hoary years I will sustain you; I have made you, and I will carry you; I will sustain you and deliver you.

אַךְ — Indeed, the righteous will extol Your Name; the upright will dwell in Your presence.

INSIGHT

אַל תִּירָא — The service concludes with verses from Proverbs and Isaiah emphasizing that no matter how long our exile may be, or what fears and anxieties beset us, God will always 'carry' us; He will surely deliver and sustain us.

MOURNER'S KADDISH D'RABBANAN
Mourners recite the Kaddish below

יִתְגַּדַּל Exalted and hallowed be His great Name. (Cong.: Amen)

בְּעָלְמָא Throughout the world which He has created according to His Will. May He establish His kingship, (Nussach Sfard: bring forth His redemption and hasten the coming of His Moshiach. (Cong.: Amen)

בְּחַיֵּיכוֹן In your lifetime and in your days and in the lifetime of the entire House of Israel, speedily and soon, and say, Amen. (Cong.: Amen. May His great Name be blessed forever and to all eternity. Blessed)

יְהֵא May His great Name be blessed forever and to all eternity. Blessed and

Yis-böraych° °v'yish-tabach, v'yispö-ayr, יִתְבָּרַךְ° °וְיִשְׁתַּבַּח, וְיִתְפָּאַר,

v'yis-romöm, v'yis-nasay, וְיִתְרוֹמָם, וְיִתְנַשֵּׂא,

v'yis-hadör, v'yis-aleh, v'yis-halöl°, וְיִתְהַדָּר, וְיִתְעַלֶּה, וְיִתְהַלָּל°,

°sh'may d'kud-shö b'rich hu°. °שְׁמֵהּ דְּקֻדְשָׁא בְּרִיךְ הוּא°.

(Cong.: Ömayn.) אמן

L'aylö min köl bir'chösö v'shi-rösö, לְעֵלָּא מִן כָּל בִּרְכָתָא וְשִׁירָתָא,

tush-b'chösö v'neche-mösö, תֻּשְׁבְּחָתָא וְנֶחֱמָתָא,

da-amirön b'öl'mö, דַּאֲמִירָן בְּעָלְמָא,

°v'im'ru ömayn°. °וְאִמְרוּ אָמֵן°:

(Cong.: Ömayn.) אמן

Al yisrö-ayl v'al rabö-nön, עַל יִשְׂרָאֵל וְעַל רַבָּנָן,

v'al tal-miday-hon, v'al köl tal-miday וְעַל תַּלְמִידֵיהוֹן וְעַל כָּל תַּלְמִידֵי

sal-miday-hon, v'al köl mön d'ös'kin תַלְמִידֵיהוֹן, וְעַל כָּל מָאן דְּעָסְקִין

b'oray'sö, di v'asrö hö-dayn, v'di v'chöl asar בְּאוֹרַיְתָא, דִּי בְאַתְרָא הָדֵין וְדִי בְכָל אֲתַר

v'asar, y'hay l'hon ul'chon וַאֲתַר, יְהֵא לְהוֹן וּלְכוֹן

sh'lömö rabö, chinö v'chisdö שְׁלָמָא רַבָּא חִנָּא וְחִסְדָּא

v'rachamin v'cha-yin ari-chin, וְרַחֲמִין וְחַיִּין אֲרִיכִין,

um'zonö r'vichö ufur-könö, וּמְזוֹנָא רְוִיחָא וּפוּרְקָנָא,

min ködöm avu-hon d'vish'ma-yö, מִן קֳדָם אֲבוּהוֹן דְּבִשְׁמַיָּא,

°v'im'ru ömayn°. °וְאִמְרוּ אָמֵן°:

(Cong: Ömayn) אמן

Y'hay sh'lömö rabö min sh'ma-yö יְהֵא שְׁלָמָא רַבָּא מִן שְׁמַיָּא

v'cha-yim tovim ölaynu v'al köl yisrö-ayl וְחַיִּים טוֹבִים עָלֵינוּ וְעַל כָּל יִשְׂרָאֵל

°v'im'ru ömayn.° °וְאִמְרוּ אָמֵן°:

(Cong: Ömayn) אמן

**The one reciting Kaddish takes three steps back and says the following,
while bowing the head to the right, straight ahead, left, straight ahead,
and bow down (as indicated):**

> O-seh *shölom (*Between Rosh Hashana and > עֹשֶׂה שָׁלוֹם (בעשי״ת:

Yom Kippur: ha- shölom) bim' romöv, ^ hu הַשָּׁלוֹם) בִּמְרוֹמָיו,^ הוּא > יַעֲשֶׂה שָׁלוֹם

< ya-aseh shölom ölaynu v'al köl yisrö-ayl, עָלֵינוּ וְעַל כָּל יִשְׂרָאֵל,

°v'im'ru ömayn.° °וְאִמְרוּ אָמֵן°:

Take three steps forward.

praised, glorified, exalted and extolled, honored, adored and lauded be the Name of the Holy One, blessed be He. (Cong.: Amen).

לְעֵלָּא Beyond all the blessings, hymns, praises and consolations that are uttered in the world; and say, Amen. (Cong.: Amen)

עַל May Upon Israel, and upon our sages, and upon their disciples, and upon all the disciples of their disciples, and upon all those who occupy themselves with the Torah, here or in any other place, upon them and upon you, may there be abundant peace, grace, kindness, compassion, long life, ample sustenance and deliverance, from their Father in heaven; and say, Amen. (Cong: Amen.)

יְהֵא May there be abundant peace from heaven, and a good life for us and for all Israel; and say, Amen. (Cong: Amen.)

עֹשֶׂה He Who makes peace (Between Rosh Hashana and Yom Kippur say: the peace) in His heavens, may He make peace for us and for all Israel; and say, Amen. (Cong: Amen.)

For *Nussach Ashkenaz*
From the first day of *Rosh Chodesh Elul*, through *Hoshana Rabbah*, it is customary to recite Psalm 27 (*L'Dovid HaShem Ori*), page 52.

THIS CONCLUDES THE EVENING SERVICES

Sefirat Haomer

The Counting
of the Omer

The Counting of the Omer

From the second night of Passover until the night before Shavuot we count the Omer. This is recited before *"Ölaynu,"* the last prayer of the Maariv (evening) service. If one forgot to count the Omer on one night, he should count it during the following day without a blessing. He can then continue counting during all remaining nights with a blessing. If he forgets an entire day, he can say the count of the Omer but should not make a blessing beforehand.

The Omer is counted while standing. As long as no days have been missed, one should recite the following blessing before counting:

STANDING

Böruch atöh adonöy, elo-haynu   בָּרוּךְ אַתָּה יְיָ, אֱלֹהֵינוּ

melech hö-olöm, asher kid'shönu   מֶלֶךְ הָעוֹלָם, אֲשֶׁר קִדְּשָׁנוּ

b'mitzvosöv, v'tzivönu al   בְּמִצְוֹתָיו, וְצִוָּנוּ עַל

s'firas hö-omer.   סְפִירַת הָעֹמֶר:

Recite the counting for today (see chart on pages 178-180), then recite the portions below.

Höracha-mön hu yacha-zir   הָרַחֲמָן הוּא יַחֲזִיר

lönu avodas bays hamik-dösh   לָנוּ עֲבוֹדַת בֵּית הַמִּקְדָּשׁ

lim'komöh, bim'hayröh   לִמְקוֹמָהּ, בִּמְהֵרָה

v'yö-maynu ömayn selöh.   בְיָמֵינוּ אָמֵן סֶלָה:

Lam'natzay-ach bin'ginos   לַמְנַצֵּחַ בִּנְגִינֹת

miz-mor shir. Elohim y'chö-naynu   מִזְמוֹר שִׁיר: אֱלֹהִים יְחָנֵּנוּ

vivö-r'chaynu, yö-ayr pönöv i-tönu   וִיבָרְכֵנוּ, יָאֵר פָּנָיו אִתָּנוּ

selöh. Löda-as bö-öretz dar-kechö,   סֶלָה: לָדַעַת בָּאָרֶץ דַּרְכֶּךָ,

b'chöl go-yim y'shu-ösechö.   בְּכָל גּוֹיִם יְשׁוּעָתֶךָ:

Yodu-chö amim elohim,   יוֹדוּךָ עַמִּים אֱלֹהִים,

yodu-chö amim kulöm. Yis-m'chu   יוֹדוּךָ עַמִּים כֻּלָּם: יִשְׂמְחוּ

The Counting of the Omer

From the second night of Passover until the night before Shavuot we count the Omer. This is recited before *"Ölaynu,"* the last prayer of the Maariv (evening) service. If one forgot to count the Omer on one night, he should count it during the following day without a blessing. He can then continue counting during all remaining nights with a blessing. If he forgets an entire day, he can say the count of the Omer but should not make a blessing beforehand.

STANDING

The Omer is counted while standing. As long as no days have been missed, one should recite the following blessing before counting:

בָּרוּךְ Blessed are You, Lord our God, King of the Universe, Who has sanctified us with His commandments, and commanded us concerning the counting of the Omer.

Recite the counting for today (see chart on **pages 178-180**), then recite the portions below.

הָרַחֲמָן May the Merciful One restore unto us the service of the Beit Hamikdosh to its place, speedily in our days; Amen, Selah.

לַמְנַצֵּחַ For the Choirmaster; a song with instrumental music; a Psalm. May God be gracious to us and bless us, may He make His countenance shine upon us forever; that Your way be known on earth, Your salvation among all nations. The nations will extol You, O God; all the nations will extol You. The nations will rejoice and sing for joy, for You will judge the peoples justly and

vira-n'nu l'umim, ki sish-pot amim	וִירַנְּנוּ לְאֻמִּים, כִּי תִשְׁפֹּט עַמִּים
mi-shor, ul'u-mim bö-öretz	מִישֹׁר, וּלְאֻמִּים בָּאָרֶץ
tan-chaym selöh. Yodu-chö amim	תַנְחֵם סֶלָה: יוֹדוּךָ עַמִּים
elohim, yodu-chö amim kulöm.	אֱלֹהִים, יוֹדוּךָ עַמִּים כֻּלָּם:
Eretz nös'nöh y'vulöh,	אֶרֶץ נָתְנָה יְבוּלָהּ,
y'vö-r'chaynu elohim elo-haynu.	יְבָרְכֵנוּ אֱלֹהִים אֱלֹהֵינוּ:
Y'vö-r'chaynu elohim, v'yi-r'u oso	יְבָרְכֵנוּ אֱלֹהִים, וְיִירְאוּ אוֹתוֹ
köl af'say öretz.	כָּל אַפְסֵי אָרֶץ:
Önö, b'cho-ach g'dulas y'min'chö,	אָנָּא, בְּכֹחַ גְּדֻלַּת יְמִינְךָ,
ta-tir tz'ruröh. Kabayl	תַּתִּיר צְרוּרָה: קַבֵּל
rinas am'chö, sag'vaynu	רִנַּת עַמְּךָ, שַׂגְּבֵנוּ,
taha-raynu, noröh. Nö gibor,	טַהֲרֵנוּ, נוֹרָא: נָא גִבּוֹר,
dor'shay yichud'chö, k'vövas	דּוֹרְשֵׁי יִחוּדְךָ, כְּבָבַת
shöm'raym. Bör'chaym taha-raym,	שָׁמְרֵם: בָּרְכֵם, טַהֲרֵם,
racha-may tzid'kös'chö tömid	רַחֲמֵי צִדְקָתְךָ תָּמִיד
göm'laym. Chasin ködosh, b'rov	גָּמְלֵם: חֲסִין קָדוֹשׁ, בְּרוֹב
tuv'chö nahayl adö-sechö. Yöchid,	טוּבְךָ נַהֵל עֲדָתֶךָ: יָחִיד,
gay-eh, l'am'chö p'nay, zoch'ray	גֵּאֶה, לְעַמְּךָ פְּנֵה, זוֹכְרֵי
k'dushö-sechö. Shav-ösaynu	קְדֻשָּׁתֶךָ: שַׁוְעָתֵנוּ
kabayl, ush'ma tza-akö-saynu,	קַבֵּל, וּשְׁמַע צַעֲקָתֵנוּ,
yoday-a ta-alumos. Böruch shaym	יוֹדֵעַ תַּעֲלֻמוֹת: בָּרוּךְ שֵׁם
k'vod mal'chuso l'olöm vö-ed.	כְּבוֹד מַלְכוּתוֹ לְעוֹלָם וָעֶד:
Ri-bono shel olöm, atöh	רִבּוֹנוֹ שֶׁל עוֹלָם, אַתָּה
tzivi-sönu al y'day mosheh	צִוִּיתָנוּ עַל יְדֵי מֹשֶׁה
av-dechö lis-por s'firas hö-omer	עַבְדֶּךָ לִסְפּוֹר סְפִירַת הָעוֹמֶר
k'day l'taha-raynu mik'lipo-saynu	כְּדֵי לְטַהֲרֵנוּ מִקְּלִפּוֹתֵינוּ

guide the nations on earth forever. The peoples will extol You, O God; all the peoples will extol You, for the earth will have yielded its produce and God, our God, will bless us. God will bless us; and all, from the farthest corners of the earth, shall fear Him.

אָנָּא We implore you, by the great power of Your right hand, release the captive. Accept the prayer of Your people; strengthen us, purify us, Awesome One. Mighty One, we beseech You, guard as the apple of the eye those Who seek Your Oneness. Bless them, cleanse them; bestow upon them forever Your merciful righteousness. Powerful, Holy One, in Your abounding goodness, guide Your congregation. Only and Exalted One, turn to Your people Who are mindful of Your holiness. Accept our supplication and hear our cry, You Who knows secret thoughts. Blessed be the name of the glory of His kingdom forever and ever.

INSIGHT

The Kabbalists explain that the 49 days that connect Passover with Shavuot correspond to the forty-nine powers of the soul. Each day, the Jewish people refined one of these soul-powers. On a national level, refining that particular soul power brought the Jews one step closer to their becoming God's chosen people.

Each year we retrace this inner journey by "Counting the Omer." When we have completed the count we celebrate Shavuot, the "Festival of Weeks." This holiday not only commemorates the giving of the Torah, it celebrates the methodical 49-step process of self-refinement of our soul-powers.

רִבּוֹנוֹ Master of the universe, You have commanded us through Moses Your servant to count Sefirat HaOmer, in order to purify

umitum-osaynu, k'mo	וּמִטֻּמְאוֹתֵינוּ, כְּמוֹ
she-kösav-tö b'sorö-sechö:	שֶׁכָּתַבְתָּ בְּתוֹרָתֶךְ:
Us'far-tem löchem mimö-chöras	וּסְפַרְתֶּם לָכֶם מִמָּחֳרַת
ha-shabös mi-yom havi-achem es	הַשַּׁבָּת מִיּוֹם הֲבִיאֲכֶם אֶת
omer ha-t'nuföh sheva shabösos	עֹמֶר הַתְּנוּפָה שֶׁבַע שַׁבָּתוֹת
t'mimos tih'yenöh.	תְּמִימֹת תִּהְיֶינָה:
Admimö-chöras ha-shabös	עַד מִמָּחֳרַת הַשַּׁבָּת
hash'vi-is tisp'ru cha-mishim	הַשְּׁבִיעִת תִּסְפְּרוּ חֲמִשִּׁים
yom, k'day she-yitö-haru naf'shos	יוֹם, כְּדֵי שֶׁיִּטָּהֲרוּ נַפְשׁוֹת
am'chö yisrö-ayl mizu-hamösöm,	עַמְּךָ יִשְׂרָאֵל מִזֻּהֲמָתָם,
uv'chayn y'hi rötzon mil'fö-nechö,	וּבְכֵן יְהִי רָצוֹן מִלְּפָנֶיךָ,
adonöy elo-haynu vay-lohay	יְיָ אֱלֹהֵינוּ וֵאלֹהֵי
avosaynu, she-biz'chus s'firas	אֲבוֹתֵינוּ, שֶׁבִּזְכוּת סְפִירַת
hö-omer shesöfar-ti ha-yom,	הָעוֹמֶר שֶׁסָּפַרְתִּי הַיּוֹם,
y'sukan mah she-pögam-ti	יְתֻקַּן מַה שֶּׁפָּגַמְתִּי
bis'firöh (say the Sefira for that day)	בִּסְפִירָה (פלונית השייך לאותו הלילה)
v'etö-hayr v'eska-daysh bik'dushöh	וְאֶטָּהֵר וְאֶתְקַדֵּשׁ בִּקְדֻשָּׁה
shel ma-löh, v'al y'day zeh	שֶׁל מַעְלָה, וְעַל יְדֵי זֶה
yush-pa shefa rav b'chöl	יֻשְׁפַּע שֶׁפַע רַב בְּכָל
hö-olömos ul'sakayn es	הָעוֹלָמוֹת וּלְתַקֵּן אֶת
naf'sho-saynu v'rucho-saynu	נַפְשׁוֹתֵינוּ וְרוּחוֹתֵינוּ
v'nish'mo-saynu mi-köl sig uf'gam	וְנִשְׁמוֹתֵינוּ מִכָּל סִיג וּפְגַם
ul'taha-raynu ul'kad'shaynu	וּלְטַהֲרֵנוּ וּלְקַדְּשֵׁנוּ
bik'dushös'chö hö-elyonöh,	בִּקְדֻשָּׁתְךָ הָעֶלְיוֹנָה,
ömayn selöh.	אָמֵן סֶלָה:

Continue with *"Ölaynu"* **(page 158).**

us from our evil and uncleanness. As You have written in Your Torah, "You shall count for yourselves from the day following the day of rest, from the day on which you bring the Omer as a wave-offering; [the counting] shall be for seven full weeks. Until the day following the seventh week shall you count fifty days," so that the souls of Your people Israel may be cleansed from their defilement. Therefore, may it be Your will, Lord our God and God of our fathers, that in the merit of the Sefirat HaOmer which I counted today, the blemish that I have caused in the Sefirah (say the *Sefirah* for that day) be rectified and I may be purified and sanctified with supernal holiness. May abundant bounty thereby be bestowed upon all the worlds. May it rectify our Nefesh, Ruach and Neshamah from every baseness and defect, and may it purify and sanctify us with Your supernal holiness. Amen, selah.

Continue with "Ölaynu" (page 158).

חסד שבחסד	הַיּוֹם יוֹם אֶחָד לָעֹמֶר:	טז בניסן
גבורה שבחסד	הַיּוֹם שְׁנֵי יָמִים לָעֹמֶר:	יז בניסן
תפארת שבחסד	הַיּוֹם שְׁלֹשָׁה יָמִים לָעֹמֶר:	יח בניסן
נצח שבחסד	הַיּוֹם אַרְבָּעָה יָמִים לָעֹמֶר:	יט בניסן
הוד שבחסד	הַיּוֹם חֲמִשָּׁה יָמִים לָעֹמֶר:	כ בניסן
יסוד שבחסד	הַיּוֹם שִׁשָּׁה יָמִים לָעֹמֶר:	כא בניסן
מלכות שבחסד	הַיּוֹם שִׁבְעָה יָמִים שֶׁהֵם שָׁבוּעַ אֶחָד לָעֹמֶר:	כב בניסן
חסד שבגבורה	הַיּוֹם שְׁמוֹנָה יָמִים שֶׁהֵם שָׁבוּעַ אֶחָד וְיוֹם אֶחָד לָעֹמֶר:	כג בניסן
גבורה שבגבורה	הַיּוֹם תִּשְׁעָה יָמִים שֶׁהֵם שָׁבוּעַ אֶחָד וּשְׁנֵי יָמִים לָעֹמֶר:	כד בניסן
תפארת שבגבורה	הַיּוֹם עֲשָׂרָה יָמִים שֶׁהֵם שָׁבוּעַ אֶחָד וּשְׁלֹשָׁה יָמִים לָעֹמֶר:	כה בניסן
נצח שבגבורה	הַיּוֹם אַחַד עָשָׂר יוֹם שֶׁהֵם שָׁבוּעַ אֶחָד וְאַרְבָּעָה יָמִים לָעֹמֶר:	כו בניסן
הוד שבגבורה	הַיּוֹם שְׁנֵים עָשָׂר יוֹם שֶׁהֵם שָׁבוּעַ אֶחָד וַחֲמִשָּׁה יָמִים לָעֹמֶר:	כז בניסן
יסוד שבגבורה	הַיּוֹם שְׁלֹשָׁה עָשָׂר יוֹם שֶׁהֵם שָׁבוּעַ אֶחָד וְשִׁשָּׁה יָמִים לָעֹמֶר:	כח בניסן
מלכות שבגבורה	הַיּוֹם אַרְבָּעָה עָשָׂר יוֹם שֶׁהֵם שְׁנֵי שָׁבוּעוֹת לָעֹמֶר:	כט בניסן
חסד שבתפארת	הַיּוֹם חֲמִשָּׁה עָשָׂר יוֹם שֶׁהֵם שְׁנֵי שָׁבוּעוֹת וְיוֹם אֶחָד לָעֹמֶר:	ל בניסן
גבורה שבתפארת	הַיּוֹם שִׁשָּׁה עָשָׂר יוֹם שֶׁהֵם שְׁנֵי שָׁבוּעוֹת וּשְׁנֵי יָמִים לָעֹמֶר:	א באייר
תפארת שבתפארת	הַיּוֹם שִׁבְעָה עָשָׂר יוֹם שֶׁהֵם שְׁנֵי שָׁבוּעוֹת וּשְׁלֹשָׁה יָמִים לָעֹמֶר:	ב באייר
נצח שבתפארת	הַיּוֹם שְׁמוֹנָה עָשָׂר יוֹם שֶׁהֵם שְׁנֵי שָׁבוּעוֹת וְאַרְבָּעָה יָמִים לָעֹמֶר:	ג באייר
הוד שבתפארת	הַיּוֹם תִּשְׁעָה עָשָׂר יוֹם שֶׁהֵם שְׁנֵי שָׁבוּעוֹת וַחֲמִשָּׁה יָמִים לָעֹמֶר:	ד באייר
יסוד שבתפארת	הַיּוֹם עֶשְׂרִים יוֹם שֶׁהֵם שְׁנֵי שָׁבוּעוֹת וְשִׁשָּׁה יָמִים לָעֹמֶר:	ה באייר
מלכות שבתפארת	הַיּוֹם אֶחָד וְעֶשְׂרִים יוֹם שֶׁהֵם שְׁלֹשָׁה שָׁבוּעוֹת לָעֹמֶר:	ו באייר
חסד שבנצח	הַיּוֹם שְׁנַיִם וְעֶשְׂרִים יוֹם שֶׁהֵם שְׁלֹשָׁה שָׁבוּעוֹת וְיוֹם אֶחָד לָעֹמֶר:	ז באייר
גבורה שבנצח	הַיּוֹם שְׁלֹשָׁה וְעֶשְׂרִים יוֹם שֶׁהֵם שְׁלֹשָׁה שָׁבוּעוֹת וּשְׁנֵי יָמִים לָעֹמֶר:	ח באייר
תפארת שבנצח	הַיּוֹם אַרְבָּעָה וְעֶשְׂרִים יוֹם שֶׁהֵם שְׁלֹשָׁה שָׁבוּעוֹת וּשְׁלֹשָׁה יָמִים לָעֹמֶר:	ט באייר
נצח שבנצח	הַיּוֹם חֲמִשָּׁה וְעֶשְׂרִים יוֹם שֶׁהֵם שְׁלֹשָׁה שָׁבוּעוֹת וְאַרְבָּעָה יָמִים לָעֹמֶר:	י באייר
הוד שבנצח	הַיּוֹם שִׁשָּׁה וְעֶשְׂרִים יוֹם שֶׁהֵם שְׁלֹשָׁה שָׁבוּעוֹת וַחֲמִשָּׁה יָמִים לָעֹמֶר:	יא באייר
יסוד שבנצח	הַיּוֹם שִׁבְעָה וְעֶשְׂרִים יוֹם שֶׁהֵם שְׁלֹשָׁה שָׁבוּעוֹת וְשִׁשָּׁה יָמִים לָעֹמֶר:	יב באייר
מלכות שבנצח	הַיּוֹם שְׁמוֹנָה וְעֶשְׂרִים יוֹם שֶׁהֵם אַרְבָּעָה שָׁבוּעוֹת לָעֹמֶר:	יג באייר
חסד שבהוד	הַיּוֹם תִּשְׁעָה וְעֶשְׂרִים יוֹם שֶׁהֵם אַרְבָּעָה שָׁבוּעוֹת וְיוֹם אֶחָד לָעֹמֶר:	יד באייר
גבורה שבהוד	הַיּוֹם שְׁלֹשִׁים יוֹם שֶׁהֵם אַרְבָּעָה שָׁבוּעוֹת וּשְׁנֵי יָמִים לָעֹמֶר:	טו באייר
תפארת שבהוד	הַיּוֹם אֶחָד וּשְׁלֹשִׁים יוֹם שֶׁהֵם אַרְבָּעָה שָׁבוּעוֹת וּשְׁלֹשָׁה יָמִים לָעֹמֶר:	טז באייר
נצח שבהוד	הַיּוֹם שְׁנַיִם וּשְׁלֹשִׁים יוֹם שֶׁהֵם אַרְבָּעָה שָׁבוּעוֹת וְאַרְבָּעָה יָמִים לָעֹמֶר:	יז באייר

16 NISAN Today is the first day of the Omer.

17 NISAN Today is the second day of the Omer.

18 NISAN Today is the third day of the Omer.

19 NISAN Today is the fourth day of the Omer.

20 NISAN Today is the fifth day of the Omer.

21 NISAN Today is the sixth day of the Omer.

22 NISAN Today is the seventh day, which is one week of the Omer.

23 NISAN Today is the eighth day, which is one week and one day of the Omer.

24 NISAN Today is the ninth day, which is one week and two days of the Omer.

25 NISAN Today is the tenth day, which is one week and three days of the Omer.

26 NISAN Today is the eleventh day, which is one week and four days of the Omer.

27 NISAN Today is the twelfth day, which is one week and five days of the Omer.

28 NISAN Today is the thirteenth day, which is one week and six days of the Omer.

29 NISAN Today is the fourteenth day, which are two weeks of the Omer.

30 NISAN Today is the fifteenth day, which are two weeks and one day of the Omer.

1 IYYAR Today is the sixteenth day, which are two weeks and two days of the Omer.

2 IYYAR Today is the seventeenth day, which are two weeks and three days of the Omer.

3 IYYAR Today is the eighteenth day, which are two weeks and four days of the Omer.

4 IYYAR Today is the nineteenth day, which are two weeks and five days of the Omer.

5 IYYAR Today is the twentieth day, which are two weeks and six days of the Omer.

6 IYYAR Today is the twenty-first day, which are three weeks of the Omer.

7 IYYAR Today is the twenty-second day, which are three weeks and one day of the Omer.

8 IYYAR Today is the twenty-third day, which are three weeks and two days of the Omer.

9 IYYAR Today is the twenty-fourth day, which are three weeks and three days of the Omer.

10 IYYAR Today is the twenty-fifth day, which are three weeks and four days of the Omer.

11 IYYAR Today is the twenty-sixth day, which are three weeks and five days of the Omer.

12 IYYAR Today is the twenty-seventh day, which are three weeks and six days of the Omer.

13 IYYAR Today is the twenty-eighth day, which are four weeks of the Omer.

14 IYYAR Today is the twenty-ninth day, which are four weeks and one day of the Omer.

15 IYYAR Today is the thirtieth day, which are four weeks and two days of the Omer.

16 IYYAR Today is the thirty-first day, which are four weeks and three days of the Omer.

17 IYYAR Today is the thirty-second day, which are four weeks and four days of the Omer.

הוד שבהוד	<u>יח באייר</u> הַיּוֹם שְׁלֹשָׁה וּשְׁלֹשִׁים יוֹם שֶׁהֵם אַרְבָּעָה שָׁבוּעוֹת וַחֲמִשָּׁה יָמִים לָעֹמֶר:	
יסוד שבהוד	<u>יט באייר</u> הַיּוֹם אַרְבָּעָה וּשְׁלֹשִׁים יוֹם שֶׁהֵם אַרְבָּעָה שָׁבוּעוֹת וְשִׁשָּׁה יָמִים לָעֹמֶר:	
מלכות שבהוד	<u>כ באייר</u> הַיּוֹם חֲמִשָּׁה וּשְׁלֹשִׁים יוֹם שֶׁהֵם חֲמִשָּׁה שָׁבוּעוֹת לָעֹמֶר:	
חסד שביסוד	<u>כא באייר</u> הַיּוֹם שִׁשָּׁה וּשְׁלֹשִׁים יוֹם שֶׁהֵם חֲמִשָּׁה שָׁבוּעוֹת וְיוֹם אֶחָד לָעֹמֶר:	
גבורה שביסוד	<u>כב באייר</u> הַיּוֹם שִׁבְעָה וּשְׁלֹשִׁים יוֹם שֶׁהֵם חֲמִשָּׁה שָׁבוּעוֹת וּשְׁנֵי יָמִים לָעֹמֶר:	
תפארת שביסוד	<u>כג באייר</u> הַיּוֹם שְׁמוֹנָה וּשְׁלֹשִׁים יוֹם שֶׁהֵם חֲמִשָּׁה שָׁבוּעוֹת וּשְׁלֹשָׁה יָמִים לָעֹמֶר:	
נצח שביסוד	<u>כד באייר</u> הַיּוֹם תִּשְׁעָה וּשְׁלֹשִׁים יוֹם שֶׁהֵם חֲמִשָּׁה שָׁבוּעוֹת וְאַרְבָּעָה יָמִים לָעֹמֶר:	
הוד שביסוד	<u>כה באייר</u> הַיּוֹם אַרְבָּעִים יוֹם שֶׁהֵם חֲמִשָּׁה שָׁבוּעוֹת וַחֲמִשָּׁה יָמִים לָעֹמֶר:	
יסוד שביסוד	<u>כו באייר</u> הַיּוֹם אֶחָד וְאַרְבָּעִים יוֹם שֶׁהֵם חֲמִשָּׁה שָׁבוּעוֹת וְשִׁשָּׁה יָמִים לָעֹמֶר:	
מלכות שביסוד	<u>כז באייר</u> הַיּוֹם שְׁנַיִם וְאַרְבָּעִים יוֹם שֶׁהֵם שִׁשָּׁה שָׁבוּעוֹת לָעֹמֶר:	
חסד שבמלכות	<u>כח באייר</u> הַיּוֹם שְׁלֹשָׁה וְאַרְבָּעִים יוֹם שֶׁהֵם שִׁשָּׁה שָׁבוּעוֹת וְיוֹם אֶחָד לָעֹמֶר:	
גבורה שבמלכות	<u>כט באייר</u> הַיּוֹם אַרְבָּעָה וְאַרְבָּעִים יוֹם שֶׁהֵם שִׁשָּׁה שָׁבוּעוֹת וּשְׁנֵי יָמִים לָעֹמֶר:	
תפארת שבמלכות	<u>א בסיון</u> הַיּוֹם חֲמִשָּׁה וְאַרְבָּעִים יוֹם שֶׁהֵם שִׁשָּׁה שָׁבוּעוֹת וּשְׁלֹשָׁה יָמִים לָעֹמֶר:	
נצח שבמלכות	<u>ב בסיון</u> הַיּוֹם שִׁשָּׁה וְאַרְבָּעִים יוֹם שֶׁהֵם שִׁשָּׁה שָׁבוּעוֹת וְאַרְבָּעָה יָמִים לָעֹמֶר:	
הוד שבמלכות	<u>ג בסיון</u> הַיּוֹם שִׁבְעָה וְאַרְבָּעִים יוֹם שֶׁהֵם שִׁשָּׁה שָׁבוּעוֹת וַחֲמִשָּׁה יָמִים לָעֹמֶר:	
יסוד שבמלכות	<u>ד בסיון</u> הַיּוֹם שְׁמוֹנָה וְאַרְבָּעִים יוֹם שֶׁהֵם שִׁשָּׁה שָׁבוּעוֹת וְשִׁשָּׁה יָמִים לָעֹמֶר:	
מלכות שבמלכות	<u>ה בסיון</u> הַיּוֹם תִּשְׁעָה וְאַרְבָּעִים יוֹם שֶׁהֵם שִׁבְעָה שָׁבוּעוֹת לָעֹמֶר:	

Continue with *"Höracha-mön"* (page 172).

18 IYYAR Today is the thirty-third day, which are four weeks and five days of the Omer.

19 IYYAR Today is the thirty-fourth day, which are four weeks and six days of the Omer.

20 IYYAR Today is the thirty-fifth day, which are five weeks of the Omer.

21 IYYAR Today is the thirty-sixth day, which are five weeks and one day of the Omer.

22 IYYAR Today is the thirty-seventh day, which are five weeks and two days of the Omer.

23 IYYAR Today is the thirty-eighth day, which are five weeks and three days of the Omer.

24 IYYAR Today is the thirty-ninth day, which are five weeks and four days of the Omer.

25 IYYAR Today is the fortieth day, which are five weeks and five days of the Omer.

26 IYYAR Today is the forty-first day, which are five weeks and six days of the Omer.

27 IYYAR Today is the forty-second day, which are six weeks of the Omer.

28 IYYAR Today is the forty-third day, which are six weeks and one day of the Omer.

29 IYYAR Today is the forty-fourth day, which are six weeks and two days of the Omer.

1 SIVAN Today is the forty-fifth day, which are six weeks and three days of the Omer.

2 SIVAN Today is the forty-sixth day, which are six weeks and four days of the Omer.

3 SIVAN Today is the forty-seventh day, which are six weeks and five days of the Omer.

4 SIVAN Today is the forty-eighth day, which are six weeks and six days of the Omer.

5 SIVAN Today is the forty-ninth day, which are seven weeks of the Omer.

Continue with *"Höracha-mön"* (page 172).

Amidah for Festivals

THE AMIDAH FOR PESACH, SHAVUOT, AND SUKKOT
The Amidah is recited while standing, with both feet together.
Before beginning, take three steps back, then three steps forward,
and say:

Adonöy, s'fösai tif-töch ufi	אֲדֹנָי, שְׂפָתַי תִּפְתָּח וּפִי
yagid t'hilö-sechö.	יַגִּיד תְּהִלָּתֶךָ:

STANDING

At the word "Böruch" bend the knee; at "Atöh" bow forward;
and at "Adonöy" straighten up.

RECALLING OUR PATRIARCHS

Böruch atöh adonöy elo-haynu	בָּרוּךְ אַתָּה יְיָ אֱלֹהֵינוּ
vay-lohay avosaynu,	וֵאלֹהֵי אֲבוֹתֵינוּ,
elo-hay avröhöm, elo-hay	אֱלֹהֵי אַבְרָהָם, אֱלֹהֵי
yitzchök, vay-lohay ya-akov,	יִצְחָק, וֵאלֹהֵי יַעֲקֹב,
hö-ayl ha-gödol ha-gibor	הָאֵל הַגָּדוֹל הַגִּבּוֹר
v'hanorö, ayl el-yon, gomayl	וְהַנּוֹרָא, אֵל עֶלְיוֹן, גּוֹמֵל
cha-södim tovim, ko-nay ha-kol,	חֲסָדִים טוֹבִים, קוֹנֵה הַכֹּל,
v'zochayr chas'day övos,	וְזוֹכֵר חַסְדֵי אָבוֹת,
umay-vi go-ayl liv'nay v'nayhem	וּמֵבִיא גוֹאֵל לִבְנֵי בְנֵיהֶם
l'ma-an sh'mo b'ahavöh.	לְמַעַן שְׁמוֹ בְּאַהֲבָה:

At the word *"Böruch"* bend the knee; at *"Atöh"* bow forward;
and at *"Adonöy"* straighten up.

Melech ozayr	מֶלֶךְ עוֹזֵר
umo-shi-a umö-gayn.	וּמוֹשִׁיעַ וּמָגֵן:
Böruch atöh adonöy,	בָּרוּךְ אַתָּה יְיָ,
mö-gayn avröhöm.	מָגֵן אַבְרָהָם:

Amidah for Festivals

INTRODUCTION

The Amidah for the *'Shalosh Regalim'* (the Three Pilgrimage Festivals), differs from the standard Shabbat Amidah in that it contains several portions pertaining to the specific Festivals celebrated.

Additions for Shabbat are included in parentheses, so that when a Festival occurs on Shabbat, these inclusions are to be recited as well.

THE AMIDAH FOR PESACH, SHAVUOT, AND SUKKOT
The Amidah is recited while standing, with both feet together.
Before beginning, take three steps back, then three steps forward,
and say:

↑
STANDING

אֲדֹנָי — My Lord, open my lips, and my mouth shall declare Your praise.

At the word "Blessed" bend the knee; at "You" bow forward;
and at "Lord" straighten up.

RECALLING OUR PATRIARCHS

בָּרוּךְ — **Blessed** are **You**, **Lord** our God and God of our fathers, God of Abraham, God of Isaac and God of Jacob, the great, mighty and awesome God, exalted God, Who bestows bountiful kindness, Who creates all things, Who remembers the piety of the Patriarchs, and Who, in love, brings a redeemer to their children's children, for the sake of His Name.

At the word "Blessed" bend the knee; at "You" bow forward;
and at "Lord" straighten up.

מֶלֶךְ — King, [You are] a helper, a savior and a shield. **Blessed** are **You Lord**, Shield of Abraham.

GOD'S MIGHT

Atöh gibor l'olöm adonöy, אַתָּה גִבּוֹר לְעוֹלָם אֲדֹנָי,

m'cha-yeh maysim atöh, מְחַיֶּה מֵתִים אַתָּה, רַב

rav l'hoshi-a. לְהוֹשִׁיעַ:

In summer say: Morid ha-töl. בקיץ: מוֹרִיד הַטָּל:

In winter say: Mashiv höru-ach בחורף: מַשִּׁיב הָרוּחַ

umo-rid ha-geshem. וּמוֹרִיד הַגֶּשֶׁם:

M'chal-kayl cha-yim b'chesed, מְכַלְכֵּל חַיִּים בְּחֶסֶד,

m'cha-yeh may-sim b'racha-mim מְחַיֶּה מֵתִים בְּרַחֲמִים

rabim, so-maych nof'lim, רַבִּים, סוֹמֵךְ נוֹפְלִים,

v'rofay cholim, uma-tir וְרוֹפֵא חוֹלִים, וּמַתִּיר

asu-rim, um'ka-yaym emu-nöso אֲסוּרִים, וּמְקַיֵּם אֱמוּנָתוֹ לִישֵׁנֵי

li-shaynay öför, mi chö-mochö עָפָר, מִי כָמוֹךָ

ba-al g'vuros umi do-meh löch, בַּעַל גְּבוּרוֹת וּמִי דוֹמֶה לָּךְ,

melech may-mis um'cha-yeh מֶלֶךְ מֵמִית וּמְחַיֶּה

umatz-mi-ach y'shu-öh. וּמַצְמִיחַ יְשׁוּעָה:

V'ne-emön atöh l'ha-cha-yos וְנֶאֱמָן אַתָּה לְהַחֲיוֹת

may-sim. Böruch atöh adonöy, מֵתִים: בָּרוּךְ אַתָּה יְיָ,

m'cha-yeh ha-amaysim. מְחַיֶּה הַמֵּתִים:

HOLINESS OF GOD'S NAME

Atöh ködosh v'shim'chö אַתָּה קָדוֹשׁ וְשִׁמְךָ

ködosh uk'doshim b'chöl yom קָדוֹשׁ וּקְדוֹשִׁים בְּכָל יוֹם

y'ha-l'luchö selöh. Böruch atöh יְהַלְלוּךָ סֶּלָה. בָּרוּךְ אַתָּה

adonöy, hö-ayl ha-ködosh. יְיָ, הָאֵל הַקָּדוֹשׁ:

184

GOD'S MIGHT

אַתָּה — You are mighty forever, my Lord; You resurrect the dead; You are powerful to save.

In summer say: He causes the dew to descend.

In winter say: He causes the wind to blow and the rain to fall.

He sustains the living with lovingkindness, resurrects the dead with great mercy, supports the falling, heals the sick, releases the bound, and fulfills His trust to those who sleep in the dust. Who is like You, mighty One! And who can be compared to You, King, Who brings death and restores life, and causes deliverance to spring forth! You are trustworthy to revive the dead. Blessed are You Lord, Who revives the dead.

INSIGHT

אַתָּה גִבּוֹר — The belief in 'the revival of the dead' is one of the thirteen principles of the Jewish faith enumerated by Maimonides.

On a deeper level, it not only refers to the physically dead but also to those who feel spiritually deadened. We beseech God to help those in need to "restore life", to rejuvenate them spiritually.

HOLINESS OF GOD'S NAME

אַתָּה — You are holy and Your Name is holy, and holy beings praise You daily for all eternity. Blessed are You Lord, the holy God.

Admidah for Pesach, Shavuot, and Sukkot

Atöh v'chartönu miköl hö-amim, אַתָּה בְחַרְתָּנוּ מִכָּל הָעַמִּים,

öhavtö osönu v'rö-tziső bönu, אָהַבְתָּ אוֹתָנוּ וְרָצִיתָ בָּנוּ,

v'ro-mamtönu miköl ha-l'shonos, וְרוֹמַמְתָּנוּ מִכָּל הַלְּשׁוֹנוֹת,

v'kidash-tönu b'mitz-vosechö, וְקִדַּשְׁתָּנוּ בְּמִצְוֹתֶיךָ,

v'kayrav-tönu malkaynu וְקֵרַבְתָּנוּ מַלְכֵּנוּ

la-avodö-sechö, v'shim'chö לַעֲבֹדָתֶךָ, וְשִׁמְךָ

ha-gödol v'haködosh הַגָּדוֹל וְהַקָּדוֹשׁ

ölaynu köröső. עָלֵינוּ קָרָאתָ:

When the festival falls on Saturday night, add the following:

Vatodi-aynu adonöy elohaynu es וַתּוֹדִיעֵנוּ יְיָ אֱלֹהֵינוּ אֶת

mish-p'tay tzidkechö, vat'lam'daynu מִשְׁפְּטֵי צִדְקֶךָ, וַתְּלַמְּדֵנוּ

la-asos chukay r'tzonechö. Vati-ten lönu, לַעֲשׂוֹת חֻקֵּי רְצוֹנֶךָ: וַתִּתֶּן לָנוּ,

adonöy elohaynu, mishpötim y'shörim יְיָ אֱלֹהֵינוּ, מִשְׁפָּטִים יְשָׁרִים

v'soros emes, chukim umitzvos tovim, וְתוֹרוֹת אֱמֶת, חֻקִּים וּמִצְוֹת טוֹבִים,

vatan-chilaynu z'manay söson וַתַּנְחִילֵנוּ זְמַנֵּי שָׂשׂוֹן

umo-aday kodesh v'chagay n'dövöh, וּמוֹעֲדֵי קֹדֶשׁ וְחַגֵּי נְדָבָה,

vatori-shaynu k'dushas shabös uch'vod וַתּוֹרִישֵׁנוּ קְדֻשַּׁת שַׁבָּת וּכְבוֹד

mo-ayd va-chagigas höregel, va-tavdayl מוֹעֵד וַחֲגִיגַת הָרֶגֶל, וַתַּבְדֵּל

adonöy elohaynu bayn kodesh l'chol, יְיָ אֱלֹהֵינוּ בֵּין קֹדֶשׁ לְחוֹל,

bayn or l'choshech, bayn yisrö-ayl בֵּין אוֹר לְחשֶׁךְ, בֵּין יִשְׂרָאֵל

lö-amim, bayn yom ha-sh'vi-i l'shayshes לָעַמִּים, בֵּין יוֹם הַשְּׁבִיעִי לְשֵׁשֶׁת

y'may hama aseh. Bayn k'dushas shabös יְמֵי הַמַּעֲשֶׂה, בֵּין קְדֻשַּׁת שַׁבָּת

lik'dushas yom tov hivdaltö, v'es yom לִקְדֻשַּׁת יוֹם טוֹב הִבְדַּלְתָּ: וְאֶת יוֹם

ha-sh'vi-i mi-shayshes y'may ha-ma-aseh הַשְּׁבִיעִי מִשֵּׁשֶׁת יְמֵי הַמַּעֲשֶׂה

kidashtö, hivdaltö v'kidashtö es am'chö קִדַּשְׁתָּ: הִבְדַּלְתָּ וְקִדַּשְׁתָּ אֶת עַמְּךָ

yisrö-ayl bik'dushösechö. יִשְׂרָאֵל בִּקְדֻשָּׁתֶךָ:

Vatiten lönu adonöy elohaynu וַתִּתֶּן לָנוּ יְיָ אֱלֹהֵינוּ

b'ahavöh (shabösos lim'nuchöh u-) בְּאַהֲבָה (שַׁבָּתוֹת לִמְנוּחָה וּ)

mo-adim l'simchöh chagim מוֹעֲדִים לְשִׂמְחָה חַגִּים

HOLINESS OF THE DAY

אַתָּה בְחַרְתָּנוּ — You have chosen us from among all the nations; You have loved us and found favor with us. You have raised us above all tongues and made us holy through Your commandments. You, our King, have drawn us near to Your service and proclaimed Your great and holy Name upon us.

INSIGHT

אַתָּה בְחַרְתָּנוּ — This blessing speaks of God's choosing the Jewish people from among all the nations to bring His light into the world. The concept of 'choice' is more of a responsibility than a mere title. It means the Jew must live his life in accordance with the Torah and be a reflection of God's benevolent and holy ways in our world.

When the festival falls on Saturday night, add the following:

וַתּוֹדִיעֵנוּ — You, Lord our God, have made known to us Your righteous statutes and taught us to carry out the decrees of Your will. You, Lord our God, have given us just statutes and teachings of truth, decrees and precepts that are good. You have given us as a heritage joyous seasons, holy festivals and holidays for [bringing] voluntary offerings. You have bequeathed to us the holiness of the Shabbat, the glory of the holiday and the celebration of the festival. You, Lord our God, have made a distinction between sacred and profane, between light and darkness, between Israel and the nations, between the Seventh Day and the six work days; between the holiness of the Shabbat and the holiness of the Festival You have made a distinction, and have sanctified the Seventh Day above the six work days. You have set apart and sanctified Your people Israel with Your holiness.

וַתִּתֶּן — And You, Lord our God, have given us in love (On Shabbat: Sabbaths for rest and) festivals for rejoicing, holidays and seasons uz'manim l'söson es yom   וּזְמַנִּים לְשָׂשׂוֹן אֶת יוֹם

(ha-shabös ha-zeh v'es yom)   (הַשַּׁבָּת הַזֶּה וְאֶת יוֹם)

On Pesach: Chag ha-matzos ha-zeh,   לפסח: חַג הַמַּצּוֹת הַזֶּה

On Shavuot: Chag ha-shövu-os ha-zeh   לשבועות: חַג הַשָּׁבוּעוֹת הַזֶּה

On Sukkot: Chag ha–sukos ha-zeh   לסוכות: חַג הַסֻּכּוֹת הַזֶּה

On Shmini Atzeret and Simchat Torah: לשמיני עצרת ולשמחת תורה:
Sh'mini atzeres ha–chag ha-zeh   שְׁמִינִי עֲצֶרֶת הַחַג הַזֶּה

V'es yom tov mikra   וְאֶת יוֹם טוֹב מִקְרָא

kodesh ha–zeh, z'man   קֹדֶשׁ הַזֶּה, זְמַן

On Pesach: chayru-saynu   לפסח: חֵרוּתֵנוּ

On Shavuot: matan tora-saynu   לשבועות: מַתַּן תּוֹרָתֵנוּ

On Sukkot: simchö-saynu   לסוכות: שִׂמְחָתֵנוּ

On Shmini Atzeret and Simchat Torah: לשמיני עצרת ולשמחת תורה:
simchö-saynu   שִׂמְחָתֵנוּ

(b'ahavöh) mikrö kodesh zaycher   (בְּאַהֲבָה) מִקְרָא קֹדֶשׁ זֵכֶר

litzi-as mitzrö-yim.   לִיצִיאַת מִצְרָיִם:

Elohaynu vay-lohay avo-saynu   אֱלֹהֵינוּ וֵאלֹהֵי אֲבוֹתֵינוּ

ya-aleh v'yövo, v'yagi-a   יַעֲלֶה וְיָבֹא, וְיַגִּיעַ

v'yayrö-eh v'yayrö-tzeh,   וְיֵרָאֶה וְיֵרָצֶה,

v'yishöma v'yipökayd v'yizöchayr,   וְיִשָּׁמַע וְיִפָּקֵד וְיִזָּכֵר,

zichro-naynu ufik'do-naynu,   זִכְרוֹנֵנוּ וּפִקְדוֹנֵנוּ,

v'zichron avosaynu, v'zichron   וְזִכְרוֹן אֲבוֹתֵינוּ, וְזִכְרוֹן

möshi-ach ben dövid avdechö,   מָשִׁיחַ בֶּן דָּוִד עַבְדֶּךָ,

188

for gladness, (On Shabbat: this Shabbat day and) this day of: On Pesach: the Festival of Matzos, and this festival of holy assembly, the season of our freedom, On Shavuot: the Festival of Shavuot, and this festival of holy assembly, the season of the giving of our Torah, On Sukkot: the Festival of Sukkot, and this festival of holy assembly, the season of our rejoicing, On Shmini Atzeret and Simchat Torah: Shmini Atzeret the Festival, and this festival of holy assembly, the season of our rejoicing, (On Shabbat: in love,) a holy assembly, commemorating the Exodus from Egypt.

INSIGHT

אֱלֹהֵינוּ — On Rosh Chodesh (the first day of each month) and on all the Festivals, this prayer is included in the Amidah and Grace After Meals. We ask God to remember us and Jerusalem and to bring deliverance and peace in our times, because on these special days it is natural to miss the Holy Temple even more.

The prayer opens with eight expressions of ascent, (Ya-aleh means Ascend). These expressions refer to the eight stages that our prayers ascend to come before God.

אֱלֹהֵינוּ — Our God and God of our fathers, may there ascend, come and reach, be seen, accepted, and heard, recalled and remembered before You, the remembrance and recollection of us, the remembrance of our fathers, the remembrance of Moshiach the son of David Your servant, the remembrance of Jerusalem Your holy city, and the remembrance of all Your people the House of Israel, for deliverance, well-being, grace,

v'zichron y'rushöla-yim ir	וְזִכְרוֹן יְרוּשָׁלַיִם עִיר
köd-shechö, v'zichron köl	קָדְשֶׁךָ, וְזִכְרוֹן כָּל
am'chö bays yisrö-ayl l'fönechö	עַמְּךָ בֵּית יִשְׂרָאֵל לְפָנֶיךָ
lif'laytöh l'tovöh, l'chayn ul'chesed	לִפְלֵיטָה לְטוֹבָה, לְחֵן וּלְחֶסֶד
ul'rachamim ul'cha-yim tovim	וּלְרַחֲמִים וּלְחַיִּים טוֹבִים
ul'shölom b'yom	וּלְשָׁלוֹם, בְּיוֹם
(ha-shabös ha-zeh v'es yom)	(הַשַּׁבָּת הַזֶּה וְאֶת יוֹם)

On Pesach: Chag ha-matzos ha-zeh,	לפסח: חַג הַמַּצּוֹת הַזֶּה
On Shavuot: Chag ha-shövu-os ha-zeh	לשבועות: חַג הַשָּׁבוּעוֹת הַזֶּה
On Sukkot: Chag ha–sukos ha-zeh	לסוכות: חַג הַסֻּכּוֹת הַזֶּה
On Shmini Atzeret and Simchat Torah:	לשמיני עצרת ולשמחת תורה:
Sh'mini atzeres ha–chag ha–zeh	שְׁמִינִי עֲצֶרֶת הַחַג הַזֶּה

b'yom tov mikrö kodesh ha-zeh:	בְּיוֹם טוֹב מִקְרָא קֹדֶשׁ הַזֶּה:
Zöch'raynu adonöy elohaynu bo	זָכְרֵנוּ יְיָ אֱלֹהֵינוּ בּוֹ
l'tovöh, ufök'daynu vo liv'röchöh,	לְטוֹבָה, וּפָקְדֵנוּ בוֹ לִבְרָכָה,
v'hoshi-aynu vo l'cha-yim tovim.	וְהוֹשִׁיעֵנוּ בוֹ לְחַיִּים טוֹבִים:
Uvid'var y'shu-öh v'rachamim	וּבִדְבַר יְשׁוּעָה וְרַחֲמִים
chus v'chönaynu v'rachaym	חוּס וְחָנֵּנוּ וְרַחֵם
ölaynu v'hoshi-aynu ki aylechö	עָלֵינוּ וְהוֹשִׁיעֵנוּ כִּי אֵלֶיךָ
aynaynu, ki ayl melech chanun	עֵינֵינוּ, כִּי אֵל מֶלֶךְ חַנּוּן
v'rachum ötöh.	וְרַחוּם אָתָּה:

V'hasi-aynu adonöy elohaynu	וְהַשִּׂיאֵנוּ יְיָ אֱלֹהֵינוּ
es birkas mo-adechö.	אֶת בִּרְכַּת מוֹעֲדֶיךָ:
L'cha-yim tovim ul'shölom,	לְחַיִּים טוֹבִים וּלְשָׁלוֹם,
l'simchöh ul'söson, ka-asher	לְשִׂמְחָה וּלְשָׂשׂוֹן, כַּאֲשֶׁר

kindness, mercy, good life and peace, on this (On Shabbat: this Shabbat day and this) day of: On Pesach: the Festival of Matzot, On Shavuot: the Festival of Shavuot, On Sukkot: the Festival of Sukkot, On Shmini Atzeret and Simchat Torah: Shmini Atzeret, the Festival, on this holy Festival day. Remember us on this [day], Lord our God, for good; be mindful of us on this [day] for blessing; help us on this [day] for good life. With the promise of deliverance and compassion, spare us and be gracious to us; have mercy upon us and deliver us; for our eyes are directed to You, for You, God, are a gracious and merciful King.

INSIGHT

וְהַשִּׂיאֵנוּ — At this point we ask God to bestow upon us the blessings of the Festivals, including blessings for a good life and peace. We also request God to sanctify us with His commandments.

Our Sages are reminding us that when we align our lives with the Torah and perform the Mitzvot properly, we bring holiness upon ourselves and our families. We also ask God to grant us our unique and special heritage in joy and gladness so we may fulfill the Mitzvot out of great joy, rather than as an unwanted burden.

וְהַשִּׂיאֵנוּ — Bestow upon us, Lord our God, the blessings of Your festivals for good life and for peace, for joy and for gladness, as You desired and promised to bless us. (On Shabbat: Our God and God of our fathers, please find favor in our rest.) Make us

rö-tzisöh v'ömarto l'vö-r'chaynu.   רָצִיתָ וְאָמַרְתָּ לְבָרְכֵנוּ:

(Elohaynu vay-lohay avosaynu   (אֱלֹהֵינוּ וֵאלֹהֵי אֲבוֹתֵינוּ

r'tzay nö vim'nuchösaynu),   רְצֵה נָא בִמְנוּחָתֵנוּ)

kad'shaynu b'mitzvosechö,   קַדְּשֵׁנוּ בְּמִצְוֹתֶיךָ,

v'sayn chel-kaynu b'sorösechö,   וְתֵן חֶלְקֵנוּ בְּתוֹרָתֶךָ,

sab'aynu mituvechö, v'samay-ach   שַׂבְּעֵנוּ מִטּוּבֶךָ, וְשַׂמַּח

naf-shaynu bishu-ösechö,   נַפְשֵׁנוּ בִּישׁוּעָתֶךָ,

v'tahayr libaynu l'öv-d'chö   וְטַהֵר לִבֵּנוּ לְעָבְדְּךָ

be-emes, v'han-chi-laynu adonöy   בֶּאֱמֶת, וְהַנְחִילֵנוּ יְיָ

elohaynu (b'ahavöh uv'rötzon)   אֱלֹהֵינוּ (בְּאַהֲבָה וּבְרָצוֹן)

b'simchöh uv'söson, (shabös u-)   בְּשִׂמְחָה וּבְשָׂשׂוֹן (שַׁבָּת וּ)

mo-aday köd-shechö, v'yis-m'chu   מוֹעֲדֵי קָדְשֶׁךָ, וְיִשְׂמְחוּ

v'chö köl yisrö-ayl m'kadshay   בְךָ כָּל יִשְׂרָאֵל מְקַדְּשֵׁי

sh'mechö. Böruch atöh adonöy,   שְׁמֶךָ: בָּרוּךְ אַתָּה יְיָ,

m'kadaysh (ha-shabös v')   מְקַדֵּשׁ (הַשַּׁבָּת וְ)

yisrö-ayl v'haz'manim.   יִשְׂרָאֵל וְהַזְּמַנִּים:

TEMPLE SERVICE

R'tzay adonöy elo-haynu b'am'chö   רְצֵה יְיָ אֱלֹהֵינוּ בְּעַמְּךָ

yisrö-ayl v'lis'filösöm sh'ay,   יִשְׂרָאֵל וְלִתְפִלָּתָם שְׁעֵה,

v'hö-shayv hö-avodöh lid'vir   וְהָשֵׁב הָעֲבוֹדָה לִדְבִיר

bay-sechö, v'ishay yisrö-ayl   בֵּיתֶךָ, וְאִשֵּׁי יִשְׂרָאֵל

us'fi-lösöm b'aha-vöh s'kabayl   וּתְפִלָּתָם בְּאַהֲבָה תְקַבֵּל

b'rö-tzon, us' hi l'rö-tzon tömid   בְּרָצוֹן, וּתְהִי לְרָצוֹן תָּמִיד

avodas yisrö-ayl a-mechö.   עֲבוֹדַת יִשְׂרָאֵל עַמֶּךָ:

V'se-chezenöh ay-naynu   וְתֶחֱזֶינָה עֵינֵינוּ

b'shuv'chö l'tziyon b'racha-mim.   בְּשׁוּבְךָ לְצִיּוֹן בְּרַחֲמִים:

holy with Your commandments and grant us our portion in Your Torah; satiate us with Your goodness, gladden our soul with Your salvation, and make our heart pure to serve You in truth. Lord our God, grant as our heritage, (On Shabbat: in love and goodwill,) in joy and gladness, Your holy (On Shabbat: Shabbat and) Festivals, and may all Israel who sanctify Your Name rejoice in You. Blessed are You Lord, who sanctifies (On Shabbat: the Shabbat and) Israel and the [festive] seasons.

TEMPLE SERVICE

רְצֵה — Look with favor, Lord our God, on Your people Israel and pay heed to their prayer; restore the service to Your Sanctuary and accept with love and favor Israel's fire-offerings and prayer; and may the service of Your people Israel always find favor.

INSIGHT

מוֹדִים — We conclude the Amidah with blessings of thanksgiving. We thank God for giving us the means to communicate with Him through prayer, and for all the miracles He does daily, irrespective, of whether we are conscious of them or not.

One of the basic values that Judaism encourages is appreciation to both God and to man, acknowledging the blessings that we have received with humility. We also bow at this prayer perhaps as a tangible expression of this sense of humility before God.

וְתֶחֱזֶינָה — May our eyes behold Your return to Zion in mercy.

Böruch atöh adonöy, ha-machazir   בָּרוּךְ אַתָּה יְיָ, הַמַּחֲזִיר

sh'chinöso l'tziyon.   שְׁכִינָתוֹ לְצִיּוֹן:

Bow forward while reciting the first five words:

THANKSGIVING

Modim anachnu löch,   מוֹדִים אֲנַחְנוּ לָךְ,

shö-atöh hu adonöy elo-haynu   שָׁאַתָּה הוּא יְיָ אֱלֹהֵינוּ

vay-lohay avo-saynu l'olöm   וֵאלֹהֵי אֲבוֹתֵינוּ לְעוֹלָם

vö-ed, tzur cha-yaynu mö-gayn   וָעֶד, צוּר חַיֵּינוּ מָגֵן

yish-aynu, atöh hu l'dor vödor,   יִשְׁעֵנוּ, אַתָּה הוּא לְדוֹר וָדוֹר,

no-deh l'chö un'sapayr   נוֹדֶה לְךָ וּנְסַפֵּר

t'hilö-sechö, al cha-yaynu   תְּהִלָּתֶךָ, עַל חַיֵּינוּ

ha-m'surim b'yödechö,   הַמְּסוּרִים בְּיָדֶךָ,

v'al nish'mosaynu ha-p'kudos   וְעַל נִשְׁמוֹתֵינוּ הַפְּקוּדוֹת

löch, v'al ni-sechö sheb'chöl   לָךְ, וְעַל נִסֶּיךָ שֶׁבְּכָל

yom imönu, v'al nif-l'ösechö   יוֹם עִמָּנוּ, וְעַל נִפְלְאוֹתֶיךָ

v'tovosechö sheb'chöl ays,   וְטוֹבוֹתֶיךָ שֶׁבְּכָל עֵת,

erev vö-voker v'tzöhö-rö-yim,   עֶרֶב וָבֹקֶר וְצָהֳרָיִם,

ha-tov, ki lo chölu racha-mechö,   הַטּוֹב, כִּי לֹא כָלוּ רַחֲמֶיךָ,

ham'rachaym, ki lo samu   הַמְרַחֵם, כִּי לֹא תַמּוּ

chasö-dechö, ki may-olöm   חֲסָדֶיךָ, כִּי מֵעוֹלָם

kivinu löch.   קִוִּינוּ לָךְ:

V'al kulöm yis-böraych   וְעַל כֻּלָּם יִתְבָּרֵךְ

v'yisromöm v'yisnasay shim'chö   וְיִתְרוֹמָם וְיִתְנַשֵּׂא שִׁמְךָ

malkaynu tömid l'olöm vö-ed.   מַלְכֵּנוּ תָּמִיד לְעוֹלָם וָעֶד:

Blessed are You Lord, Who restores His Divine Presence to Zion.

Bow forward while reciting the words in bold below:

THANKSGIVING

מוֹדִים **We thankfully acknowledge that You are** the Lord our God and God of our fathers forever. You are the strength of our life, the shield of our salvation in every generation. We will give thanks to You and recount Your praise, evening, morning and noon, for our lives which are committed into Your hand, for our souls which are entrusted to You, for Your miracles which are with us daily, and for Your continual wonders and beneficence. You are the Beneficent One, for Your mercies never cease; and the Merciful One, for Your kindnesses never end; for we always place our hope in You.

INSIGHT

וְעַל כֻּלָּם — Here we recapitulate and bring to a close all our thanks for the many blessings that God gives to us on a constant basis. After recounting all the goodness that comes from Him, both the revealed and hidden, we are overcome with gratitude and thanks.

We show appreciation to God by heeding to His will, as expounded in the Torah. In this prayer we give voice to our appreciation and gratitude.

וְעַל — And for all these, may Your Name, our King, be continually blessed, exalted and extolled forever and all time.

Admidah for Pesach, Shavuot, and Sukkot

At the word "Böruch" bend the knee; at "Atöh" bow forward; and at "Adonöy" straighten up.

V'chöl ha-cha-yim yo-duchö selöh   וְכֹל הַחַיִּים יוֹדוּךָ סֶּלָה

viha-l'lu shim'chö ha-gödol l'olöm   וִיהַלְלוּ שִׁמְךָ הַגָּדוֹל לְעוֹלָם

ki tov, hö-ayl y'shu-ösaynu   כִּי טוֹב, הָאֵל יְשׁוּעָתֵנוּ

v'ezrö-saynu selöh, hö-ayl ha-tov.   וְעֶזְרָתֵנוּ סֶלָה, הָאֵל הַטּוֹב:

Böruch atöh adonöy,   בָּרוּךְ אַתָּה יְיָ,

ha-tov shim'chö ul'chö   הַטּוֹב שִׁמְךָ וּלְךָ

nö-eh l'hodos.   נָאֶה לְהוֹדוֹת:

PEACE

Sim shölom tovöh uv'röchöh,   שִׂים שָׁלוֹם, טוֹבָה וּבְרָכָה,

cha-yim chayn vö-chesed   חַיִּים חֵן וָחֶסֶד

v'rachamim, ölaynu v'al köl   וְרַחֲמִים, עָלֵינוּ וְעַל כָּל

yisrö-ayl amechö. Bö-r'chaynu   יִשְׂרָאֵל עַמֶּךָ: בָּרְכֵנוּ

övinu kulönu k'echöd b'or   אָבִינוּ כֻּלָּנוּ כְּאֶחָד, בְּאוֹר

pönechö, ki v'or pönechö,   פָּנֶיךָ, כִּי בְאוֹר פָּנֶיךָ,

nösatö lönu, adonöy el-ohaynu,   נָתַתָּ לָנוּ יְיָ אֱלֹהֵינוּ

toras cha-yim v'ahavas   תּוֹרַת חַיִּים, וְאַהֲבַת

chesed utz'dököh uv'röchöh   חֶסֶד, וּצְדָקָה וּבְרָכָה

v'rachamim v'cha-yim v'shölom.   וְרַחֲמִים וְחַיִּים וְשָׁלוֹם:

V'tov b'aynechö l'vöraych   וְטוֹב בְּעֵינֶיךָ לְבָרֵךְ

es am'chö yisrö-ayl b'chöl ays   אֶת עַמְּךָ יִשְׂרָאֵל בְּכָל עֵת

uv'chöl shö-öh bish'lomechö.   וּבְכָל שָׁעָה בִּשְׁלוֹמֶךָ:

Böruch atöh adonöy,   בָּרוּךְ אַתָּה יְיָ,

ha-m'vöraych es amo   הַמְבָרֵךְ אֶת עַמּוֹ

yisrö-ayl ba-shölom.   יִשְׂרָאֵל בַּשָּׁלוֹם:

**At the word "Blessed" bend the knee; at "You" bow forward;
and at "Lord" straighten up.**

וְכָל — And all living things shall forever thank You, and praise Your great Name eternally, for You are good. God, You are our everlasting salvation and help, O benevolent God. **Blessed** are **You Lord**, Beneficent is Your Name, and to You it is fitting to offer thanks.

INSIGHT

שִׂים שָׁלוֹם — This prayer contains the essence of the Priestly Blessing, *"Peace, goodness, life, graciousness, kindness and mercy."* We all want these blessings in our personal lives and we ask God to bestow them upon us and upon all of Israel.

The blessing also reminds us of our communal responsibility to each other. Despite the fact that we are scattered around the world, we are one nation, and one body.

PEACE

שִׂים — Bestow peace, goodness and blessing, life, graciousness, kindness and mercy, upon us and upon all Your people Israel. Bless us, our Father, all of us as one, with the light of Your countenance. For by the light of Your countenance You gave us, Lord our God, the Torah of life and lovingkindness, righteousness, blessing, mercy, life and peace. May it be favorable in Your eyes to bless Your people Israel, at all times and at every moment, with Your peace. Blessed are You Lord, Who blesses His people Israel with peace.

Admidah for Pesach, Shavuot, and Sukkot

Yih-yu l'rö-tzon im'ray fi,	יִהְיוּ לְרָצוֹן אִמְרֵי פִי,
v'heg-yon libi l'fönechö,	וְהֶגְיוֹן לִבִּי לְפָנֶיךָ,
adonöy tzuri v'go- ali.	יְיָ צוּרִי וְגוֹאֲלִי:

Elohai, n'tzor l'shoni may-rö,	אֱלֹהַי, נְצוֹר לְשׁוֹנִי מֵרָע,
us'fösai midabayr mirmöh.	וּשְׂפָתַי מִדַּבֵּר מִרְמָה:
V'lim'kal'lai, nafshi sidom,	וְלִמְקַלְלַי, נַפְשִׁי תִדּוֹם,
v'nafshi ke- öför la-kol tih-yeh.	וְנַפְשִׁי כֶּעָפָר לַכֹּל תִּהְיֶה:
P'sach libi b'sorö-sechö,	פְּתַח לִבִּי בְּתוֹרָתֶךָ,
uv'mitzvosechö tirdof nafshi,	וּבְמִצְוֹתֶיךָ תִּרְדּוֹף נַפְשִׁי,
v'chöl ha-chosh'vim ölai	וְכָל הַחוֹשְׁבִים עָלַי
rö-öh, m'hayröh hö-fayr atz-ösöm	רָעָה, מְהֵרָה הָפֵר עֲצָתָם
v'kalkayl ma-chashavtöm.	וְקַלְקֵל מַחֲשַׁבְתָּם:
Yih-yu k'motz lif'nay ru-ach	יִהְיוּ כְּמוֹץ לִפְנֵי רוּחַ
umal-ach adonöy do-cheh.	וּמַלְאַךְ יְיָ דּוֹחֶה:
L'ma-an yay-chöl'tzun y'didechö,	לְמַעַן יֵחָלְצוּן יְדִידֶיךָ,
hoshi-öh y'min'chö va-anayni.	הוֹשִׁיעָה יְמִינְךָ וַעֲנֵנִי:
Asay l'ma-an sh'mechö,	עֲשֵׂה לְמַעַן שְׁמֶךָ,
asay l'ma-an y'minechö,	עֲשֵׂה לְמַעַן יְמִינֶךָ,
asay l'ma-an torösechö,	עֲשֵׂה לְמַעַן תּוֹרָתֶךָ,
asay l'ma-an k'dusho-sechö.	עֲשֵׂה לְמַעַן קְדֻשָּׁתֶךָ:
Yih-yu l'rö-tzon im'ray fi,	יִהְיוּ לְרָצוֹן אִמְרֵי פִי,
v'heg-yon libi l'fönechö,	וְהֶגְיוֹן לִבִּי לְפָנֶיךָ,
adonöy tzuri v'go- ali.	יְיָ צוּרִי וְגוֹאֲלִי:

Take three steps back and say the following, while bowing the head to the left, straight ahead, right, straight ahead, and bow down (as indicated):

< O-seh* shölom bim' romöv, hu	‹עֹשֶׂה שָׁלוֹם בִּמְרוֹמָיו, הוּא
> ya-aseh shölom ölaynu v'al köl	›יַעֲשֶׂה שָׁלוֹם עָלֵינוּ וְעַל כָּל

יְהְיוּ — May the words of my mouth and the meditation of my heart be acceptable before You, Lord, my Strength and my Redeemer.

INSIGHT

אֱלֹהַי — This prayer was composed by the Sage Mar the son of Ravina, who used to conclude his prayer with this petition.

The Torah places a great emphasis on creating harmony between people. Therefore it is critical that we constantly train ourselves and pray to God to "guard my tongue from evil and my lips from speaking with deceit." However, it is insufficient to only abstain from evil, we must also strive to do good and add light through the lessons of the Torah and therefore we beseech God to "open my heart to Your Torah."

אֱלֹהַי — My God, guard my tongue from evil and my lips from speaking deceitfully. Let my soul be silent to those who curse me; let my soul be as dust to all. Open my heart to Your Torah, and let my soul eagerly pursue Your commandments. As for all those who plot evil against me, hasten to annul their counsel and frustrate their design. Let them be as chaff before the wind; let the angel of the Lord thrust them away. That Your beloved ones may be delivered, help with Your right hand and answer me. Do it for the sake of Your Name; do it for the sake of Your right hand; do it for the sake of Your Torah; do it for the sake of Your holiness. May the words of my mouth and the meditation of my heart be acceptable before You, Lord, my Strength and my Redeemer.

Take three steps back and say the following, while bowing the head to the left, straight ahead, right, straight ahead, and bow down (as indicated):

<He Who makes peace in His heavens, may He >make peace for

Admidah for Pesach, Shavuot, and Sukkot

yisrö-ayl, °v'im'ru ömayn.° °יִשְׂרָאֵל, °וְאִמְרוּ אָמֵן:

Y'hi rö-tzon mil'fö-nechö, adonöy יְהִי רָצוֹן מִלְּפָנֶיךָ, יְיָ

elo-haynu vay-lohay avo-saynu, אֱלֹהֵינוּ וֵאלֹהֵי אֲבוֹתֵינוּ,

she-yibö- neh bays ha-mikdösh שֶׁיִּבָּנֶה בֵּית הַמִּקְדָּשׁ

bim' hayröh v'yö-maynu, בִּמְהֵרָה בְיָמֵינוּ,

v'sayn chel-kaynu b'sorö-sechö. וְתֵן חֶלְקֵנוּ בְּתוֹרָתֶךָ:

Take three steps forward. This concludes the Amidah.

On Shavuot and Sukkot: The Amidah is followed by **Whole-Kaddish** on page 152, and *Olaynu* (It is Incumbent...) on page 158.

On Shabbat: Continue with *Vayechulu* (The Heavens...) on page 148.

On the first night of Pesach: Add the whole *Hallel* (not included in this prayerbook).

On the second night of Pesach: Add the whole *Hallel* (not included in this prayerbook), and the **Counting of the *Omer*,** on page 171.

us and for all Israel; °and say: Amen°.

יְהִי — May it be Your will, Lord our God and God of our fathers, that the *Beit Hamikdash* (Holy Temple) be speedily rebuilt in our days, and grant us our portion in Your Torah.

Take three steps forward. This concludes the Amidah.

On Shavuot and Sukkot: The Amidah is followed by **Whole-Kaddish** on page 152, and *Olaynu* **(It is Incumbent...)** on page 158.

On Shabbat: Continue with *Vayechulu* **(The Heavens...)** on page 148.

On the first night of Pesach: Add the whole *Hallel* (not included in this prayerbook).

On the second night of Pesach: Add the whole *Hallel* (not included in this prayerbook), and the **Counting of the** *Omer*, on page 171.

Selected Prayers

THREE CORE PRAYERS
FOR THE FRIDAY NIGHT SERVICE

If, for whatever reason, you cannot join a service, you are encouraged to recite three of the essential prayers of the Friday night service privately. Of course, you may pray the entire service on your own as well, omitting the parts marked for the prayer leader.

Lecha Dodi

One of the pearls of Jewish sacred poetry, *Lecha Dodi* was composed by Rabbi Sholmo Halevi Alkabetz (1505 – 1585). This song of praise compares the Jewish people to a bridegroom calling to his beloved, the Shabbat bride. See 2nd paragraph page **88**.

The Shema

"Hear O Israel the Lord our God, the Lord is One" is the clarion call of the Jewish people. The foundation of our belief and deep devotion to God and His commandments, the three chapters of the Shema are found in the Book of Deuteronomy. See page **116**.

The Amidah

Unlike the weekly Amidah which has eighteen benedictions, the Shabbat Amidah has only seven — in honor of the seventh day. The Amidah is the central prayer of all our services. See page **130** (on Festivals page 182).

Selected Songs

1. Ilu ho-tzi-önu אִלּוּ הוֹצִיאָנוּ .1

mimitzra-yim da-yaynu. מִמִּצְרַיִם דַּיֵּנוּ.

Had He [only] brought us out of Egypt,
it would have sufficed us.

2. Ayli-yöhu ha-növi, ayli-yöhu אֵלִיָּהוּ הַנָּבִיא, אֵלִיָּהוּ .2

ha-tishbi, ayli-yöhu hagil-ödi, הַתִּשְׁבִּי, אֵלִיָּהוּ הַגִּלְעָדִי,

bim'hayröh yövo aylaynu im בִּמְהֵרָה יָבֹא אֵלֵינוּ עִם

möshi-ach ben dövid. מָשִׁיחַ בֶּן דָּוִד:

Elijah the prophet, Elijah the Tishbi, Elijah the Gilodi,
will swiftly come to us with Moshiach the son of David.

3. Dövid melech yisrö-ayl דָּוִד מֶלֶךְ יִשְׂרָאֵל .3

chai v'ka-yöm. חַי וְקַיָּם:

David, King of Israel, is living and enduring.

4. Hinay mah tov umah nö-im הִנֵּה מַה טּוֹב וּמַה נָּעִים .4

sheves achim gam yöchad. שֶׁבֶת אַחִים גַּם יָחַד:

How good and pleasant it is when
brothers live together in harmony.

5. Yachad kulöm k'dushö l'chö
y'shalei-shu, ka-dövör hö-ömur
al yad n'viechö, v'köroö zeh
el zeh v'ömar.

5. יַחַד כֻּלָּם קְדֻשָּׁה לְךָ
יְשַׁלֵּשׁוּ, כַּדָּבָר הָאָמוּר
עַל יַד נְבִיאֶךָ, וְקָרָא זֶה
אֶל זֶה וְאָמַר:

Together, everyone will thrice repeat Holy onto You,
according to the words communicated through
Your prophet, "and they said to one another.

6. Köl hö-olöm kulo gesher tzar
m'od. V'hö-ikör lo l'fachayd k'lal.

6. כָּל הָעוֹלָם כֻּלּוֹ גֶּשֶׁר צַר
מְאֹד. וְהָעִקָּר לֹא לְפַחֵד כְּלָל:

The whole world is a very narrow bridge,
but the main thing is not to fear at all.

7. Min ha-maytzar körösi köh,
önöni vamerchöv köh.

7. מִן הַמֵּצַר קָרָאתִי קָּהּ,
עָנָנִי בַמֶּרְחָב קָהּ:

From out of distress I called to God;
with abounding relief, God answered me.

8. Mitzvöh g'dolöh lih-yös
b'simchöh tömid.

8. מִצְוָה גְדוֹלָה לִהְיוֹת
בְּשִׂמְחָה תָּמִיד:

It is a great Mitzvah to be happy always.

3. Am yisrö-ayl chai. ‎3. עַם יִשְׂרָאֵל חַי:

Od övinu chai. ‎עוֹד אָבִינוּ חַי:

The people of Israel live. Our Father still lives.

18. O-seh shölom bim'romöv, ‎18. עֹשֶׂה שָׁלוֹם בִּמְרוֹמָיו,

hu ya-aseh shölom ölaynu, ‎הוּא יַעֲשֶׂה שָׁלוֹם עָלֵינוּ,

v'al köl yisrö-ayl v'im'ru ömayn. ‎וְעַל כָּל יִשְׂרָאֵל וְאִמְרוּ אָמֵן:

He Who makes peace in His heavens,
may He make peace for us and for all Israel;
and say, Amen.

22. Simön tov umazöl tov y'hay ‎22. סִמָּן טוֹב וּמַזָּל טוֹב יְהֵא

lönu ul'chöl yisrö-ayl ömayn. ‎לָנוּ וּלְכָל יִשְׂרָאֵל אָמֵן:

May there be a good omen and good mazal
for us and for all Israel. Amen.

21. She-yibö-neh bays ha-mikdösh ‎21. שֶׁיִּבָּנֶה בֵּית הַמִּקְדָּשׁ

bim'hayröh v'yömaynu, v'sayn ‎בִּמְהֵרָה בְיָמֵינוּ, וְתֵן

chelkaynu b'sorö-sechö. ‎חֶלְקֵנוּ בְּתוֹרָתֶךְ:

[May it be your will] that the Beit Hamikdash
be speedily rebuilt in our days, and grant us
our portion in Your Torah.

About the Kotel

About the Kotel

"The Divine Presence Has Never Departed From the Western Wall"

What is the significance of the Western Wall?

The Western Wall has been the center of Jewish yearning and memory for more than 2,000 years. The only fragment of the Great Temple to survive the Roman destruction, the Divine Presence has never departed from The Western Wall. Built to support the western side of the Temple Mount, it is known as the Western Wall (in Hebrew, *HaKotel HaMa'aravi*), and it is the most sacred structure of the Jewish people. Its ancient stones stand testimony to a glorious Jewish past, a proud heritage, and an extraordinary national rebirth. It is a focus of Jewish longing and prayer for redemption and renewal.

Why is the Temple Mount sacred?

Long before the Temple stood on this mount, Jewish tradition tells us that Abraham came here to sacrifice his son Isaac, and Jacob slept here, dreaming of a ladder to heaven. Then called Mount Moriah, its summit was where Solomon built the Temple on the land which his father King David purchased from Aravnah, the Jebusite, approximately 3,000 years ago. That Temple was destroyed by the Babylonian conqueror Nebuchadnezzar about 2,500 years ago. Seventy years after that destruction, the Returnees to Zion constructed the Second Temple, and about three hundred and fifty years later the Hasmonean kings expanded this work.

Later, the great builder of Jerusalem, King Herod, enlarged the Temple complex, surrounded it with huge walls, and rebuilt the Temple within these walls. Such was its splendor, it was said that "he who has not seen the Temple of Herod has not seen a building of true beauty." Approximately two millennia ago, the Romans set the Temple on fire and destroyed its surrounding walls. Only the Western Wall remained standing, its original length intact.

What does the Temple mean to Jews and non-Jews?

The prophet Isaiah called the Temple a "House for all nations." A universal center of spirituality, it stirs the thoughts and emotions of Jew and non-Jew and energizes the inner connection between the individual and God. Even with the Temple destroyed, the holiness of the place is such that it remains sacred, which is why Jews everywhere around the world continue to face it while praying. Throughout history and today, people from all over the world converge here to see, feel, pray, and to place notes, requests and pleas between its timeless stones.

What is the Western Wall Plaza?

The Western Wall Plaza is the cleared area in front of part of the Western Wall. Since the site is first and foremost a place of prayer, the Plaza provides worshippers a dignified approach to this holy Wall. Because the Western Wall is the national and spiritual center of the Jewish nation, the Plaza is a setting for national events: the Priests' Blessing (*Birkat Cohanim*) on Pesach and Sukkot, candle-lighting on Chanukah, the swearing-in of Israel's police and armed forces recruits, and IDF Memorial Day and Jerusalem Day ceremonies. It is also the most significant and popular location for bar and bat mitzvahs of youngsters from Israel and abroad, as well the official site of the bar and bat mitzvah ceremonies of young victims of terror.

Until some 700 years ago, the entire length of the Western Wall (1,600 feet; 488 meters) was accessible. Gradually, the city's Mamluk and Moslem conquerors built against it, leaving only this small section of the Wall (187 feet, 57 meters) visible. Jews who continued to pray at the Wall began winding their way through narrow alleys to reach it until Jordan occupied Jerusalem's Old City in 1948 (5708) and Jews were denied access to the Wall. With Jerusalem reunified in 1967 (5727), and the Wall joyously restored to the Jewish people, the plaza in front of it was cleared, allowing all to approach. The Wall, which had always been a symbol of national unity, returned to being a unique place of prayer.

Do we see the entire Western Wall from the Plaza?

Though just over an eighth of the Wall lines the Prayer Plaza, another 80-plus meters (262 feet) stretch to the right as you face the Wall, and some 320 meters (1,050 feet) continue to the left, into the Western Wall Tunnels.

What is special about being at the Western Wall?

All stand equal in front of the Wall. Jews sense their Judaism, often for the first time. Touching its stones links us with our nation and heritage, with the Jewish people and our long, turbulent history. Standing at the Wall, perspectives, thoughts and feelings crystallize and the insignificant fades away. The Wall has withstood time; it has witnessed war and peace, destruction and revival. For generations, it has absorbed the prayers and yearnings of those near and far. Today, it is the most visited site in Israel.

To feel, to understand, to experience true awe, come to Jerusalem, to the Western Wall.